LIBERTY
DEFINED

LIBERTY
DEFINED

50 Essential Issues
That Affect Our Freedom

RON PAUL

GRAND CENTRAL
PUBLISHING

NEW YORK   BOSTON

Grand Central Publishing
Hachette Book Group
237 Park Avenue
New York, NY 10017
www.HachetteBookGroup.com

Printed in the United States of America

First Edition: April 2011

10   9   8   7   6   5   4   3   2   1

Grand Central Publishing is a division of Hachette Book Group, Inc.

The Grand Central Publishing name and logo is a trademark of Hachette Book Group, Inc.

The publisher is not responsible for websites (or their content) that are not owned by the publisher.

Library of Congress Cataloging-in-Publication Data
Paul, Ron
    Liberty defined : 50 essential issues that affect our freedom / Ron Paul.
        p. cm.
    ISBN 978-1-4555-0145-8 (regular ed.)—ISBN 978-1-4555-0177-9
(large print ed.)   1. Liberty—United States.   2. United States—Politics
and government—2009–   I. Title.   II. Title: 50 essential issues that
affect our freedom.   III. Title: Fifty essential issues that affect our freedom.
    JC599.U5P372 2011
    320.01'1—dc22

                                                            2011000852

This book is dedicated to the great intellectuals of freedom
who taught and inspired me and so many others:

Ludwig von Mises, F. A. Hayek, Leonard E. Read,
Murray N. Rothbard, and Hans F. Sennholz.

CONTENTS

INTRODUCTION

America's history and political ethos are all about liberty. The Declaration of Independence declares that life, liberty, and the pursuit of happiness are unalienable rights, but I believe that both life and the pursuit of happiness also depend on liberty as a fundamental bedrock of our country. We use the word almost as a cliché. But do we know what it means? Can we recognize it when we see it? More importantly, can we recognize the opposite of liberty when it is sold to us as a form of freedom?

Liberty means to exercise human rights in any manner a person chooses so long as it does not interfere with the exercise of the rights of others. This means, above all else, keeping government out of our lives. Only this path leads to the unleashing of human energies that build civilization, provide security, generate wealth, and protect the people from systematic rights violations. In this sense, only liberty can truly ward off tyranny, the great and eternal foe of mankind.

The definition of liberty I use is the same one that was accepted by Thomas Jefferson and his generation. It is the understanding derived from the great freedom tradition, for Jefferson himself took his understanding from John Locke (1632–1704). I use the term "liberal" without irony or contempt, for the liberal tradition in the true sense, dating from the late Middle Ages until the early part of the twentieth century,[1] was devoted to freeing society from the shackles of the state. This is an agenda I embrace, and one that I believe all Americans should embrace.

To believe in liberty is not to believe in any particular social and economic outcome. It is to trust in the spontaneous order that emerges when the state does not intervene in human volition and human cooperation. It permits people to work out their problems for themselves, build lives for themselves, take risks and accept responsibility for the results, and make their own decisions.

Do our leaders in Washington believe in liberty? They sometimes say they do. I don't think they are telling the truth. The existence of the wealth-extracting leviathan state in Washington, DC, a cartoonishly massive machinery that no one can control and yet few ever seriously challenge, a monster that is a constant presence in every aspect of our lives, is proof enough that our leaders do not believe. Neither party is truly dedicated to the classical, fundamental ideals that gave rise to the American Revolution.

Of course, the costs of this leviathan are incalculably large. The twentieth century endured two world wars, a worldwide

1. An excellent overview of the history of the idea of liberty and its right is Rodney Stark, *The Victory of Reason: How Christianity Led to Freedom, Capitalism, and Western Success* (Random House, 2005) and Ludwig von Mises, *Liberalism* (Mises Institute [1929] 2010)

depression, and a forty-five-year "Cold War" with two super-powers facing off with tens of thousands of intercontinental missiles armed with nuclear warheads. And yet the threat of government today, all over the world, may well present a greater danger than anything that occurred in the twentieth century. We are policed everywhere we go: work, shopping, home, and church. Nothing is private anymore: not property, not family, not even our houses of worship. We are encouraged to spy on each other and to stand passively as government agents scan us, harass us, and put us in our place day after day. If you object, you are put on a hit list. If you fight to reveal the truth, as WikiLeaks or other websites have done, you are targeted and can be crushed. Sometimes it seems as if we are living in a dystopian novel like *1984* or *Brave New World*, complete with ever less economic freedom. Some will say that this is hyperbole; others will understand exactly what I'm talking about.

What is at stake is the American dream itself, which in turn is wrapped up with our standard of living. Too often, we underestimate what the phrase "standard of living" really means. In my mind, it deals directly with all issues that affect our material well-being, and therefore affects our outlook on life itself: whether we are hopeful or despairing, whether we expect progression or regression, whether we think our children will be better off or worse off than we are. All of these considerations go to the heart of the idea of happiness. The phrase "standard of living" comprises nearly all we expect out of life on this earth. It is, simply, how we are able to define our lives.

Our standards of living are made possible by the blessed

institution of liberty. When liberty is under attack, everything we hold dear is under attack. Governments, by their very nature, notoriously compete with liberty, even when the stated purpose for establishing a particular government is to protect liberty.

Take the United States, for example. Our country was established with the greatest ideals and respect for individual freedom ever known. Yet look at where we are today: runaway spending and uncontrollable debt; a monstrous bureaucracy regulating our every move; total disregard for private property, free markets, sound money, and personal privacy; and a foreign policy of military expansionism. The restraints placed on our government in the Constitution by the Founders did not work. Powerful special interests rule, and there seems to be no way to fight against them. While the middle class is being destroyed, the poor suffer, the justly rich are being looted, and the unjustly rich are getting richer. The wealth of the country has fallen into the hands of a few at the expense of the many. Some say this is because of a lack of regulations on Wall Street, but that is not right. The root of this issue reaches far deeper than that.

The threat to liberty is not limited to the United States. Dollar hegemony has globalized the crisis. Nothing like this has ever happened before. All economies are interrelated and dependent on the dollar's maintaining its value, while at the same time the endless expansion of the dollar money supply is expected to bail out everyone.

This dollar globalization is made more dangerous by nearly all governments acting irresponsibly by expanding their powers and living beyond their means. Worldwide debt is a problem that will continue to grow if we continue on this path. Yet all governments, and especially ours, do not hesitate to further expand their powers at the expense of liberty in a futile effort to force an outcome of their design on us. They simply expand and plummet further into debt.

Understanding how governments always compete with liberty and destroy progress, creativity, and prosperity is crucial to our effort to reverse the course on which we find ourselves. The contest between abusive government power and individual freedom is an age-old problem. The concept of liberty, recognized as a natural right, has required thousands of years to be understood by the masses in reaction to the tyranny imposed by those whose only desire is to rule over others and live off their enslavement.

This conflict was understood by the defenders of the Roman Republic, the Israelites of the Old Testament, the rebellious barons of 1215 who demanded the right of habeas corpus, and certainly by the Founders of this country, who imagined the possibility of a society without kings and despots and thereby established a framework that has inspired liberation movements ever since. It is understood by growing numbers of Americans who are crying out for answers and demanding an end to Washington's hegemony over the country and the world.

And yet even among the friends of liberty, many people are deceived into believing that government can make them safe from all harm, provide fairly distributed economic security, and improve individual moral behavior. If the government is granted a monopoly on the use of force to achieve these goals, history shows that that power is always abused. Every single time.

Over the centuries, progress has been made in understanding the concept of individual liberty and the need to constantly remain vigilant in order to limit government's abuse of its powers. Though steady progress has been made, periodic setbacks and stagnations have occurred. For the past one hundred years, the United States and most of the world have witnessed a setback for the cause of liberty. Despite all the advances in technology, despite a more refined understanding of the rights of minorities, despite all the economic advances, the individual has far less protection against the state than a century ago.

Since the beginning of the last century, many seeds of destruction have been planted that are now maturing into a systematic assault on our freedoms. With a horrendous financial and currency crisis both upon us and looming into the future as far as the eye can see, it has become quite apparent that the national debt is unsustainable, liberty is threatened, and the people's anger and fears are growing. Most importantly, it is now clear that government promises and panaceas are worthless. Government has once again failed and the demand for change is growing louder by the day. Just witness the dramatic back-and-forth swings of the parties in power.

The only thing that the promises of government did was to delude the people into a false sense of security. Complacency and mistrust generated a tremendous moral hazard, causing dangerous behavior by a large number of people. Self-reliance and individual responsibility were replaced by organized thugs who weaseled their way into achieving control over the process whereby the looted wealth of the country was distributed.

The choice we now face: further steps toward authoritarianism or a renewed effort in promoting the cause of liberty. There is no third option. This course must incorporate a modern and more sophisticated understanding of the magnificence of the market economy, especially the moral and practical urgency of monetary reform. The abysmal shortcomings of a government power that undermines the creative genius of free minds and private property must be fully understood.

This conflict between government and liberty, brought to a boiling point by the world's biggest bankruptcy in history, has generated the angry protests that have spontaneously broken out around the country—and the world. The producers are rebelling and the recipients of largess are angry and restless.

The crisis demands an intellectual revolution. Fortunately, this revolution is under way, and if one earnestly looks for it, it can be found. Participation in it is open to everyone. Not only have our ideas of liberty developed over centuries, they are currently being eagerly debated, and a modern, advanced understanding of the concept is on the horizon. The Revolution is alive and well.

The idea of this book is not to provide a blueprint for the future or an all-encompassing defense of a libertarian program. What I offer here are thoughts on a series of controversial topics that tend to confuse people, and these are interpreted in light of my own experience and my thinking. I present not final answers but rather guideposts for thinking seriously about these topics. I certainly do not expect every reader to agree with my beliefs, but I do hope that I can inspire serious, fundamental, and independent-minded thinking and debate on them.

Above all, the theme is liberty. The goal is liberty. The results of liberty are all the things we love, none of which can be finally provided by government. We must have the opportunity to provide them for ourselves, as individuals, as families, as a society, and as a country. Off we go: A to Z.

LIBERTY
DEFINED

ABORTION

On one occasion in the 1960s when abortion was still illegal, I witnessed, while visiting a surgical suite as an OB/GYN resident, the abortion of a fetus that weighed approximately two pounds. It was placed in a bucket, crying and struggling to breathe, and the medical personnel pretended not to notice. Soon the crying stopped. This harrowing event forced me to think more seriously about this important issue.

That same day in the OB suite, an early delivery occurred and the infant born was only slightly larger than the one that was just aborted. But in this room everybody did everything conceivable to save this child's life. My conclusion that day was that we were overstepping the bounds of morality by picking and choosing who should live and who should die. These were human lives. There was no consistent moral basis to the value of life under these circumstances.

Some people believe that being pro-choice is being on the side of freedom. I've never understood how an act of violence, killing a human being, albeit a small one in a special place, is portrayed as a precious right. To speak only of the mother's cost in carrying a baby to term ignores all thought of any legal rights of the unborn. I believe that the moral consequence of cavalierly accepting abortion diminishes the value of all life.

It is now widely accepted that there's a constitutional right to abort a human fetus. Of course, the Constitution says nothing about abortion, murder, manslaughter, or any other acts of violence. There are only four crimes listed in the Constitution: counterfeiting, piracy, treason, and slavery. Criminal and civil laws were deliberately left to the states. It's a giant leap for the federal courts to declare abortion a constitutional right and overrule all state laws regulating the procedure. If anything, the federal government has a responsibility to protect life—not grant permission to destroy it. If a state were to legalize infanticide, it could be charged with not maintaining a republican form of government, which is required by the Constitution.

If we, for the sake of discussion, ignore the legal arguments for or against abortion and have no laws prohibiting it, serious social ramifications would remain. There are still profound moral issues, issues of consent, and fundamental questions about the origin of life and the rights of individuals. There are two arguments that clash. Some argue that any abortion after conception should be illegal. Others argue that the mother has a right to her body and no one should interfere with her decision. It's amazing to me that many people I have spoken to in the pro-choice group rarely care about choice in other circumstances. Almost all regulations by the federal government to protect us from ourselves (laws against smoking, bans on narcotics, and mandatory seat belts, for example) are readily supported by the left/liberals who demand "choice." Of course, to the pro-choice group, the precious choice we debate is limited to the mother and not to the unborn.

The fact is that the fetus has legal rights—inheritance, a right not to be injured or aborted by unwise medical treatment, violence, or accidents. Ignoring these rights is arbitrary and places relative rights on a small, living human being. The only issue that should be debated is the moral one: whether or not a fetus has any right to life. Scientifically, there's no debate over whether the fetus is alive and human—if not killed, it matures into an adult human being. It is that simple. So the time line of when we consider a fetus "human" is arbitrary after conception, in my mind.

It's interesting to hear the strongest supporters of abortion squirm when asked if they support the mother's right to an abortion in the ninth month of pregnancy. They inevitably don't support such an act, but every argument that is made for abortion in the first month is applicable to late pregnancy as well. It's still the mother's body. It's still her choice. Due to changed circumstances, she may well have strong compelling social reasons to prevent a live birth and assume its obligations, even in the third trimester. This is a dilemma for the proponents of choice and they should be challenged as to where the line should be drawn.

Another aspect of this debate needs to be resolved: If an abortion doctor performs a third-trimester abortion for whatever reason, a handsome fee is paid and it's perfectly legal in some states. If a frightened teenager, possibly not even knowing she was pregnant, delivers a baby and she kills it, the police are out en masse to charge her with a homicide. What really is so different between the fetus one minute before birth and a newborn one minute after birth? Biologically and morally, nothing. We must also answer the grim question of what should be done with a newborn that inadvertently survives an abortion. It happens more than you might think. Doctors have been accused of murder since the baby died after delivery, but that hardly seems just. The real question is, how can a human infant have such relative value attached to it?

In the age of abortion, with nearly a million being performed each year in the United States, society sends a signal that we place a lower value on the small and the weak. Most young people choose abortions for economic reasons; they believe that they cannot afford to bear the child and would rather wait.[1] Why is it that moral considerations do not trump such fears? Why do these women not consider other options, such as adoption, more seriously? They've been taught by society that an unwanted fetus-baby has no right to life and therefore has no real value. And why do so many young women put themselves at risk for having to make such choices in the first place? Availability of abortion, most likely, changes behavior and actually increases unwanted pregnancies.

The difference or lack thereof between a baby one minute after birth and one minute before needs to be quantified. The Congress or the courts are incapable of doing this. This is a profound issue to be determined by society itself based on the moral value it espouses.

1. Akinrinola Bankole, et al., "Reasons Why Women Have Induced Abortions: Evidence from 27 Countries." International Family Planning Perspectives (1998).

Abortion is rarely a long-term answer. A woman who has had one abortion is more likely to have another.[2] It's an easier solution than a change in long-developed personal behavior. My argument is that the abortion problem is more of a social and moral issue than it is a legal one. In the 1960s, when I was in my OB/GYN residency training, abortions were being done in defiance of the law. Society had changed and the majority agreed the laws should be changed as well. The Supreme Court in 1973 in *Roe v. Wade* caught up with the changes in moral standards.

So if we are ever to have fewer abortions, society must change again. The law will not accomplish that. However, that does not mean that the states shouldn't be allowed to write laws dealing with abortion. Very early pregnancies and victims of rape can be treated with the day after pill, which is nothing more than using birth control pills in a special manner. These very early pregnancies could never be policed, regardless. Such circumstances would be dealt with by each individual making his or her own moral choice.

As a bankrupt government takes over more of our health care, rationing of care by government mandates is unavoidable. Picking and choosing who should live and who should die may sound morally repugnant, but this is where we end up in a world with scarce means and politically driven decisions about how those means are going to be employed. The federal government will remain very much involved in the abortion business either directly or indirectly by financing it.

---

2. Susan A. Cohen, "Repeat Abortion, Repeat Unintended Pregnancy, Repeated and Misguided Government Policies." *Guttmacher Policy Review*, Spring 2007, Volume 10, Number 2.

One thing I believe for certain is that the federal government should *never* tax pro-life citizens to pay for abortions. The constant effort by the pro-choice crowd to fund abortion must rank among the stupidest policies ever, even from their viewpoint. All they accomplish is to give valiant motivation for all pro-life forces as well as the antitax supporters of abortion to fight against them.

A society that readily condones abortion invites attacks on personal liberty. If all life is not precious, how can all liberty be held up as important? It seems that if some life can be thrown away, our right to personally choose what is best for us is more difficult to defend. I've become convinced that resolving the abortion issue is required for a healthy defense of a free society.

The availability and frequent use of abortion has caused many young people to change their behavior. Its legalization and general acceptance has not had a favorable influence on society. Instead, it has resulted in a diminished respect for both life and liberty.

Strangely, given that my moral views are akin to theirs, various national pro-life groups have been hostile to my position on this issue. But I also believe in the Constitution, and therefore, I consider it a *state-level* responsibility to restrain violence against any human being. I disagree with the nationalization of the issue and reject the *Roe v. Wade* decision that legalized abortion in all fifty states. Legislation that I have proposed would limit federal court jurisdiction of abortion. Legislation of this sort would probably allow state prohibition of abortion on demand as well as in all trimesters. It will not stop all abortions. Only a truly moral society can do that.

The pro-life opponents to my approach are less respectful of the rule of law and the Constitution. Instead of admitting that my position allows the states to minimize or ban abortions, they claim that my position supports the legalization of abortion by the states. This is twisted logic. Demanding a national and only a national solution, as some do, gives credence to the very process that made abortions so prevalent. Ending nationally legalized abortions by federal court order is neither a practical answer to the problem nor a constitutionally sound argument.

Removing jurisdiction from the federal courts can be done with a majority vote in the Congress and the signature of the President. This is much simpler than waiting for the Supreme Court to repeal *Roe v. Wade* or for a constitutional amendment. My guess is that the scurrilous attacks by these groups are intended more to discredit my entire defense of liberty and the Constitution than they are to deal with the issue of abortion. These same groups have very little interest in being pro-life when it comes to fighting illegal, undeclared wars in the Middle East or preventive (aggressive) wars for religious reasons. An interesting paradox!

My position does not oppose looking for certain judges to be appointed to the Supreme Court, or even having a constitutional definition of life. Removing the jurisdiction from the federal courts would result in fewer abortions much sooner, but it wouldn't prevent a national effort to change the Supreme Court or the Constitution by amendment. It makes one wonder why the resistance to a practical and constitutional approach to this problem is so strong.

Just about everyone knows that the Hippocratic oath includes the pledge not to do abortions. In the 1960s, most medical schools, rather than face the issue, just dropped the tradition of medical-school graduating seniors repeating the oath. My class of 1961 ignored the oath at graduation. Just think, the oath survived for so many years and then ended right before the drug and Vietnam War culture, when it was most desperately needed.

By 1988, when my son Dr. Rand Paul graduated, the oath was made voluntary in a special baccalaureate ceremony. But strangely, the oath was edited to exclude the provision pledging not to do an abortion. Today, sadly, medical school applicants in some schools are screened and can be rejected or at least intimidated on this issue.

As a pro-life libertarian physician, my strong advice, regardless of what is legal, is for medical personnel to just say no to participation in any procedure or process that is pro-death or diminishes respect for life in any way. Let the lawyers and the politicians and mercenary, unethical doctors deal with implementing laws regulating death.

Deregulating the adoption market would also make a margin of difference in reducing abortion. This would make it easier for nonprofit groups to arrange for adoptive parents and for them to compensate the mother enough to absorb the expenses and opportunity costs associated with carrying the child to term. Small changes could make a large difference here.

Finally, here is my program for pro-life MDs and medical personnel:

- Do not perform abortions for convenience or social reasons.
- Do not be the agent of active euthanasia.

- Do not participate in any manner—directly or indirectly—in torture.
- Do not participate in human experimentation. I'm not referring to testing new drugs with the patient's consent. I'm speaking of our long history of military participation in human experimentation. The Tuskegee experiment, in which black soldiers who had syphilis were deliberately mistreated, is one example.
- Do not be involved with the state in executing criminals or in any way approve the carrying out of the death penalty.
- Do not participate in government-run programs where medical care is rationed for economic or social reasons that place relative value on life.
- Do not give political or philosophical support for wars of aggression, referred to as preventive wars.

Paul, Ron. 1983. *Abortion and Liberty*. Lake Jackson: Foundation for Rational Economics and Education.

Assassination

A foreign policy that endorses worldwide intervention and occupation requires that people live in perpetual fear of supposed enemies. In the post–9/11 period, proponents of such policies have been quite able to promote the fear needed for the American people to accept policies they otherwise would have rebelled against. Fear has enabled permanent runaway domestic surveillance and the sacrifice of privacy through legislation such as the Patriot Act. A citizen walking through the airport today is bombarded with *1984*-style propaganda messages that are designed to make us fear some amorphous threat and also be suspicious of others. The government designs these messages to make us feel dependent and heavily lorded over in every aspect of our lives. These messages are becoming ever more pervasive, hitting us even in grocery stores when we are shopping.

If we are fearful enough, we are willing to tolerate what might otherwise be regarded as immoral means of dealing with the enemy. For example, the use of torture to combat evildoers has been accepted by a large number of otherwise reasonable Americans as a result of those who purposely, successfully used fear as a tactic to achieve their mischievous goals. And now we are moving toward the acceptance of assassinations of American citizens as necessary to provide national security, as I will show below. This, to me, signifies that we are no longer a nation of laws but rather a nation of people who act outside the law without restraint. The corruption in ideals has been so grave that many conservatives regard criticism of assassination as a sign of liberal wimpiness and sentimentality. In fact, we are dealing with a fundamental issue of human rights here.

We are told we are at war—against terrorism. Yet terrorism is a tactic and described in federal law as a crime. The war is "worldwide," so lawlessness by our government can be perpetuated anywhere in the world, including within the borders of the United States. In wartime, the government assumes greater emergency powers to make secret arrests, build secret prisons, torture, and use secret rendition allowing other, more ruthless countries to do our dirty work.

The term "war on terror" should never be used as anything more than a cliché, like "war on" drugs, poverty, illiteracy, etc. But its use is deliberate, even in these symbolic usages, to con the people into thinking that all citizens must cooperate and sacrifice our liberties to "win" the war. Though these violations are fully endorsed by the Obama administration, they were introduced and generally used by the Bush administration.

We've moved much further along in the disintegration of American jurisprudence. Indefinite detention without charges or a right to counsel is now an established precedent for anyone in the world, including an American citizen, declared "an enemy combatant" by a single U.S. official. It has been acknowledged by the Obama administration that the current policy permits the assassination of any suspect anywhere in the world, including an American citizen.[1] This, they argue, is crucial to keep all Americans safe. Somewhere along the way we forgot that the enemies of our Constitution are both foreign and domestic. It appears that many people in government want us to believe that the greater danger is coming from people like the underwear bomber rather than from our own government.

Our government has, for years, been involved in "regime change" around the world, which includes the use of assassination. But up until February 3, 2010, there was no admission to such a policy or recognition of its illegality. On this date, before the House Intelligence Committee, the Director of National Intelligence (DNI) Dennis C. Blair admitted that indeed such a policy existed. American citizens can be assassinated at the direction of the U.S. government with the authority probably coming from the DNI. As he put it: "Being a U.S. citizen will not spare an American from getting assassinated by military or intelligence operatives."[2]

No longer trying to keep assassination top secret and even admitting it can involve an American citizen is a bold and scary change in attitude. Many people now believe that it is proper under the law, necessary for our security, and condoned

---

1. Glenn Greenwald, "Confirmed: Obama authorizes assassination of U.S. citizen." *Salon*, April 7, 2010. Salon.com.
2. This statement was made in Congressional testimony and is widely documented. See, e.g., http://www.democracynow.org/.

by both the people and their elected representatives in the Congress. Even more frightening is that the previously ridiculous notion that torture is legal is now more or less true—a rather sorry state of affairs.

Who would have ever believed that we could fall so far? The basic principle of the writ of habeas corpus has been around for 800 years, and so has the right not be in indefinite detention without charges. The justification for such abuse of the rule of law is all based on concocted fear by false claims associated with a lack of respect and understanding of what liberty is all about. It is constantly argued that danger in this post–9/11 period demands a different code of conduct to assure the people's safety. Possibly so. But it is further argued that only a few Americans are on the target list for assassination.

Possibly so, but so what? Tyranny always begins with oppression of unpopular minorities. If we wait for tyranny to target the mainstream and the majority, it will be too late. These targeted individuals are "suspects," not convicted criminals; nor, for the most part, are they even charged with a crime. Many innocent people have been held in secret prisons and tortured without legal counsel.

The perpetrators of the first Twin Towers bombing in 1993 were arrested, tried in New York City, and sentenced to life in prison. It is important that even the guilty have their day in court—not so much out of sympathy, for many are known to be evil, wicked men, but to keep us from ever slipping into a situation in which American citizens lose their right to have their day in court. Literally hundreds of terrorists have been tried in civilian courts in this country and convicted and did not have to be tried in secret military courts.

According to Dennis Blair, the justification for deciding who is to be assassinated is to declare an individual a "threat." No charges of a crime or plan to commit a crime are needed. Being a "threat" is a purely subjective term and is totally ambiguous. Casual acquaintance or associations based on false information can easily lead to deadly mistakes.

Certainly, speech that does not echo the party line or information that truthfully explains the nature and cause of anti-American activity can easily be construed as a threat to American policy overseas and a challenge to the current government. Blair claims that no one will be targeted for "free speech." I guess that is supposed to make us all rest more peacefully.

Anwar-al-Awlaki, the American citizen targeted by a CIA drone in Yemen, was never charged with a crime. The attack against Awlaki failed to kill him, but several others who were killed are now listed as statistics of collateral damage. More hatred of Americans will surely be generated by these constant events.

Government, once given power thought to be very limited in scope, is never restrained in expanding the use of its new-gotten power. Some people have perpetual desires for expanding government power and they frankly admit that, to achieve their goals, they never want any crisis to go to waste.

Enough Americans need to wake up and change this dangerous trend. But first they have to come to understand why no person should be exempt from the Bill of Rights when charged with violating U.S. law. The Constitution protects "persons," not just "citizens."

The war on terror slogan says "we are at war," and therefore protection of civil liberties is to be forfeited. But here is a fact: No war has been declared. The executive branch cannot ordain a war. The Congress and the courts are derelict in their duty if they do nothing to stop the madness of targeting American citizens for assassination before this evil precedent is perpetuated and more frequently used.

Belfield, Richard. 2005. *The Assassination Business: A History of State-Sponsored Murder.* New York: Carroll & Graf.

Napolitano, Andrew. 2006. *The Constitution in Exile: How the Federal Government Has Seized Power by Rewriting the Supreme Law of the Land.* Nashville, TN: Thomas Nelson.

AUSTRIAN ECONOMICS

The phrase "Austrian School" or "Austrian economics" is not something I ever expected would enter into the vocabulary of politics or media culture. But since 2008, it has. Reporters use it with some degree of understanding, and with an expectation that readers and viewers will understand it too. This is just thrilling to me, for I am a long-time student of the Austrian tradition of thought.

The phrase is often used as a synonym for free market economics. I don't object to this characterization, but it isn't exactly precise. It is possible to appreciate the role of markets without actually embracing the Austrian tradition, and it is possible to learn from the Austrian tradition without holding a particular political position. Nonetheless, the tradition has much to teach us and it goes far beyond the mere appreciation and defense of free enterprise.

The school of thought is named for the country of its modern founder, Carl Menger (1840–1921), an economist at the University of Vienna who made great contributions to the theory of value. He wrote that economic value extends from the human mind alone and is not something that exists as an inherent part of goods and services; valuation changes according to social needs and circumstances. We need markets to reveal to us the valuations of consumers and producers in the form of the price system that works within a market setting. In saying these things, he was really recapturing lost wisdom that had earlier been understood by Frédéric Bastiat (1801–1850), J. B. Say (1767–1832), A. R. J. Turgot (1727–1781), and many more throughout history. But history needs people like Menger to rediscover forgotten wisdom.

Menger built up a new school of thought in Austria with thinkers such as Eugen von Böhm-Bawerk (1851–1914), F. A. Hayek (1899–1992), Ludwig von Mises (1881–1973), Henry Hazlitt (1894–1993), Murray Rothbard (1926–1995), and Hans Sennholz (1922–2007) and gave rise to a huge number of philosophers, writers, financial analysts, and many others today who have learned from the tradition. The Austrian School champions private property, free markets, sound money, and the liberal society generally. It provides a way of looking at economics that takes into account the unpredictability of human action (absolutely no one can quantitatively know the future) and the huge role of human choice in the way economies work (in markets, consumers drive decisions over production), and explains how it is that order can emerge out of the seeming chaos of individual action. In short, the Austrian School provides the most robust defense of the economic system of the free society that has ever been made. This is why I often refer people to the Austrian School rather than speak about Adam Smith and the classical school, much less other schools of thought such as the Keynesian or Marxist schools.

People often forget that economists are not mere technicians who follow numbers. They are philosophers of sorts, thinkers who carry around certain assumptions about the way the economy works and society is built. The Austrian School had achieved mainstream status before the so-called Keynesian Revolution of the 1930s swept away the older wisdom. John Maynard Keynes turned truth on its head, arguing that saving is not a precursor to investment but rather a drag on the economy. He conceived of the various sectors of the economy (saving, investment, consumption, production, borrowing, lending) not as integrated through the price system but as homogeneous aggregates that are constantly colliding with one another. He imagined that wise central planners could know more than irrational market participants and correct for macroeconomic imbalances through manipulating market signals. More often than not, he proposed credit expansion as the solution to all that ails us. This entire agenda presumes the existence of a wise activist state that is involved in every level of economic life. Liberty was not an issue that concerned him.

He wrote at a time when the world fell in love with the idea of a planned economy and a planned society and lost its attachment to liberty as an ideal. From that point on through today, the Keynesian system has been in charge. But in our own times, the Austrian School has made a massive comeback in many different sectors, including academia, and this is in large part due to the work of private institutions such as the Ludwig von Mises Institute to show that the Austrian paradigm makes more sense of the way the world works than the bundle of fallacies that characterize the Keynesian system.

Ideas are very important to the shaping of society. In fact, they are far more powerful than bombs or armies or guns. And this is because ideas are capable of spreading without limit. They are behind all the choices we make. They can transform the world in a way that governments and armies cannot. Fighting for liberty with ideas makes much more sense to me than fighting with guns or politics or political power. With ideas, we can make real change that lasts.

The Austrian School believes this too, because it places such a high value on the subjective element of economics and on the individual as the primary economic unit. We are not cogs in a macroeconomic machine; people will always resist being treated as such. Economics should be as humanitarian as ethics or aesthetics or any other field of study.

Mises, Ludwig von. [1949] 1998. *Human Action: The Scholars Edition*. Auburn, AL: Mises Institute.

Paul, Ron. [1982] 2004. *Mises and Austrian Economics: A Personal View*. Auburn, AL: Mises Institute.

Rothbard, Murray. 1995. *An Austrian Perspective on the History of Economic Thought*. Auburn, AL: Mises Institute.

Bipartisanship

People often say that what this country needs is for people in Washington to stop fighting and just get the job done. To achieve that, we need more "bipartisanship." I don't agree. If two parties with two sets of bad ideas cooperate, the result is not good policy but policy that is extremely bad. What we really need are correct economic and political ideas, regardless of the party that pushes them.

For more than 100 years, the dominant views that have influenced our politicians have undermined the principles of personal liberty and private property. The tragedy is these bad policies have had strong bipartisan support. There has been no real opposition to the steady increase in the size and scope of government. Democrats are largely and openly for government expansion, and if we were to judge the Republicans by their actions and not their rhetoric, we would come to pretty much the same conclusion about them. When the ideas of both parties are bad, there is really only one hope: that they will continue fighting and not pass any new legislation. Gridlock can be the friend of liberty.

Some argue that what I say can't be true because Republicans are fighting with Democrats all the time, and legislation still gets passed. True, but all the fighting, despite the rhetoric, is only over which faction will control the power to pass out the benefits. The scramble to serve various special interests is real. Yet when it comes to any significant differences on foreign policy, economic intervention, the Federal Reserve, a strong executive branch, or welfarism mixed with corporatism, both parties are very much alike.

The major arguments and "hotly contested" presidential races are mostly for public consumption, to convince the people they actually have a choice. Republicans have been great at expanding the welfare state and running up the deficit despite their campaign promises. Democrats remain champions of foreign adventurism despite their effort to portray themselves as the peace party.

We have had way too much bipartisanship that promotes an agenda that has ignored constitutional restraints and free market principles. Many Republicans will argue that they stood strong against Obama's expansion of government-run medical care. It is true that they did, and that helped perpetuate the belief that the two parties are radically different. But we must remember that when Republicans were in charge just a few years ago, the government still expanded its role in medical care, and in very similar ways. The biggest difference is that the Republicans didn't advertise it.

So-called moderate politicians who compromise and seek bipartisanship are the most dangerous among the entire crew in Washington. Compromise is too often synonymous with "selling out," but it sounds a lot better. Honest politicians who state that their goal is total socialized medicine (or education, etc.) are met with a greater resistance; while people who favor the same thing but sell it as moderate bipartisanism slip by unnoticed. They are the ones who destroy our liberties incrementally, in the name of compromise and civility.

Incrementalism can only be justified if we regain some of our liberties and if the size and scope of government shrinks. The medical care debate of 2010 concluded with the radicals being held in check by the moderates who got them to back off from a single-payer system—i.e., socialized medicine. Yet the result was that we again moved significantly closer to that position. President Obama and the Congress agreed on a tax bill in late 2010 that retained some existing tax laws plus expanded unemployment insurance so that people could continue to stay off the labor rolls—and this was sold as a bipartisan "tax cut"!

Moderates are somehow convinced that they are the saviors of the country, rescuing us all from the effects of philosophical differences. In fact, philosophical differences are healthy because they lead to the clarification of principles. Genuine progress is going to require more confrontation, partisanship, and serious and honest discussion of the truth about government, the economy, and every sector of American life. It also needs politicians who can hold strong to their beliefs and do not compromise their core values. How sad a state we are in when it seems like such a stretch to expect that from a politician! We need to bring back some understanding of the idea of liberty and what it means. Bipartisanship will not help that process along, mainly because there are so few things on which the two parties agree that would be good for the country.

Higgs, Robert. 1989. *Crisis and Leviathan: Critical Episodes in the Growth of American Government*. New York: Oxford University Press.

Rothbard, Murray. 2006. *For a New Liberty*. Auburn, AL: Mises Institute.

BUSINESS CYCLE

In the midst of the "great recession" that began in earnest in 2008, there was no end to the talk about stimulus, yet hardly any talk about what causes recessions in the first place. The answer involves looking not at the downturn itself but at the structure of the preceding boom. Here is where the economic balance is tipped and production gets distorted. Rather than look at the recession as the disaster, we are better off looking at it as a period of healing following a false sense of prosperity generated by the boom times.

So what causes these economic booms—periods in which productivity expands in some sectors far beyond what the economic fundamentals seem to justify? Here we can draw on the Austrian theory of the business cycle, which was first sketched by Ludwig von Mises in the early days of central banking. He wrote that the central bank posed a serious danger due to its ability to manipulate the interest rate. Because artificially low rates cause an expansion of the money supply, these invented rates are central to understanding what causes booms. Mises wrote in 1923: "The first condition of any monetary reform is to halt the printing presses."[1]

The interest rate is a signal that tells bankers and businesses about the best times to expand production. When interest rates fall below their market rate, a false signal is sent out that there are more saved funds available for lending, so naturally, everyone starts to do more business and expand production. They feel they are getting a good deal. The mere process of simple lending acts to create new forms of money in the economy and thus create an economic boom. This boom is usually worsened by government promising bailouts to banks, loan guarantors, and enterprises, thereby encouraging bad investment and business by removing the fear of failure.

The combination of these factors is precisely what led to the wild housing boom from the 1990s and forward that came crashing down in 2008. There was nothing particularly new in this except that this time it happened to affect housing. In previous times, it had affected the stock market, the dot-com market, the oil market, and other sectors, all the way back to when the Federal Reserve Bank was created in 1913. Of course there were business cycles before that time, but they were not as severe and not as widespread, precisely because banking was not as centrally controlled as it has since become. But even back then, people understood the dangers of credit creation by banks and the false signals that they send to producers.

The problems of the business cycle are then exacerbated by

1. The Causes of the Economic Crisis, "Stabilization of the Monetary Unit," (Auburn, AL: Mises Institute, 2006), p. 14.

the attempt to prevent the bust from leveling out as the market would dictate. In other words, when a bust is looming, a frantic scrambling and even more artificial attempts to inflate the economy occur, which only worsens the inevitable correction. This tendency to use macroeconomic measures began under Herbert Hoover in 1930, a pattern that was continued by FDR. Hoover and FDR actually pushed the same agenda of high spending, attempted monetary expansion, controls on business, and efforts to keep wages high. FDR managed to take us farther down the road to serfdom only because he had longer in office.

One might suppose that the incredible failures of those efforts to work as planned would have discredited countercyclical policy forever. One might suppose that the same failures of Japanese policies that led to a twenty-year recession in Japan would also discredit these efforts. But not so: Both the Bush and Obama administrations (just like Hoover and FDR) have attempted to stimulate the economy through artifice and ended up causing enormous damage to the economy and to economic liberty.

We are currently at a crossroads, deciding which political and economic path to take. It all boils down to two choices: either more government or less. The true believers, still in charge, remain fully committed to central economic planning; others argue that enough is enough, the evidence is clear, and it's freedom we need, not more government interference.

The misguided remain adamant that to solve the problems of huge malinvestment and debt that have been caused by Federal Reserve–orchestrated low interest rates, the government's obligation is to come up with more creative regulations.

They aim for even lower interest rates by creating trillions of dollars of new money, all while increasing spending and debt. Grade-school math can show you why this won't work. I am dumbfounded to hear serious, highly educated political leaders enthusiastically endorse such a program with straight faces.

Over the decades, Keynesianism has generated a false confidence—a moral hazard of immense proportion, as former Fed chairman Paul Volcker has admitted. The Federal Reserve, the regulatory agencies, and Congress have systematically taught the American people to trust the government to be there when trouble strikes and that caution in investing, spending, and debt is harmful to the economy.

All the mistakes of the past decades are now clearly revealing themselves. And yet, since Washington has not changed its ways in the slightest, the needed corrections will be long in coming. If blame is to be placed for the mess we're in, don't just pick on George Bush and Barack Obama. Blame Lord Keynes and all his followers who rejected the Austrian theory of the business cycle. It is bad theory that is the root of the problem, the belief that the central banks can turn stones into bread.

Simply put: If we want to cure the bust, don't create the boom. Economic growth must be based on real factors, not phony stimulus provided by the central bank.

Mises, Ludwig von. [1912] 2009. *The Theory of Money and Credit.* Auburn, AL: Mises Institute.

Schiff, Peter D., and Andrew J. 2010. *How an Economy Grows and Why It Crashes.* Hoboken, NJ: John Wiley and Sons.

Campaign Finance Reform

O ur ongoing political agenda is filled with phony reforms that purport to curb the influence of "bad people" in Washington, and campaign finance reform is always one of these issues. The incentive is so great to buy influence, even before it becomes necessary to lobby for favors, that the "investment" in government begins with elections. All the reforms in the world will not eliminate the corruption in this system. Certainly, regulating elections will not do so, and the attempt alone threatens our liberties to work within the system in order to change the system.

The McCain-Feingold Act, or the Bipartisan Campaign Reform Act, of 2002 was the most recent attack on the First Amendment's protection of political speech. Twice in lower courts the restrictions on corporations and unions were upheld. The Supreme Court dropped a bombshell in January 2010 when it ruled by a five-to-four margin (*Citizens United v. Federal Election Commission*) that McCain-Feingold was unconstitutionally restricting free speech. That brought loud dissent from those who don't mind using government power to restrict political activity; these same people do not even entertain the thought that excessive spending on campaigning is a symptom of corrupt big government.

If there were less to buy through influencing campaigns, there would be a lot less incentive to invest so much in the process. The size of government violates the Constitution and, in particular, its rather narrow enumerated powers (read the Constitution for yourself and see how few there really are); and the problem is further compounded by regulating free speech, which also undermines the Constitution. Those who attack the court's decision say that corporations and unions have no rights of free speech, following the flawed belief that government can regulate commercial speech in advertising. This is especially harmful when it comes to producers of vitamins and nutritional products, companies that aren't even permitted to explain what they believe are the health benefits that come from the use of their products, thereby denying consumers useful information. The notion that political speech and commercial speech are two different entities must be rejected. Speech should not be subject to prior restraint.

Corporations don't have rights per se, but the individual who happens to own a corporation or belong to a union does have rights, and these rights are not lost by merely acting through another organization.

If the right of free speech is lost because individuals belong to corporations, then radio and TV stations, newspapers and magazines, and various groups on the Internet would be subject to prior restraint by the government. Those who argue against permitting corporations to spend money on elections would never argue that corporate media entities like CNN should be legally barred from influencing opinion. The rights of the media are not inconsequential considering how the media can make or destroy a candidate with biased reporting, especially close to elections.

This whole complex issue is nothing more than a predictable consequence of government overreach and a flawed attempt to rectify what appears to be an injustice. Sadly, any effort to remove the incentive to buy government simply by sharply reducing the size and scope of government (thereby making less available to buy in the first place) would be met with great resistance from both liberals and conservatives.

The $2,400 campaign donation limit per person in federal elections makes no sense. How could it be that the right to support a candidate is arbitrarily limited to a dollar amount? And why that dollar amount? Yes, it is correct that the amount of money being spent on elections is obscene, but it's understandable to me, since much is to be gained by financially participating in the process. Government is a growth industry, and tragically so. The real obscenity is the size of government and its intrusion into every aspect of our economic and personal lives, which generates the financial interest and involvement in the elections.

Campaign laws simply won't solve the problem. Even if stricter laws were passed, the stakes are so great that the financing would just go underground (or under the table), as is not infrequently done under current conditions. The corruption is not eliminated; it merely takes other forms.

As bad as the process is, there is an even worse solution offered: taxpayer-financed elections. Talk about abusing rights! Can one imagine the eruption of the Tea Party's anger if those who are disgusted and angry have to pay out of pocket for the campaign of two individuals they find grossly offensive?

———•———

Fridson, Martin. 2006. *Unwarranted Intrusions: The Case Against Government Intervention in the Marketplace.* New York: John Wiley & Sons.

Higgs, Robert. 1997. "The Futility of Campaign Finance Reform." Independent Institute. http://www.independent.org.

CAPITAL PUNISHMENT

B elievers in the omnipotence of state military power are
enthusiastic supporters of the death penalty. It's strange
to me that those who champion best the rights of pre-born
are generally the strongest supporters of the death penalty and
preventive, that is, aggressive, war. Ironically, those who find
the death penalty an affront to life are usually the strongest
supporters of abortion.

I grant that there certainly is a difference in the life being
protected; one is totally innocent—the unborn—and the other
usually a person convicted of a horrible crime, like murder or
rape. The difference of opinion is usually along the lines of
conservative versus liberal.

This is one issue in which my views have shifted in recent
years, especially since being elected to Congress. There was a
time I simply stated that I supported the death penalty. Now
my views are not so clearly defined. I do not support the federal death penalty, but constitutionally I cannot, as a federal
official, interfere with the individual states that impose it.

After years spent in Washington, I have become more

aware than ever of the government's ineptness and the likelihood of its making mistakes. I no longer trust the U.S. government to invoke and carry out a death sentence under any conditions. Too many convictions, not necessarily federal, have been found to be in error, but only after years of incarcerating innocent people who later were released on DNA evidence.

Rich people when guilty are rarely found guilty and sentenced to death. Most people believe O. J. Simpson was guilty of murder but went free. This leads to a situation where innocent people without enough money are more likely to get the death penalty while the guilty rich people with good lawyers get off.

For me it's much easier just to eliminate the ultimate penalty and incarcerate the guilty for life—in case later evidence proves a mistaken conviction. The cost of incarceration is likely less than it is for death penalty appeals drawn out not for years but for decades.

This issue is not only about mistakes that governments make. It is about the power they wield. If the government can legally kill, it can do just about anything else short of that. I no longer believe that government should be trusted with this power. All power is likely to be abused, and disproportionately so against the government's own enemies.

This is not to argue that some of the convicted are not truly guilty of the charges and deserve the death penalty, which they might have received instantaneously if caught in the midst of a violent life-threatening act against a loved one in someone's home.

The ineptness of government, the mistakes it is capable of

making, the innocent people convicted, the power rush that judges might get from taking away life, the advantage of the rich over the poor are not the only things that influenced my change in attitude. The numbing effect on the executioner—that is, society—is also a factor. It contributes to the dehumanizing of society and the casual acceptance of the relative value of life. People realize this and most want no part of the process, except maybe out of vengeance.

Why are executions made sterile and easy, nothing more than a medical procedure? Would the public support execution by beheading on TV? No way. Killing in a deliberate manner, not out of immediate self-defense, fortunately, is not something most people want to gloat over. If individuals don't want to watch it or participate in it, it indicates there's something uncivilized about it.

Even the killing by our soldiers, though they have been conditioned to be killers, is a significant cause of psychological devastation and mental illness, which is obviously made worse when those killed are innocent bystanders written off as collateral damage. This is all tragic and indicates that taking life has consequences, even on the living.

The death penalty does have an effect on the society that endorses it. The more civilized the society is, the more likely it has moved away from a casual or careless administration of the death penalty. The more authoritarian a government becomes, the greater is the number of executions.

Those who are vocal supporters of the right to life of the unborn should be encouraged to rethink the issue of blanket support of the death penalty and their militant support for aggressive wars.

The Founders of this country, I would assume, supported the death penalty, though the way the Constitution was written, that decision was left to the individual states. They wrote only three federal crimes into the Constitution: counterfeiting, treason, and piracy, with slavery, including involuntary servitude, being added by the Thirteenth Amendment. In the Coinage Act of 1792, the death penalty was authorized for counterfeiting the currency. This is not an unexpected application of government power over life and death; too often it is used not against actual criminals but rather enemies of the state.

Consider the case of Julian Assange, the founder of Wiki-Leaks. After he spread diplomatic documents, the long knives came out. Bill O'Reilly said that Assange was a traitor and "should be executed." Sarah Palin said that he ought to be targeted "like the Taliban." Ralph Peters of Fox News said, "I would execute leakers." Mike Huckabee said, "I think anything less than execution is too kind a penalty." Glenn Beck said Assange should be executed. G. Gordon Liddy said he should be put on a kill list.[1]

In the end, Assange is just one man with a laptop and he was merely releasing what is true, information that embarrassed many but harmed no one. And this is the man that so many think ought to be subject to the death penalty? Government always uses its power to punish its own enemies, but its enemies are not necessarily our enemies.

Plus, there is a terrible hypocrisy at work here. Is the

1. There are many, many more examples of this archived at FreedomRadio .com, with complete citations to each case.

government really the institution to stand in judgment? Just think of what it would be like if all those individuals in Washington responsible for counterfeiting our currency or forcing unconstitutional penalties on us through the tax system were to be punished with the death penalty. It wouldn't be pretty. It's best we change our system rather than think people such as Assange, or others digging for the truth, are treasonous and should be executed.

Though the individual states have discretion on how to punish those who commit violent crimes, at the national level the consistent right-to-life position should be to protect the unborn and oppose abortion, to reject the death penalty, and to firmly oppose our foreign policy that promotes an empire requiring aggressive wars that involve thousands of innocent people being killed. We would all be better off for it, and a society dedicated to peace, human life, and prosperity would more likely to be achieved.

———————

Bedau, Hugo Adam. 2005. *Debating the Death Penalty: Should America Have Capital Punishment? The Experts on Both Sides Make Their Case.* New York: Oxford University Press.

Jacquette, Dale. 2009. *Dialogues on the Ethics of Capital Punishment.* New York: Rowman & Littlefield.

CENTRAL INTELLIGENCE AGENCY

M ost Americans know little about the Central Intelligence Agency. Too many of those who do know falsely believe it serves our national security interest. Today, if anyone criticizes the CIA or the principle of its existence, he is portrayed as being sympathetic to the terrorists.

But the CIA, for the most part, has had a failed record. Its credibility deservedly dropped after its participation in the lies told by the administration regarding the weapons of mass destruction that Saddam Hussein was supposed to have possessed. This is not to say there aren't many agents in the CIA with very good intentions and a good record. Some have resigned in disgust. Others who have retired have been willing to speak out objectively and have been helpful in providing vital information about how the CIA has gone astray.

Intelligence gathering by governments about their enemies and potential enemies is an old practice that will continue as long as governments exist. Such intelligence gathering is a completely separate issue from the secret activities of the

CIA that involve assassination, regime change, torture, secret rendition, and rigging foreign elections.

Legitimate intelligence should be a narrowly defined and tightly controlled process. If it isn't, by its very nature it can get totally out of control with clandestine operations. An all-powerful, all-secret intelligence agency can become a government unto itself.

The CIA was officially established in 1947 by the National Security Act. It replaced the Office of Strategic Services, which was started during World War II. Intelligence gathering as we know it today was never part of our early history; especially when a declared war was not being fought. Since its creation, the CIA has been responsible for instigating every manner of political instability abroad, wildly exaggerating threats to the United States (as it did with the Soviet Union), and going around both Congress and the White House to achieve its own bureaucratic and political priorities. Today, the intelligence operation is huge, complex, and out of control.

The first major use of the CIA to interfere in the election process of a country was in 1953 with the overthrow of the duly elected leader of Iran, Mohammad Mosadeck. Our numerous CIA involvements have included assassination, assisting coups, rigging elections, and holding mock elections.[1] Overthrowing foreign governments is illegal under international law and common law. It's illegal under U.S. law and the Constitution. Morally it has no place in a country that professes to be a constitutional republic.

The CIA's involvement abroad is unbelievably complex and

---

1. "Secrets of History: The CIA in Iran," *New York Times*, April 16, 2000.

pervasive. It is not thoroughly monitored by Congress and even our presidents don't have full knowledge of what the CIA does, since it has the ability to self-finance. The CIA is an active participant in waging wars, with control of the drone bombing of any country seen as a potential enemy in the future. Obviously, this is a dangerous power to wield, especially in secret. Rigging elections and secretly killing our supposed enemies is now seen as a relatively acceptable policy. Using contractors to carry out clandestine operations makes it even harder for the CIA's activities to be monitored or understood. To say the least, with its ability to self-finance, the CIA, including its parent organization and sister agencies, is a uniquely powerful entity.

In 2004, as a consequence of 9/11, Congress created the office of the Director of National Intelligence (DNI). This office is theoretically supposed to be in charge of the CIA and sixteen agencies of the U.S. intelligence community. Its size and scope make it virtually impossible for the DNI to be an efficient protector of all our interests and to supervise all the agencies' activities.

To operate all these spy agencies costs American taxpayers an estimated $80 billion per year.[2] I say "estimated" because precise numbers are secret information and difficult even for members of Congress to get. Yet when these agencies get a significant lead like a phone call from the father of a potential terrorist, as was the case with Umar Farouk Abdulmutallab, no one acts on it. It seems we're not getting our money's worth when it comes to the intelligence we're paying for.

---

2. "Total U.S. Intelligence Bill Revealed for First Time," Associated Press, October 28, 2010.

As always, whenever anything fails in Washington, the answer is more government and more money. We certainly did that after 9/11 with the establishment of the Department of Homeland Security. One thing is for certain: The intelligence agencies may not improve, but the American people will *not only* lose more of their money through higher taxes, but personal liberties will also be attacked. Legislation like the Patriot Act can be passed easily after any attack—serious like 9/11 or almost silly ones, like the underwear bomber.

Intelligence-gathering shortcomings are met with ever more panic and spending mania. Eighty billion dollars is not enough. We need much more. We don't have too many bureaucrats involved; we need more. Where does it end? At total government control and utter bankruptcy? They never want to ask or admit that we're endangered as a *consequence* of our foreign policy. They don't want to change that. They believe that with greater and more pervasive spying we can compensate for a policy that will inevitably generate more people around the world who will want to harm us. Treating the symptoms will not cure the disease.

In a truly free republic, there would be no need for super-spy agencies. The threats would be fewer and concern for violating the civil liberties and privacy of citizens would be paramount. I don't argue for a complete abolishment of intelligence gathering, but I do strongly object to the size and scope of what has developed in this country. Most of the time, common sense, warnings that come to us, and information in the public domain can do as well as the current ineptness or deliberate deception of the proactive activities of the CIA and its involvement in the affairs of other nations.

Countries such as Sweden and Switzerland spend minuscule amounts on military preparation. Costa Rica has no military at all. These countries are not threatened, because they are regarded as nonaggressive. They naturally are far less threatened—though they are "free and prosperous"—by outsiders wanting to terrorize their citizens.

The failure of our spy agencies to warn us of major events is an obvious shortcoming and to be expected from a complex, massively bureaucratic system. But what occurred leading up to the Iraq War and how the CIA was used to produce false intelligence at the urging of the politicians who wanted the war is more than a disgrace. It's immoral—and illegal. It's amazing to me that the outrage over this is not more palpable.

Today, the United States beats the war drums against a host of countries that we are antagonizing and provoking. Intelligence assessments claim that countries from Pakistan to Yemen, Iran, and North Korea are all planning to do us harm one way or another. The CIA is not serving our security interests by participating in this charade of overblown danger.

The old fallback has always been that the Congress has ultimate control through the appropriations process. There's evidence that the CIA can do its own funding through illegal drug trafficking.[3] Instead of trying to stop drugs, the CIA is capable of benefiting from the size of drug operations around the world. Congress in these circumstances is totally ineffective on oversight.

3. Coletta Youngers, Eileen Rosin, eds. *Drugs and Democracy in Latin America: The Impact of U.S. Policy* (Boulder, CO: Lynne Rienner Publishers, 2005), p. 206.

Generally, though, Congress never cuts back on the CIA budget, even when members suspect corruption and waste. Not supporting the CIA and its activities is considered un-American and unpatriotic. It's similar to the continued appropriations of money for illegal undeclared wars. Many of the antiwar members of Congress who want the wars to end can't vote against the funding or they will be accused of "not supporting the troops." Political pressure from whomever is President prompts his party members to support bad wars and intelligence operations even if they are out of control.

The suicide bombing attack against the CIA outpost on a military base in Khost, Afghanistan, on December 30, 2009, should have surprised no one. Seven CIA agents were killed. The agents were only following orders, doing what they were told to do. The tragedy is that the people who ordered the CIA to drone-bomb North Waziristan (Pakistan) are implementing a deeply flawed, immoral policy of preventive war against the people of Pakistan.

It's the ultimate tragedy to see any American killed. It's quite rare for a CIA agent to be killed, yet hundreds if not thousands of people are killed around the world by our CIA agents and military, supposedly making us all "safe and secure" here at home. Some people are being murdered on orders of our own government around the world, so we can expect the violence to continue and the retaliation against the CIA to increase.[4]

Changing the whole notion of the intelligence agencies is

---

4. Jacob Hornberg, "More CIA Killings, Lies, and Cover-Ups," November 21, 2008, FFF.org.

crucial. Since the motivation and acceptance of CIA activity is to protect us from potential suicide bombers, this cannot be reversed unless we get an answer to this question: Why are some willing to commit suicide to do us harm? I believe the answer relates directly to the recklessness of U.S. foreign policy. If we don't get this answer, the fix is in—tyranny. If the truth be known, we would all be safer if the CIA in its current form were to be abolished.

———◦———

Faddis, Charles S. 2010. *Beyond Repair: The Decline and Fall of the CIA*. Guilford, CT: Lyons Press.

Weiner, Tim. 2008. *Legacy of Ashes: The History of the CIA*. New York: Anchor Books.

CIVIL DISOBEDIENCE

I strongly believe in the principle of peaceful civil disobedience. It is one way that the impulse to liberty checks the powerful. I have not participated in it—except by refusing to participate in the usual congressional vote-trading games—but I support those who have, from both the left and the right of the political spectrum. Many war resisters have been arrested and imprisoned all the way back to the Civil War and even all the way back to the Whiskey Rebellion. Protests against slavery and segregation have prompted many to peacefully demonstrate and challenge the law. Protests against the tax code and the unconstitutional monetary system are growing more frequent.

Any protest, even when protected by the Constitution, is regarded by those in power as a dangerous challenge to the authority of the state. It is indeed that. Much good has come from these protests, and sadly, many good people have been imprisoned for years and sometimes for life because of their protests.

Though I have not chosen this method of protest and instead have chosen to promote change through education and political action, I admire people who do so as long as it's nonviolent and the participants understand exactly what is at stake. It's conceivable that someday I might consider it the only option. What tactic one chooses is strictly a personal choice. The greatest benefit of civil disobedience is the publicity it generates. This serves as an educational tool, so eventually it will help to change bad laws or stop an ill-conceived war. Although limited, it is more practical to believe that just because a protester is morally and constitutionally right, justice will be achieved in the courts.

However, our courts are just as "corrupted" with bad ideas as are the executive and the legislative branches of our government. Great changes have been achieved through civil disobedience, and the heroes who engaged in it deserve our gratitude. Their real reward comes from the inner satisfaction of pursuing the truth as they see it—not from a sense of sacrificing for the greater good.

Admiring someone who practices peaceful civil disobedience and perseveres for long periods doesn't mean that one has to agree with that individual's entire philosophy. I like what Martin Luther King, Jr., did to eliminate state-enforced segregation; the use of the boycott is a great tool to promote peaceful change, and King spoke out brilliantly against the unconstitutional and pointless slaughter of the Vietnam War. I do not believe, however, that his economic views were supportive of the free market. Even as he became more radical, and correct, on the Vietnam War, he moved to the left on economic issues.

This is regrettable but also highly conventional. In my view, there is a general tendency for people who are correct on war to be wrong on economics, and the same tendency for people who are correct on economics to be wrong on war. As sure as a person is willing to stand up against the Iraq war for its cost and militarization, he will be arguing for expanded and tax-paid health care at home. And sure as a person denounces big government at home, he will argue for dramatic expansions of military power. If we had a consistent philosophy of peace and freedom, we would oppose both socialism and war and be willing to fight against all forms of statism, whether domestic or international.

Sometimes the domestic and international intersect in ways that remind us of this truth. This is when disobedience is especially necessary. There are many unsung heroes who have stood up against the involuntary servitude of the draft, especially when fighting in undeclared and unconstitutional wars. One of the best known to suffer prosecution for his beliefs and resistance was Muhammad Ali. Though he had joined the Nation of Islam and argued he was a conscientious objector, he was still arrested for refusing to serve and go to Vietnam in 1966. His summation of his beliefs as to why he refused became classic. Simply, he said: "I ain't got no quarrel with the Viet Cong."[1] No other American did either!

Ali was found guilty in a Houston court in 1967, sentenced to five years in prison, and fined $10,000—the jury took twenty-one minutes. He lost his title and was banned from boxing for seven years. After five years, the Supreme Court unanimously ruled in favor of Ali. He never served a day in prison but nevertheless paid a high price for his convictions.

Sports writer Harold Conrad said after the conviction and

1. "Muhammad Ali: The Greatest," *Time*, June 14, 1999.

sentencing: "He threw this life away on one toss of the dice for something he believed in. Not many folks do that."[2] True, "not many folks do that," but I disagree that he threw his life away. That fight, against the state, he eventually won, though at a cost, and history may show that it was the best of all his fights and the one that should have given him the greatest sense of dignity and pride.

At the time, Ali's resistance to war and the military draft was seen by a majority of Americans to be "unpatriotic." But they did not understand that patriotism is the act of standing up to the government when the government is wrong, and at great risk stand firmly on principles that protect the freedoms of all people. Those who resist the state nonviolently, based on their own principles, deserve our support.

The opposite approach to protest is the use of violence. Violence is a terrible agent of social change. Individuals advocating or participating in violence, on occasion, will associate with certain groups and falsely give the impression that they are acting as a bona fide member of the group. The media rarely have any desire to sort out the facts, especially if the group that is being wrongly blamed represents anti–big government views. FBI agents will infiltrate certain groups they deem dangerous. Government itself, spying on any private group, is dangerous to our Fourth Amendment rights, which is something people tend to forget. The argument usually is that it's necessary to keep the American people safe. There have been many examples where the government official not

2. "The Greatest Is Gone," *Time*, February 27, 1978.

only urges the breaking of the law but participates in it so the suspects can be caught red-handed. It was this abuse of the law that led to the tragedy of Ruby Ridge (where the government killed a man's wife in a pointless hunt in 1992[3]) and the entrapment of various "militia" groups. It has been used in drug investigations as well. The use of government agents to encourage the breaking of laws in a sting operation represents government violence that can surpass the violence of the suspected criminals.

I personally don't know of any organized group that is calling for the violent overthrow of our government. There are many individuals demanding a more just system that doesn't reward the well connected with bailouts, nor punish those who ask only to be totally self-reliant and not be forced to be a ward or victim of the state.

The vast majority of Americans detest the mere thought of violence as a legitimate tool for bringing about political changes. Nearly everyone still believes that changes are available through the political process. Many who feel helpless working in the very messy political system still see the benefits of working to change attitudes through education and understanding. Others endorse the principle of peaceful civil disobedience as a means for bringing about political changes. This is a legitimate tool that was practiced by many in the civil rights movement in order to eliminate arcane laws that forced segregation.

Martin Luther King, Jr., understood its merit and the obvious risk of imprisonment and becoming the victim of government

---

3. A good roundup of the case can be found at Wikipedia /Ruby_Ridge, accessed December 15, 2010.

violence. Civil disobedience is a form of personal nullification of unfair and unconstitutional laws. Even the current left-wing pundits, who condemn all nullification arguments by strict constitutionalists, would hardly fail to see this comparison.

Civil disobedience is a process whereby the weak and defenseless can resist the violence perpetuated by the state. The great danger is that when government gets too powerful and abusive, a greater number of citizens give up on education, politics, and peaceful resistance to bring about change and drift toward violent resistance to the state. The line between them is always murky, and some people are always overly anxious to resort to combating government violence with citizen violence. Though this type of conflict resulted in our own revolution against Britain, my personal nature compels me to argue for peaceful persuasion to bring about the understanding necessary to advance the cause of liberty.

People must understand that we can't use violence to have our own way over others—nor should the agents of our government have that power. Even a majority vote should never be accepted as legitimatizing government's use of violence against the people.

King, Martin Luther, Jr. 2001. *The Autobiography of Martin Luther King*. New York: Grand Central Publishing.

Rockwell, Llewellyn H., Jr. 2008. *The Left, the Right, and the State*. Auburn, AL: Mises Institute.

Thoreau, Henry David. [1849] 1998. *Civil Disobedience*. Amherst, NY: Prometheus Books.

CONSCRIPTION

D o we own our bodies and ourselves? We do, and it is based on this belief that we, as a country and society, reject slavery. We are not shy about saying it: Slavery is immoral. In the same way, moral law should be all that is needed to prohibit the state from forcing certain individuals into involuntary servitude in the military for the purpose of waging wars against an enemy, real or imaginary.

The Constitution provides no authority to draft certain groups of young people to serve in the military. Conscription was not used in the Revolutionary War and it was soundly rejected by the Congress in the midst of the British attack on Washington in the War of 1812.

Lincoln precipitated draft riots during the Civil War, and the effort to force conscription on the American people hurt the war effort and offered no benefit. It was Woodrow Wilson in his holy war to promote worldwide democracy who established the principle of the draft as a patriotic duty. The Thirteenth Amendment outlawing involuntary servitude has been a narrowly construed amendment, not applying to the eighteen-to-thirty-five-year-olds most susceptible to military slavery.

Just as an income tax sends the message about who owns us and the fruits of our labor (even when the tax is only 1 percent), the draft and the registration for it remind every eighteen-year-old that ultimately the government controls his fate. The state can kidnap you at any time. This is an outrage that should never be tolerated in any society.

A free society, valued by the people, would be adequately defended by volunteers, without age, sex, or any other restrictions. It is the unpopular wars, the big ones, that require conscription, and the state wants always to be prepared. It is great that we haven't had a draft for nearly forty years, but the requirement that all young people register for a possible draft persists.[1] If we are to regain our liberties, one change that should be made is to repeal draft registration. Getting rid of the need for a standing voluntary army or armies backed up by the draft requires, in addition to honoring individual rights, a foreign policy of nonintervention that diminishes the chances of war.

Military historians have shown that a conscripted army has no economic advantage over a volunteer army. Likewise, there

---

1. SSS.gov says: "Almost all male U.S. citizens, and male aliens living in the U.S., who are 18 through 25, are required to register with Selective Service. It's important to know that even though he is registered, a man will not automatically be inducted into the military. In a crisis requiring a draft, men would be called in sequence determined by random lottery number and year of birth. Then, they would be examined for mental, physical and moral fitness by the military before being deferred or exempted from military service or inducted into the Armed Forces."

are no military advantages for using conscripted soldiers for conflict.[2]

A draft can never be fair; it can't be universal since there's never a need for everyone to be put on active duty. Discrimination by age is the first tool used to pick and choose those who must go. In our times, someone over thirty-five is just as capable of serving in the military as someone eighteen. Yet rarely are those over thirty-five, forty-five, or fifty-five ever forced into the military. And there are also many other reasons for deferrals or exemptions: health, student status, religious beliefs, needs in a family business, needs in industry, etc.

There are always plans to make the next draft fair and without exemptions, but it has never worked that way in the past. The rich were allowed to pay a substitute to fight in their place in the Civil War, and ever since then there have always been exceptions, many of them political. The wars since World War II were never declared, and Korea and Vietnam were fought with draftees. The example set by some famous "chicken-hawks" not only should draw severe criticism from all Americans but show how a draft can be manipulated by privileged individuals.

Chicken-hawks are individuals who dodged the draft when their numbers came up but who later became champions of senseless and undeclared wars when they were influencing foreign policy. Former Vice President Cheney is the best example of this disgraceful behavior. When it became known

2. Jeffrey Rogers Hummel, "The American Militia and the Origin of Conscription: A Reassessment," *Journal of Libertarian Studies*, Volume 15, Number 4 (Fall 2001): pp. 29–77.

that Cheney got five student deferrals and never served in the 1960s, he was quizzed about it and blew it off by saying that he had "other priorities." At the time he said this he was the chief architect of the war in Iraq, and he has remained dedicated to our omnipresence in the Middle East for the purpose of remaking it in our and Israel's interest.

In Congress, at this time, there is essentially no interest in reinstating the draft, but neither is there any interest in my legislation to repeal the Selective Service Act. The strongest current support for the draft comes from the Congressional Black Caucus, which is a bit ironic since minorities were discriminated against in the 1960s in implementing the draft. Minorities served in greater numbers during the Vietnam and the Korean wars and suffered a greater percentage of fatalities and casualties than whites. At times there were justified outcries from minority groups because the Dick Cheneys of the world were able to evade the draft while minorities suffered disproportionately.

Now the argument against this position is that, though it's a voluntary army, blacks disproportionately serve and suffer casualties compared to whites. And this is true. But today no one serves who doesn't volunteer. It hardly makes sense that the draft is the salvation to this dilemma since it was and always has been arbitrary. But the proponents argue that the next time there's a draft it will be different. It never is.

One thing that has helped recent recruitment has been the weak economy; people join for economic reasons, possibly explaining why minorities volunteer in greater proportion than whites. But even before the recent downturn, a weaker economy than the government admits to over the past decade pushed a lot of people into augmenting their pay by joining the Reserves and the Guard units, never expecting that Bush and Obama would be so dependent on the reservists for multiple tours of duty to the Middle East.

Prohibiting members of the military to leave when their tours are up is essentially a de facto draft—this stop-loss program has been severely criticized by the personnel and the families who suffer from it.

With the current military exhausted and the increasing odds of armed conflict, the specter of the draft is once again raised. For now, though, the disastrously weak economy will serve the interest of the state by prompting many individuals to volunteer, despite the risks involved.

Conscription should never be part of a free society. It's not permitted in the United States since our Constitution does not provide the authority to force someone into involuntary duty to fight a war. Slavery is precisely forbidden, and that's what involuntary service is.

Countries that conscript or have the capacity to conscript are more likely to get involved in unnecessary political wars. Much more important than having a military made up of massive standing armies, navies, air forces, marines, military contractors, and the CIA to make us "safe" would be to have a foreign policy that makes sense. It would be a lot cheaper, and we would never have to resort to the draft to defend the country and keep us safe.

Ronald Reagan, among other conservatives, opposed the draft. Robert Taft ("Mr. Republican") was a strong opponent. Hanging in my congressional office is the following quote from Taft: "A compulsory draft is . . . far more typical of a totalitarian nation than of a democratic nation. The theory behind it leads directly to totalitarianism. It is absolutely opposed to the principle of individual liberty which has always been considered a part of American democracy" (August 14, 1940).

Henderson, David R. 2010. "From 'Porous' to 'Ruthless' Conscription, 1776–1917." *Independent Review.* http://www.independent.org.

Higgs, Robert. 2005. *Against Leviathan: Government Power and a Free Society.* Independent Institute. http://www.independent.org.

Webster, Daniel. 1814. "On Conscription," reprinted in *Left and Right*, Volume 1, Number 2, Spring 1965.

DEMAGOGUES

Politics breeds demagogues—politicians and media pundits alike. The word "demagogue" itself dates to the ancient world because the phenomenon is that old. Demagogues seek influence and political power by appealing to the prejudices, emotions, fears, and expectations of the public. They do not enlighten; they browbeat and play rhetorical games.

Demagoguery is the enemy of liberty and serves the interest of power seekers across the political spectrum. Government attracts all those who enjoy using power over others and those who convince themselves that average people need "smart" people to take care of them. And only the demagogues can provide the "wisdom" to appoint those who should rule over us. When the goal of political action is no longer the defense of liberty, no word other than demagoguery can describe the despicable nature of politics.

Demagogues manipulate a political issue in a manner to obscure or distort truth with emotionalism and prejudice. The goal of all demagogues is to achieve power at all costs.

Dictators accomplish this by brute force; in democracies,

demagogues do it the same way but camouflage the brute force with idealistic declarations of being humanitarian saviors. Even brutal dictators must convince a gullible public that the violence is required to do good for the people. This is true whether it's Soviet-style communism, French Jacobinism, the environmental alarmists, the current neoconservatives, or the cradle-to-grave welfarists.

Though the demagogues on the right and left are true competitors for power, they share a belief in state power and the techniques and tools of the demagogue. The purpose is to take a principled stand by the proponents of liberty and reason and turn it into support for something ugly and mean by gross distortion of the truth.

The right is vocal in condemning opposition to the Bush-Obama doctrine of preventive war as being unpatriotic, un-American, and against the troops. If one opposes a constitutional amendment to ban flag burning, it's considered unpatriotic and un-American. If one lacks enthusiasm for the war on drugs, it's charged that that person doesn't care about kids and would promote drug use for them. Opposing foreign aid draws charges, from right and left, of nefarious motivations. Also, among this crowd, if you have doubts about using the federal government as an instrument for imposing a particular cultural or religious agenda, you are regarded with suspicion and called an opponent of uprightness and morality.

The left is every bit as aggressive in impugning their opponents' character when criticizing a principled stand for private property. Defending states' rights and the Tenth Amendment, according to the left, is to flirt with racism and even support slavery. But they get tongue-tied when challenged on the issue by a state like California legalizing medicinal mari-juana, whether or not they endorse the heavy hand of the Federal Drug Administration's overriding of all state laws on the drug issue.

The great heinous thought crime related to race relations is to argue that private property owners have a right to use that property as they please, as long as they do not commit violence against another person. Strict private property control is now seen as the most evil position anyone can take. To argue for the freedom to choose, which necessarily means the freedom to include or exclude others, is seen as evidence of malice. Evidently, property can only be used by permission from the state. International, national, state, and local governments along with various courts "own" the land and all businesses, and we must answer to the bureaucrats to get legal permits to use it.

To suggest that, in a free society where property is owned by the people, the owners of a business establishment have a right to pick and choose customers and workers and to make only mutually agreed-to economic transactions is seen as the worst possible gaffe. In fact, this right is at the core of the libertarian position. It is the essence of the freedom of association. There is no getting around it: Freedom of association also implies the freedom not to associate. To restrict this association based on some subjective evaluation of a person's motivations is necessarily to impose on the freedom and rights of others.

A serious-minded liberal or progressive, not the demagogue, should consider the analogy of the First Amendment. It is a well-known and accepted tenet of the left that the First

Amendment is designed to protect controversial and disagreeable speech. Benign conversation needs no protection. All religions and political beliefs are protected, even those considered bizarre, as long as they are nonviolent in nature.

Use of property should be viewed the same way. In fact, free speech is protected by a clear right of private property. The properties that house magazines, newspapers, electronic media, the Internet, and churches are (supposed to be) immune from government surveillance and control. Prior restraint in the propagation of information is prohibited. If property is protected for these purposes, it shouldn't be such a giant leap to understand why all property should be equally protected.

For this reason, people who burn American flags, provided that they own them and burn them on their own property, are deserving of defense. I'm never so embarrassed by the Republican Party than when it demagogues issues like flag burning and saying the Pledge of Allegiance. These are despicable campaign tactics.

Americans should be willing to stand up for the rights of all. So it is with many private acts we might otherwise object to. The home must be protected. We pick our friends, our partners, our guests, and our sexual practices. We decide who enters and who must leave, and we set the rules of behavior.

What's the magic difference between a church, a school, a home, a newspaper, or a radio or TV station, and a commercial business? From my point of view, these are all institutions rooted in private property. The authoritarian disagrees and wants to dictate all the rules regarding both hiring practices and who must be served in private commercial establishments; at the same time, conservative authoritarians never hesitate to dictate smoking, drinking, drug use, and sexual habits on private property.

What liberal authoritarians don't quite understand is that, if government has the power to control business establishments and all their decisions, they have justified the intrusion of government in every social aspect of our lives—an authority that they now essentially assume.

But the character of the demagogue explains the inconsistent position. If a political enemy can be accused of racism or as supporting drugs for children, demagoguing the issue is a convenient tool for maintaining or gaining power in the political process. The principle of private ownership and personal choice is of no interest to the demagogues. In the long run, though, the goals of honest liberals, conservatives, and progressives alike are undermined.

The politicians and friendly media work together to promote an agreed-to agenda. Though the demagogic process is of epidemic proportions, fortunately for the future of mankind, there are honest, decent people who disagree and have the integrity to not resort to the dishonesty of a demagogue and who abhor the process. Instead they use rational discourse in an attempt to influence others. The common use of demagoguing by politicians and their media allies keeps many decent people from getting their hands dirty in the political process. However, there's still a lot of room outside of politics for these decent individuals to use their talents in education and journalism to influence change.

Anyone who even questions the drug war, the war on pornography, the Civil Rights Act of 1964, or any war is regarded as an evil opponent of law and order and civilization. These are perfect examples of how honest discussions are kept at bay by the demagogue. The shutting down of discussion of these topics is all about trying to maintain bugaboos that people can blame their problems on.

H. L. Mencken offered the following harsh judgment of Americans and their willingness to listen to demagogues:

> Politics under democracy consists almost wholly of the discovery, chase, and scotching of bugaboos. The statesman becomes, in the last analysis, a mere witch-hunter, a glorified smeller and snooper, eternally chanting "Fe, Fi, Fo, Fum!" It has been so in the United States since the earliest days. The whole history of the country has been a history of melodramatic pursuits of horrendous monsters, most of them imaginary: the red-coats, the Hessians, the monocrats, again the red-coats, the Bank, the Catholics, Simon Legree, the Slave Power, Jeff Davis, Mormonism, Wall Street, the rum demon, John Bull, the hell hounds of plutocracy, the trusts, General Weyler, Pancho Villa, German spies, hyphenates, the Kaiser, Bolshevism. The list might be lengthened indefinitely; a complete chronicle of the Republic could be written in terms of it, and without omitting a single important episode.

The influence that the religious, intellectual, and political demagogues have in a free society poses a much greater danger to mankind than the risk of allowing a businessman to use his property as he chooses. Yet the left is hysterical over the "grave" danger they envision from business people "owning" their property without regulations and control by bureaucrats and politicians.

———•••———

La Boétie, Étienne de. [1553] 2008. *The Politics of Obedience: The Discourse of Voluntary Servitude.* Auburn, AL: Mises Institute.

Mencken, H. L. [1926] 2009. *Notes on Democracy.* New York: Dissident Books.

DEMOCRACY

History has proven it again and again: No system of government is a good one once the government grows too big and powerful. If the government is small and unintrusive, the form of government doesn't matter that much. No one is seeking to overthrow the monarchy of Liechtenstein, for example, or uproot the system of oligarchical rotation of Costa Rica. The trouble with democracy is not so much its workings at any one time; the trouble is the dynamic it sets in place that gradually changes a small government into a big one. It was precisely to prevent that from happening that the founding generation in the United States borrowed the idea of a republic from the Roman experience. Not everything was to be subjected to mob rule; voting was in place to rotate the management of a small government that operated under strict rules.

Today that has changed, and not for the better. As much as I defend the freedoms of everyone, those freedoms should be limited in the following sense: People should not be able to vote to take away the rights of others. And yet this is what the slogan democracy has come to mean domestically. It does not mean that the people prevail over the government; it means that the government prevails over the people by claiming the blessing of mass opinion. This form of government has no limit. Tyranny is not ruled out. Nothing is ruled out.

Perhaps more dangerous is the idea of exporting democracy. We've been told that one of the main reasons we're in the Middle East and Central Asia is to spread America's goodness and our political system of democracy. Among other lies, this justification for the occupation of Iraq and Afghanistan has led to a huge sacrifice of American lives and wealth.

This argument fails to address the inconsistency of the United States in continuing to support many dictatorial governments, both past and present. I doubt many Americans truly believe that "spreading democracy" is the real reason we invade, occupy, and threaten numerous countries around the world. How could it be when you look at those we support around the world?

Less often, we hear that these invasions and occupations are necessary for national security purposes. Even if spreading democracy is the goal, we need to question the religious defense of the political system of democracy. It was Woodrow Wilson who originated this policy when he bluntly stated that World War I was a noble cause in our effort "to make the world safe for democracy."

A noble cause of spreading liberty, not democracy, would make a lot more sense, if it was understood that violence and intimidation would never be used to pursue this goal. Besides, if it's liberty we want to promote, it's a republic that we should seek—not a democracy—and only persuasion and education would be used to spread this message. Threats and violence are diametrically opposed to the message we would purport to be spreading.

The difference between a democracy and a republic is important. Pure democracy, in which the law itself is up for grabs based on legislative maneuvering, is the enemy of individual rights, and it victimizes the minority. Dictatorial powers, by gaining acceptance by 51 percent of voters and colluding to suppress minorities, are every bit as harmful as a single dictator. The "democratic mandate" is more seductive since the people too often are conditioned to accept the notion that as long as the consensus of 51 percent agree, something is morally acceptable. A militant dictator is more suspect, and when he abuses the rights of individuals, it is easier to understand who the abuser is. A republic, on the other hand, is a non-monarchical system that makes no claim to somehow embody the will of the people; it is a system merely for the appointment of leaders and the administration of law.

This does not mean that democratic elections can't be used to choose leaders whose job it should be is to promote liberty. But that is a far cry from allowing minorities to be victimized by a coalition making up the majority.

Even so, there are many practical concerns about the democratic election of leaders. Unfortunately, quite frequently, elections are not honest. Texas, Louisiana, Chicago, and others have had examples where the political machine not the votes, controls the outcome. Most historians acknowledge that the LBJ race for the Senate in 1948 against Coke Stevenson was stolen. The election was decided on eighty-seven votes, and though it was highly disputed, most people now concede that it was not a fair election. Without this victory, LBJ most likely would have never been elected President, meaning the disastrous escalation of the Vietnam War might not have occurred.

I had my own experience with a "stolen election." In 1976, I lost a race for Congress by more than 300 votes after a recount. Though we had proof of more than 1,300 fraudulent votes, we were never able to present the evidence in court. There are dozens, if not hundreds, of cases of questionable vote counts in our history.

Our CIA has been implicated many times in influencing elections around the world. It is not unusual for the United States to preach democratic elections to others. When they occur, if we are unhappy with the outcome, we refuse to recognize the winners and continue to support the losers.

We have spent billions of dollars supporting elections in Iraq. Many American lives have been lost in the process and massive casualties have been inflicted on the Iraqi people, all in the name of democratic elections. At the same time we continue to support dictators in Egypt, Jordan, Saudi Arabia, Libya, and other places around the world. Though we accept the premise that there's not much choice in how to pick our leaders other than elections, elections are far from perfect. But the real danger of democracy is the ability of the majority to arbitrarily redefine individual rights.

Our Constitution was designed to protect individual rights, and the Founders knew clearly that they wanted a republic, not a democracy, where the majority could not dictate the definition of rights of the minority. They did a reasonably good job in writing the Constitution but yielded to the principle of democracy in compromising on the slavery issue. The majority voted for supporting second-class citizenship for blacks, a compromise that we paid heavily for, not only in the 1860s but more than a hundred years later as well. It would have been better if we had stayed a loose-knit confederation and not allowed the failed principles of democracy and slavery to infect the Constitution.

From early on the principle of a republic was undermined, which unfortunately allowed the concept of democracy to flourish. How many times in the past ten years have we heard our leaders brag about our wonderful effort to institute democracy in the Middle East, while hearing nothing about promoting personal liberty, property rights, sound money, and free markets, or a republic?

How can we "spread our goodness" around the world through occupation and violence when here at home we have squandered our liberties and wealth? American political culture, unfortunately, has come to worship at the altar of democratic majoritarianism. This has made the concept of rights arbitrary and capricious, and individual and natural rights are no longer cherished or understood.

It is this failed understanding that permits the welfare-warfare state while destroying the concept of civil liberties and personal self-ownership and responsibility.

Today the majority can do just about anything it wants. If the majority, or a well-organized minority that buys votes, wants to use government force to dictate to every American what they can eat or smoke, they are now able to do it. Voluntary associations, economic and social, are routinely regulated by government even when force and fraud are not involved. Victimless crimes are routinely punished by government, while it pays less attention to those individuals committing violent acts.

One tragic example came to my attention when a funda-
mentalist Christian minister came to my office to ask for help
for his son, who had been imprisoned by federal authorities.
He knew the typical conservative member of Congress would
have no sympathy for his plight. His adult son, in his twen-
ties, who from birth suffered from a mental deficiency, was
completely dependent on his parents. He had access to a computer and visited child pornography web pages. The authorities found out and he was arrested, tried, convicted, and
imprisoned. His father's request to me was to get the prison
officials to allow his son to take his hormonal medications
that he had been dependent on since birth. This needless prohibition made the situation much worse for the prisoner and
devastated his family. He never committed an act of violence
and had no real understanding of the "crime" he committed,
but a lot of money was spent investigating, trying, and impris-
oning an individual who was no threat to anyone. Surely a
free society can distinguish between a crime of producing and
distributing child pornography and happening across random
images on a digital delivery system. Surely we can grant that
the producer is the problem here, not the casual web surfer.

The majority, or what people see as the majority, or even
just what people perceive as conventional wisdom, now defines
what rights are: What people want, demand, need, or wish for
can be declared a right by merely writing a law. This breeds
coalition building and incestuous bipartisanship where various groups get together and push for their handouts. That's
why the loot is passed out to the special interest groups in the
"pork barrel."

A precise definition and understanding of what our rights

are would prevent this. Since both the rich and the poor endorse this principle, they share in the benefits. Trouble is, the poor are deceived into believing taxes on the rich will serve their interest. The rich, symbolized by the Goldman Sachs elite, end up the winners in the scramble to sit at the table where the "free lunch" is served.

Some say that members of Congress should listen to the people and vote accordingly. Listening to the people when they are right makes sense, but if the majority of the people demand unconstitutional and immoral transfer programs, the member of Congress has an obligation to live up to his or her oath of office and campaign promises. If ten thousand people in a district can be organized to demand that a member of Congress support a special handout, and the rest of the people in the district are apathetic and pay no attention to the lobbying effort of a pressure group, "listening to his constituents" would invite legalized looting (as it already has).

Even if a true majority of a district demanded support for unconstitutional spending, the rule of law is undermined if the member of Congress complies with the demands. Unfortunately, that's what has been happening for a long time. The "will of the people" is being invoked to pass unconstitutional measures. The majority (all the various interest groups) gangs up on the minority as it rewrites the rules that were supposed to have been written in the Constitution to constrain the arbitrary dictatorial powers of the government, the majority, and the special interests. The result is that pure democracy replaces the supposedly strict restraints placed in the Constitution on the ability of the majority to rule at will. This limitation on the power of the federal government was put there with the belief that "their just powers" were only those consented to by the governed.

Nineteenth-century lawyer Lysander Spooner carried this argument one step further. He believed that only a "few" consented.[1] Therefore, the Constitution should not apply to those who did not give their personal consent to cede any personal liberty (power) to the state. This is an interesting argument, but it's not likely to make much headway at this stage in our history. Enforcing the Tenth Amendment is a big enough challenge to us for now.

Today, as a result of our careless thinking, our desire for government assistance, and the emphasis on unearned economic benefits over free markets and self-reliance, we have a society made up of various special interest groups demanding their "rights."

My guess is that the majority of Americans believe that citizens—especially if in need—have a "right" to medical care, free education, a house, subsidized food, and endless other services. What they don't want to hear is that governments have nothing to pass out, since they produce nothing. Anytime government provides a benefit, it must first steal it from someone else who is producing it, thus violating the rights of that individual. It is important to remember that.

A majority vote should never be used to justify the undermining of human rights. That is what the philosophy of socialism, welfarism, and all other forms of authoritarianism depend on. This same principle allows wars to be fought for reasons

---

1. All of Spooner's writings are worthy of study. George H. Smith, *The Lysander Spooner Reader* (San Francisco: Fox & Wilkes, 1992).

unrelated to national defense. Governments are very sophisticated in confiscating wealth from one segment of society and transferring it to another. When the country is wealthy, the victims are complacent and allow the process to expand massively. Taxation, borrowing, and inflating are all used as the deceptive tactics to disguise who is the actual victim, but the complacency ends when the productive capacity of a nation can no longer keep up with the demands and promises made.

This dilemma elicits many suggestions on how to solve the problem of diminished resources. But the real solution requires a revolutionary change in understanding what individual rights are, and why the obsession with democracy is not the same as freedom and prosperity. In the nearly two-year debate on revamping a failed health-care system, almost no one in Washington was willing to entertain the thought that medical care is not a right and should not be provided by government. I've never heard a major politician state this truth. Even those who oppose President Obama's health-care plan do so on less principled grounds and do not question the fundamental assumption that government is somehow responsible for providing a system of universal health-care delivery.

Preventive wars, as our recent wars have been called, depend on tacit support by the majority of our citizens and the assumption that our motivations and goals are all that matters. This attitude permits us to violate the individual rights of the victims of our occupation and those who suffer collateral damage from our constant bombing of countries that never attacked us and are even incapable of doing so if they wanted. This is a far cry from the justified defense of one's country if invaded.

A majority vote may gain the politicians cover for what they do, but this vote has no moral authority to violate the right to life and liberty of any individual. This means that government, even with the consent of the governed via democratic vote, should not mold personal behavior, supervise economic transactions, or try to make the world a better place by using our armies to "make the world safe for democracy."

———

Caplan, Bryan. 2007. *The Myth of the Rational Voter*. Princeton: Princeton University Press.

Hoppe, Hans-Hermann. 2001. *Democracy: The God That Failed*. New Brunswick, NJ: Transaction Publishers.

Spooner, Lysander. [1972] 2008. *Let's Abolish Government*. Auburn, AL: Mises Institute.

DISCRIMINATION

I f we are going to stick to the dictionary definition of the term "discrimination," there is nothing wrong with it at all. It means merely to choose this over that. We can speak of "discriminating tastes" and regard this as a compliment. At one time the word merely meant "the power of making fine distinctions; discriminating judgment; to differentiate."

Choosing friends of good character is discrimination that we should all endorse. We all discriminate on whom we invite into our homes and whom we date and marry, go to church and generally socialize with. It's a right we all cherish and we should understand exactly what it is. This is positive discrimination and should never be regulated by government.

But it is a different matter when it comes to politics. Here is where the word "discrimination" indicates some sin against the civic religion. To be sure, banning blatant discrimination in all government programs makes perfect sense. Government programs are constructed for public access. But forcing people to integrate and avoid discrimination in all private transactions through affirmative action laws is a different matter.

Forced integration in private affairs, instead of bringing people together, actually exacerbates the conflicts that many are trying to eliminate.

Governments have notoriously written laws that segregated people whether by race, gender, or sexual orientation. This practice was common from the time of slavery until the policy was replaced with affirmative action and forced association in private affairs, thus substituting one set of violations of individual rights with another. Evidence is slim that the hostility between the various groups has been diminished with all the legislation of the past fifty years.

Voluntary associations are better, are more authentic, and are longer lasting, than associations forced by legislation and imposed by bureaucrats. Martin Luther King, Jr., advised that a person's character should be the only measure of a person's worth and the color of one's skin should be irrelevant. Yet quotas and affirmative action programs are based on certain groups qualifying for special privileges. Reversing the discrimination hasn't brought people together. Resentment remains in many areas but not where character and talent are the tests of one's ability. This is true in sports, entertainment, finance, politics, and in the professions.

Even more appalling is the presumption that wherever blacks and whites and others associate freely and to their mutual benefit, and whenever a person makes accommodation for disability—and this is far more common than one would think from the media—it is due solely to government laws that have forced the issue. The idea here is that if people are left to their own devices, they will always and everywhere choose homogeneity in their social associations. I can't imagine a stranger view of the human condition. To me it demonstrates that the supporters of antidiscrimination have an extremely low view of people and their choices.

Getting ahead because of special privileges granted by government is the same as falling behind because of arbitrary penalties. Both violate the principles of individual rights and private property ownership. In a free society, individuals *are* allowed to be creeps and pick and choose all their associations. That is, they can discriminate even when the majority disapproves of their choices.

Outright foolish discrimination in business and elsewhere can be quickly punished by social and economic disapproval; the iron fist of government is not required to force integration and thereby undermine the principles of liberty. The use of the economic boycott in the civil rights struggle was a powerful weapon and an appropriate one.

Instead, the antidiscrimination fanatics want laws mandating rules for all associations insofar as race, age, gender, employment, sexual orientation, etc., are concerned. These laws never improve social relationships, even when the superficial goal of no "discrimination" is achieved. What is lost is freedom of choice. Property rights are rejected and resentment intensifies. Forced hiring practices have no place in a free society.

On the other hand, I've often observed that the voluntary association approach, with no laws mandating integration, does not achieve integration in the churches. Almost all churchgoers attend segregated churches by pure choice. And even after decades of school integration by federal mandates, the vast majority of black and white children are still in segregated schools. In other words, when left to choice in areas of life not driven by commercial considerations, separation frequently seems to be the chosen preference. We can regret this but not deny that some homogeneous voluntary groupings are the result of choice. Some might also regret that some heterogeneous voluntary groupings are the result of choice. Such is life under liberty.

If we could see only the individual and not groups of individuals, it wouldn't matter whom people associated with as long as no force or prohibitions were imposed by government. This is the way all civilized people should think. Unfortunately, friction remains among the various groups because of the call for forced integration based on political priorities. This replaces the proper goal of seeking equal justice before the law and making skin color, age, sex, and sexual orientation irrelevant. Outlawing discrimination has made for a less free and less prosperous society without bringing the various groups closer together.

The argument is sometimes made that because of past injury, racial or otherwise, even hundreds of years ago, privileges and special favors are fair compensation needed to make up for past injustices. The problem is, those who must pay are not themselves guilty parties, and making up for some earlier injustice merely discriminates against another group. This only exacerbates hostilities between groups and ends up working against the desired goal. Falsely and loudly accusing someone of racism or anti-Semitism if the person is not in agreement with reparations is the worst form of bigotry. Such hypocrisy has destroyed a lot of people's reputations and lives and does great harm to any effort to bring people together voluntarily.

If reparations are available, it's hardly a surprise that the line of eager recipients grows quickly. Even those who don't qualify under the rules get in line. Many times those demanding reparations were never personally injured. The result is that undeserving recipients demand financial benefits for something they did not suffer from people who had nothing to do with the injustice. It doesn't sound very fair to me.

Behavior quickly changes when government benefits are offered. The mere offer of financial giveaways to victims of hurricanes, for example, invites every manner of public corruption; it creates a moral hazard as well. Government financial programs also benefit financial and business interests the same way. It's not only the welfare poor who line up for benefits, whether after a natural disaster or during a financial crisis. Government force, illegally and illogically used to stop all discrimination, results in a multiplicity of unintended consequences, altered behavior, and fraud.

Epstein, Richard. 1995. *Forbidden Grounds: The Case Against Employment Discrimination Laws*. Boston: Harvard University Press.

Sowell, Thomas. 1995. *Race and Culture*. New York: Basic Books.

EDUCATION

It's quite clear that there's no constitutional authority for the federal government to be involved in education, regardless of what the Supreme Court has claimed. Ideally, education in a free society would be the responsibility of the parents or the individual or local community, not the government. There is no constitutional prohibition for states or local communities to be involved in education, and up until the mid-twentieth century, education was the responsibility of the church, the family, and the local community.

In the past sixty years especially, the federal government has become very much involved in financing and directing education at all levels. There is no evidence that quality of education has improved. There is evidence that more people go to college and that the cost has skyrocketed. At the grade school and high school levels, where local schools and parents have ever less control over the curriculum and administration of schools, there's definitely been more violence, more drugs, and more dropouts associated with more centralized control.

Competition is helpful in any endeavor. And this is true

in education. The near monopoly control over the indoctrination of young people in our public school systems is counterbalanced by homeschooling, private schooling, and education readily available on the Internet. The regulations on starting a variety of alternatives to public schools are extremely tight and keep the market from operating as it might.

The effort to provide more competition to the public school system has not solved the problem, though there are always a few who benefit from vouchers, tax credits, and charter schools. Too often these efforts are unfairly made available and do not eliminate the power of the state to control the curriculum. The best interim option for reform would be to give a tax credit for all educational expenses. Vouchers invite bureaucratic control of their usage and are unfairly distributed.

The textbook argument is unsolvable in a government-run school. All social science books are biased toward different viewpoints. Science books are usually more objective and are not influenced by prejudiced bureaucrats. There's no way a book on social or political science can be nondiscriminatory and offend no one. It's equivalent to finding a religion satisfactory to all groups.

In private schools or homeschools the issue is moot. The decisions are made by the parents and the school operators, secular or religious. Attendees come with the understanding of any particular bias.

Problems associated with emphasis on history and politics in public schools will never be solved by electing a new group of book editors who remove one textbook and replace it with another. In the private system, prayers or Bible reading are not debatable issues, and no one's rights are abused.

Most people today accept the idea that the Department of

Education is a legitimate federal institution. Not too many years ago, however, the Republican Party platform argued for getting rid of the Department of Education. This pretense was removed with the election of George W. Bush in the year 2000. With both Democratic and Republican support, he massively increased the Department of Education with the disastrous No Child Left Behind program. Now national control of all public schools is firmly a bipartisan effort. It doesn't seem to matter that students, parents, administrators, and teachers generally disapprove of No Child Left Behind. Once an institution is hooked on federal financing, it's virtually impossible to stop the bureaucratic regulations and mandates that routinely follow subsidies.

The judiciary hasn't helped matters either. Court rulings on discipline, decorum, and political correctness have intimidated many dedicated teachers and curtailed any creativity they might have. Lawsuits and threats stifle a good educational environment—something homeschoolers and private schoolers don't have to worry about.

The founders of this country were well educated, mostly by being homeschooled or taught in schools associated with a church. In early times in new settlements, the families would band together to hire a teacher to come and teach. Under those rather crude conditions—without palaces in which to teach—the children were taught the classics as well as foreign languages. Today, our children can get through eight or even twelve grades without even touching on these subjects.

But everybody passes—no *single* child is left behind. Instead, they are all left behind in *large groups*. Washington, DC, the only city that Congress has jurisdiction over, has one of the most expensive, most violent, most crime- and drug-ridden school systems in the country. And the only complaint Congress gets from District of Columbia teachers and administrators is that they need more money.

The current system has driven many state school systems into bankruptcy. Extravagance in building ornate physical structures while neglecting quality education has added greatly to the debt burden of local and state budgets. This is all in addition to the contribution of the huge sums of money eaten up by the federal bureaucracy and the Department of Education, which contributes to the national debt.

The NEA (National Education Association), one of the most powerful lobby groups in the country, not only successfully agitates for structural and bureaucratic excesses, it is responsible for teacher salaries and retirement benefits that far exceed those of the private sector. The future obligation to pay all the retirement and health benefits will require a constant inflow of revenues.

Many pension funds are not solvent. With an economy that is likely to remain weak for a long time, assuring that the retired teachers will receive their benefits is questionable. This will probably prompt federal assistance in time. When the conditions in the large cities and states present a major crisis, I'm certain the federal government will bail them out with printing press money. The only question then will be the value of the dollars they receive.

Even with the mess we have created with our schools, we are not on the verge of undoing our public school system or wisely reforming it. There is no serious effort to deal with the problem of vastly inefficient, underperforming schools. In reality, the whole system may self-destruct by both poor performance and runaway costs. The grandiose structures built by so many government-run schools resulted from the huge subsidies from the federal government financed by debt and outrageous taxes.

It's a huge problem to deal with under today's circumstances. The majority of the American people assume the public school system is a "sacred" institution. We have been told that our "free" public school education made America what it is today. Soon they will be forced to quit making that claim. Eliminating federal controls someday may be achievable.

If government schools were maintained by local control, the problem of monopoly control of education for the entire school-age population would be greatly reduced. The "owners" of the school could be the local school boards, which could set curriculum and discipline standards and taxes. This solution is not perfect, but it is vastly better than a Washington-based economic czar using the educational system for propaganda, perpetuating the falsehoods of the state and the so-called benefits of a powerful central government. Thank goodness for the Internet, Amazon, and the thirst for truth that no government is big enough to silence.

———•◦•———

Burleigh, Anne Husted. 1979. *Education in a Free Society*. Indianapolis: Liberty Fund.

Rothbard, Murray N. 1999. *Education: Free and Compulsory*. Auburn, AL: Mises Institute.

West, E. G. 1994. *Education and the State: A Study in Political Economy*. Indianapolis: Liberty Fund.

EMPIRE

The majority of Americans, most likely, do not believe we are an empire. They believe we are a free people and enjoy the benefits of living in a democratic republic. Most people do not read the international news. Even wars are only interesting to people at the very outset. But most Americans lose interest after a few weeks.

As a result, most people remain blissfully unaware of the activities of the American global empire. This really came home to me on 9/11, when most Americans expressed shock and amazement that anyone would have a reason to deliver a message to the United States in the form of a bloody and destructive attack. Most people asked what we ever did to incite such a thing. George Bush explained that these crazy people must have "hated us for our freedoms."

Well, it's a bit more complicated than that, to say the least. There are lots of people who hate us for invading their countries, supporting dictatorships, starving people through sanctions, and maintaining an unprecedented military empire of global reach. Truly, the United States is an empire by any definition, and quite possibly the most aggressive, extended, and expansionist in the history of the world. Do we really find it shocking that some people in the world don't like this? Would we, as American citizens, like it if some superpower were doing this to us?

The transition from a republican form of government to an authoritarian empire is most often insidious. Yet history has recorded quite a precipitous shift that dated the end of the Roman Republic and the beginning of its empire. The date is etched in history when Julius Caesar boldly marched with his legions and crossed the Rubicon. The rules were clear. A proconsul in charge of a province outside of Rome was not permitted to enter Rome with his troops. The Rubicon, a twenty-nine-kilometer river running east and west in northern Italy, was the line that separated the militarily run provinces and the Roman Republic. It was a small river but a mighty barrier; it provided a symbolic wall of defense against any internal military threat by an ambitious Roman general.

But Julius Caesar successfully crossed the Rubicon with his legions and defeated Pompey's effort to defend the Republic. Caesar quickly secured Asia Minor and within three years the Senate appointed him dictator for life, which was the final blow to the Roman Republic.

Cicero failed to save the Republic, but he left a great legacy in his effort and influenced generations to come—including the Founders of our own republic. Though the crossing of the Rubicon is considered the seminal event in the fall of the Roman Republic, militarism had already been in place outside of Rome itself. The destruction of the Republic came as a consequence of the growth and expansion of Roman military power throughout the Mediterranean region.

The Romans assumed that as long as the proconsuls and their military forces did not take over the republican Senate in Rome, the status quo of the Republic would be maintained.

Julius Caesar's military genius, his loyal troops, and the material benefits they received though conquest, along with the Senate's forbearance, permitted him to annex essentially all of Europe and part of Great Britain. Eventually, most of the known civilized world became part of the Roman Empire.

Some analogies can be made between the fall of the Roman Empire and the problems we face today in America. One thing for certain, though, is that the duration of the American republic and empire compared to those of the Romans will be much shorter. Geopolitical events today are moving rather swiftly compared to ancient times due to modern technology—weapons, speed of travel, and communications.

The Roman Republic lasted approximately 450 years before Octavius Caesar brought it to an end. The Roman Empire, if dated from time when Octavian was called the Exalted One in 29 BC, lasted until AD 476. Today's military and CIA efforts are almost totally unrestrained by the U.S. Congress. The extent of our modern-day worldwide empire strongly suggests a similar pattern of the military independence enjoyed by Julius Caesar.

Much more sophisticated today, the CIA along with our military might have orchestrated military coups against governments we find dispensable. Iran-Contra-type financing is a tool used to circumvent any effort by Congress to restrain clandestine activity that promotes our empire.

Eighty billion dollars are spent on intelligence gathering to protect the American people, without much to show for it.

Possible secret financing by the Federal Reserve, with loans and guarantees to our friends to assist empire building, is unconfirmed but would not be surprising.

Money spent by the CIA and other security agencies receives virtually no oversight by the U.S. Congress. When problems result as a consequence, the military is frequently called upon to bring about order and Congress is coerced into supporting the effort for supposed national security reasons.

These efforts have led to a worldwide presence of American troops. The American people have been brainwashed into accepting this for various reasons. Some Americans believe a great danger is lurking and have become convinced that security demands our ever-growing presence around the world.

Others, less fearful, believe we are only spreading our "goodness" and democracy out of a spirit of benevolence. Even if this were true, why would we spread such a message with armed military? Some still believe in a modern-day mercantilism that requires us to protect natural resources—such as oil—for national survival. Too few understand that the much greater threat to us is the deeply flawed policy that condones military occupation and a world empire.

But just as the military of Julius Caesar and the empire he forcefully implemented eventually led to the destruction of the 450-year-old Roman Republic, our current worldwide military presence invites the same result.

Though it took years for the Roman military empire to be built, it was clear that "passing the point of no return" was when the republic was doomed and the empire would reign. The question for us is, Have we crossed our Rubicon? Our future depends on a proper assessment and wise discussions as to what actions we should take. History will determine the outcome and the wisdom of our actions. We have only the present in which to decide on our course of action. History and an understanding of human nature should be used to guide us, but they do not provide all the answers.

We don't have a geographic boundary to delineate our republic from the imminent danger of becoming an empire. But I cannot conceive how anyone can deny that the American Empire is not in charge of the world today. With the demise of the Soviet Empire in 1989, the United States quickly assumed the role of the worldwide administrator of military power, and the domination continues to expand and grow. Even with the financial crisis and our shrinking wealth and the exponential growth of debt, we remain the economic powerhouse of the world. The dollar still reigns as king for now. We have more military might than all the rest of the world put together. No one dares attack us in a conventional manner. The danger lies within, with our military and our economic excesses and our lost liberties.

If we indeed are an empire, is our republican form of government salvageable? If so, one thing is certain: it won't take hundreds of years to complete the transition as it did with the Roman Republic and Empire. It's more likely to be like the dissolution of the British Empire or the quick disappearance of the Soviet system.

All governments reflect the people's attitude; no system lasts that cannot maintain popular support. Welfare and warfare brought us to where we are, and the majority remains enthralled with promises of bliss.

Pompey fought a military battle in an attempt to stop Caesar and lost his life for it. Today, we can still resist without a military or violent confrontation. To acquiesce and not resist in any way and escape to another part of the world is not a realistic option for most Americans. To confront the opposition and defend the rightness of the grand experiment in liberty is the only choice we have.

I am encouraged by Victor Hugo's frequently quoted assessment regarding ideas and military powers: "There is nothing more powerful than an idea whose time has come." We're in an ideological struggle and one that is winnable, but it cannot be won without addressing the status of the American Empire. An empire, which requires perpetual war and preparation for war, is incompatible with a free society. Those who consider themselves to be opponents of big government and yet have an uncritical attitude toward militarism and war are either fooling themselves or haven't thought enough about the problem. War feeds the growth of the state. The state is nourished on the liberties of the people. The choice is liberty or dictatorship (authoritarianism), republic or empire. The notion that we can cut government and maintain the empire is preposterous.

A country that supports preventive war, allows assassination of its own citizens, and endorses torture can hardly be called a republic. We now have troops stationed around the world. Our empire is every bit as pervasive as was the British Empire at its zenith. Though it was based on colonialism, ours is a military client-run empire, with troops in 135 countries and with more than 900 bases.

It is the atmosphere surrounding empires that prompts a redefinition of patriotism. Those who are critical of the policies of preventive wars and occupation are dismissed as being unpatriotic, and part of the "blame America" crowd. Interestingly, though, the soldiers who must fight the wars do not necessarily join in this chorus of discontents. There was a time when a willingness to criticize one's own government when it was wrong was the very definition of patriotism.

Our foreign policy of interventionism has brought the worst out in those who support the empire.

One of the most disturbing incidents was when President George W. Bush made fun of himself at the Annual Radio and Television Correspondents' Dinner, May 3, 2004. At this dinner he had a slide show mocking his running around the White House pretending to search for weapons of mass destruction, obviously referring to those that were never found in Iraq. To treat with such levity such a serious blunder (some call it a lie) that has caused so much death and destruction is beyond the pale. And those present at the dinner all had a good laugh over it.

Another episode of callous disregard for decency relating to foreign policy occurred when negative ads against Max Cleland were run by a bunch of chicken-hawks in his 2002 Senate reelection race. Depicting an individual who had lost two legs and an arm in Vietnam as being weak on defense was about as low as one can get in politics. The ad had Senator Cleland's face morphed into Saddam Hussein's while it implied that Cleland didn't care about the security of the American people because he didn't always vote with President Bush. Some Republicans even insisted that Max Cleland not be referred to as a war hero though he had been awarded a Silver Star for gallantry in action.

It can't get much worse. To this day, it's remarkable that

Max Cleland has a positive attitude about life and America despite the vitriol that spewed from those who, in the name of patriotism, supported America's aggressive wars.

Empires redefine patriotism just as welfare redefines charity; the two go together. The two ideas are but one idea: that the state should be master. When empires are rich—whether by looting the conquered or inflating the currency—the people grow dependent, work and produce less, and enjoy the "bread and circuses" or their "guns and butter" while drowning in consumer excesses, encouraged by moral decay and financed by debt. All this hastens the day of reckoning when the bills come due and the empire collapses. The republic dies unless a new generation is reinvigorated to secure our lost liberties and reject the addictive notion of empire.

Empires require the support of the people. In ancient times, glorious celebrations of military victory and conquest unified and were welcomed by the people. Conquering others meant slaves and confiscated wealth from the defeated. This meant less work, more leisure and personal excesses, and national prestige. A residual of this sentiment persists today. Death and injury are seen as a small price to pay for the "benefits" of our empire.

The endless praise offered to those who serve in the military—"thank you for your service" in defending the empire—is a required politically correct salutation to our "universal" soldiers. No, they never say thank you for "defending the empire"; it's much more decent—it's thank you for defending our freedoms, our Constitution, and for fighting "them" over there so we don't have to fight them here at home. Though the wars we fight are now unconstitutional, the military is end-lessly praised for defending our liberties and Constitution.

Many on the right who endorse the preventive-war men-tality of overseas aggression are sincere in their belief that this effort is required to defeat the enemies of liberty. They refuse to see any connection between a policy of perpetual war and the loss of civil liberties at home. They believe their own rhetoric. This deception only facilitates big government, defi-cits, and the diminishment of individual liberty they say they are fighting to preserve. Tea Party activists will often claim to oppose the system of tax and spend, bailouts and socialism, but to the extent that they uncritically defend U.S. foreign policy, they are supporting all the policies they claim to be against.

To inspire a nation's support and individual sacrifice for a flawed policy requires a dangerous enemy. But what happens when there is but one superpower and no hated enemy with which to incite the people and gain their support for constant militarism? In the Cold War, the U.S. government used the Soviets to generate the people's support of empire building for "national security purposes." And throughout the Cold War, the U.S. empire grew, liberty suffered, and debt skyrocketed. In the past decade, the real wealth of the middle class has declined as a consequence.

After the collapse of the Soviet system—a result of its flawed economic system, not a military defeat—instead of our getting a "peace dividend," we were introduced to a new enemy, mili-tant Islam, and a new place for building the American empire throughout the Middle East. In order to define our new nemesis, our government needed to schizophrenically flip-flop on previous alliances.

Our "friend" and ally Saddam Hussein had to be turned into a Hitlerian monster about to attack us with nonexistent nuclear weapons. After U.S. Ambassador to Iraq April Glaspie gave him a green light to invade Kuwait over a border dispute and mineral rights, it became easy for the war propagandists to excite the American people into supporting what is a twenty-year war in the Middle East, redesigning the Middle East by fomenting civil wars and regime change and constant turmoil.

Why wouldn't Saddam Hussein trust the United States in his military answer to an old conflict with a rival neighbor, since the United States supported him in his decadelong war against Iran? Various special interest groups joined this concerted effort. To create a new enemy against which we can unite, many interest groups came together: oil interests, neocon intellectuals, pro-war Christians, and "patriotic" Americans convinced that a great danger to our security existed and had to be stopped. Protecting "our" oil and our military presence around the world to prevent a new superpower from developing was an easy-to-sell policy to the American people.

The republic is on its last legs and the military approach of brute force is impractical and unsustainable for the twenty-first century. Though our weapons have become more sophisticated and more numerous, current warfare has changed from state control to stateless resistance, al Qaeda and Taliban style—a modern-day form of guerrilla resistance.

We are now faced with what William S. Lind has referred to as fourth-generation warfare. The idea is that those who see themselves as defending their homeland can, in fact, compete with the overweening force of a world power with a nuclear arsenal. We have more weapons and spend more money on our military and sophisticated surveillance technology than all the other nations put together; yet after ten years we have not located Osama bin Laden nor have we brought peace and stability to Iraq or Afghanistan.

We have spent a couple trillion dollars, and most importantly, sacrificed a lot more Americans than died on 9/11. Nearly 6,000 have been killed, and hundreds of thousands of physical and mental casualties have been sustained, in addition to hundreds of thousands of Iraqi and Afghani citizens, only to see the Taliban and al Qaeda moving into Pakistan, Yemen, and Somalia. We have created a very unstable Iraq, now more aligned with the Iranians, as we turn control over to the Shiite Muslims. If our threats against Iran lead to a U.S.–Israeli preventive war against her, it will only drive Iran and Iraq closer to a growing financial giant—China.

Every time there's a military confrontation, whether in Iraq, Afghanistan, Pakistan, or Yemen, even Somalia, "victory" is reported since so many "insurgents" were killed, and when examined closely there is an admission that many civilian casualties resulted as well, referred to as collateral damage. If it was always reported that we killed "freedom fighters" defending their homeland, which is closer to the truth, the American people would be outraged.

In the 1980s, at the urging of Ronald Reagan, the United States supported the mujahedeen in Afghanistan with which bin Laden aligned himself in an effort to defeat the Soviet invaders and occupiers. They were called freedom fighters.

The Taliban is an outgrowth of this organization. It is a certainty that with every death of an Afghan citizen, many more are motivated to join the effort to rid their land of all foreign troops while boosting support for the Taliban, al Qaeda, and the recruiting of suicide bombers. The longer the wars go on, the greater is the danger to our nation's security and our financial well-being.

Americans today, by a large majority, support the Republican and Democratic policy that hinges on fighting the global war on terrorism. But it's actually not a war in the military or constitutional sense. There's no precise enemy. There's been no declaration of war. Terrorism is a tactic of criminals. Terrorism defined by the United States and international laws is a criminal act—not an act of war. Nevertheless, U.S. citizens have been conditioned to condone almost any action, including the first use of nuclear weapons against third-world countries, to pursue the war on terrorism out of fear that is deliberately generated by those who desire empire and despise liberty.

The war on terror is no more a true war than the wars on poverty, illiteracy, or drugs. It's a mere metaphor to provide fear and intimidate people into sacrificing their liberties. I have actually heard a member of Congress say it's all justified because "the people are too stupid to take care of themselves." Stretching the truth and lying are permissible under the code of the "noble lie" endorsed by neoconservatives in order to secure the people's support. Some members of Congress moan a little, but the funds are always made available for fear of being called un-American or a member of the "blame America" crowd and being characterized as weak on national defense.

Even imminent, national bankruptcy does not persuade

Congress to resist the media and government propaganda promoting constant expansion of the worldwide military presence "defending" the empire. Supplemental war-funding bills are never defeated and are used to add on additional welfare spending.

The linchpin of the fearmongering is the hate and fear that can be generated by providing an explanation of why "they" hate us and why "they," the terrorists, want to attack us. We are told that it's because militant Islam is preoccupied with hate for and envy of Americans because of our freedoms and prosperity.

It is not infrequently that I hear members of Congress express their unqualified opinion that it is only the hate-filled Muslim religion that is the source of our problems, and we must pursue the war on terrorism at all costs, even if it does mean preventive war.

Some well-known neocons say they have never heard any other explanation than the religious hatred that they claim Islam generates. They stick to their argument that anyone who would suggest that our own policies contribute to suicide terrorism is committing virtual treason. Sadly, many Americans have been conditioned to believe this.

Demagoguing, lying, or denying that no unintentional consequences or blowback result from our invasion, occupation, and bombing of other nations, especially Arab and Muslim countries, presents the greatest danger to our security, freedom, and prosperity.

In all criminal acts, law enforcement officers immediately look for the motives that may have been involved, yet the neocons insist that the motivation is solely religious in nature. Those who want to blame only the Muslim religion absolutely don't want to hear or even entertain the thought that terrorist attacks against us are related to the blowback phenomenon the CIA identified many years ago.

One group calls terrorist attacks vicious criminal acts against innocent civilians in an attempt to draw attention to injustices for which the perpetrators see no resolution. The intensity of their conviction becomes so great that they sacrifice their lives for a cause they believe in. The horrendous tragedy is that many innocent bystanders are killed on purpose as the terrorists vent their anger and frustration.

Presidential war powers, already excessive, are tolerated as our Presidents use signing statements on new legislation (written pronouncements issued by a President upon the signing of a bill into law), executive orders, departmental regulations, and abuse of the powers of the CIA and FBI. The constant exaggeration of the dangers that are said to be coming from third-world nations that cannot even feed themselves or refine oil nevertheless convince many Americans that it's necessary for the President—whether a Republican or Democrat—to keep us safe at all costs.

Even ignoring the real cause of the threat from foreigners who want to terrorize us, few want to put the danger in proper perspective. Nine years without a single terrorist attack in the United States and with innumerable deaths on the highways and homicides in this country is a lot of misplaced effort to "fight" terrorism in the Middle East for which we suffer horrendous casualties and financial burdens.

It's impossible to make our country safer, freer, and wealthier if we aren't willing to admit the mistake and come to understand how flawed our policies are. This is a far cry from "blaming America." Bad policy by a few of our leaders motivated by ignorance, special interests, and self-serving desires is not equivalent to blaming the American people. Closing one's eyes to this truth is the biggest part of the problem. The American people have to become informed and reject the bad policies of the few who are driven by the special interests. That's what true patriotism requires—not blind obedience to government-driven war propaganda.

For a little bit of reassurance—even with all the bad mistakes that contributed to the terrorist dangers—it is more likely an American will die from being hit by lightning than from a terrorist attack. I recognize this is a dangerous statement to make—surely there will be someone in Washington who will write legislation to declare a "war on lightning."

Another way to put this danger in perspective is by noting that out of the 14,000 homicides committed in the United States last year, only fourteen were attributed to terrorism. Between 35,000 and 40,000 deaths occur every year on our government-owned and -operated highways, with minimal concern compared to the danger of terrorism.

Years ago, a member of Congress slipped a laminated quote into my hand that he must have thought I would find meaningful. I paid little attention at first and unfortunately I don't recall just who gave me the quote. I placed it next to my voting card and have carried it ever since. The quote came from Elie Wiesel's book *One Generation After*.[1] The quote was entitled "Why I Protest."

1. Elie Wiesel, *One Generation After* (New York: Random House, 1970), p. 72.

Author Elie Wiesel tells the story of the one righteous man of Sodom, who walked the streets protesting against the injustice of this city. People made fun of him, derided him. Finally, a young person asked: "Why do you continue your protest against evil; can't you see no one is paying attention to you?" He answered, "I'll tell you why I continue. In the beginning I thought I would change people. Today, I know I cannot. Yet, if I continue my protest, at least I will prevent others from changing me."

I'm not that pessimistic that we can't change people's beliefs or that people will not respond to the message of liberty and peace. But we must always be on guard not to have others change us once we gain the confidence that we are on the right track in the search for truth.

Cicero lost his struggle to save the Roman Republic and was assassinated for his efforts. Though imperfect in his political career, he left a great legacy known to this day. He heroically refused to join Julius Caesar's betrayal of the Roman constitution and the rule of law. Caesar's personal triumph was solidified and he was appointed dictator for three years. Two years later he was appointed dictator for life and was assassinated soon afterward on the Ides of March.

At the age of sixty and in the year Caesar was crowned dictator, Cicero started writing a series of books on history and politics up until that time. Intellectual study for Cicero was every bit as important as politics and war. By this time in his life, especially since the end of the Republic was at hand, Cicero opted for documenting his thoughts on the significance of a republic that honored the rule of law. He wrote compulsively and once remarked that he wrote more in that short three-year period knowing the republic was doomed than during his lifetime when the republic was in place.

Cicero would have been remembered for what he did actively as a politician and orator in his effort to save the Roman constitution and the republic. But his legacy was sealed for more than 2,000 years by his philosophic dissertations that, once it was clear to him that the Roman Republic was dead, sprang from his effort to reflect on it.

We cannot know exactly what tomorrow will bring, nor in what time the consequences of bad policy will evolve, so we must strive for truth and the preservation of those values that we are convinced have benefited mankind. We could be successful and preserve the American Republic as it was intended, giving up the militarism of the American Empire. The odds are slim that that will occur without a bloody reaction from those who wield the power over the military-industrial complex, our political process, the media, our economy, our monetary system, and our personal lives. But regardless, since the principles of liberty are based on morally correct ideas, anything we do to preserve them will benefit mankind.

Making progress in promoting civilization is a much higher goal than the limited desire to "save the Republic." Technological advances, the consequences of economic liberty, have far surpassed our ability and concerns for understanding the importance of the moral values required to maintain the process. Concentration on our material well-being and neglect of the moral principles that underpin material abundance will result in the loss of prosperity, peace, and liberty. Already the signs are ominous: a sharply decreasing standard of living for millions worldwide.

The American Empire is the enemy of American freedom. It is every bit as much the enemy of American citizens as it is of its victims around the world.

———•———

Denson, John. 2006. *A Century of War.* Auburn, AL: Mises Institute.

Eland, Ivan. 2004. *The Empire Has No Clothes: U.S. Foreign Policy Exposed.* Independent Institute. http://www.independent.org.

Mises, Ludwig von. 1945. *Omnipotent Government.* New Haven: Yale University Press.

ENVY

E nvy is the painful awareness of another's good fortune.
It is usually associated with the desire to bring an end
to that good fortune through some means. Thus is it worse
than jealousy, which is wanting what another has. Envy seeks
to take away what another has out of spite and hatred, and
is driven by the desire to destroy. It is an extremely destructive emotion, one that cannot bring personal happiness and
is sure to bring social harm. The exercise of envy only ends
in satisfying a kind of lust for bad to come to others. All the
world religions condemn the impulse. It is one of the seven
deadly sins. It is something we train our children not to feel.
No good can come of it.

I raise it in this context because envy is one of the driving forces of redistributionist politics in the United States,
an emotion and motivation endorsed every day on the edi-
torial pages. It is the secret motivation behind the unrelent-
ing attacks on the rich heard every day inside Washington, a
town whose population includes some of the most well-to-do
people in the entire country. The emotion that is behind the

attacks on the justly rich, and the emotion that such attacks seek to stir within the population, is envy.

Envy is sometimes called the green-eyed monster. Many religious traditions have given rise to charms and methods for warding it off. That's because the envious will stop at nothing in order to achieve their goals of harming those who succeed, even when achieving that goal is itself personally harmful. Policies driven by envy, such as the progressive income tax and the inheritance tax, do not help society. They gather revenue but arguably less than would be gathered if all taxes were low and friendly to overall production. But such policies do accomplish the goal of harming people who are rich and successful.

There are dangerous social consequences to the private exercise of envy. People fear driving a nice car or living in a nice home because these behaviors might elicit reprisal. So it is in public policy. Policies rooted in envy discourage the accumulation of wealth, punish success, and cause people to pull back from doing great things. People who might otherwise pursue wealth think twice, knowing full well that the force of law stands waiting to crush success.

To hate is always injurious to the soul. To hate because another person or class of people has done well for itself compounds the injury. But that is precisely what policies that survive solely to punish people for making money, or for living well, are really all about. It's been going on for a very long time. It strikes me as a form of institutionalized immorality. Under ideal conditions, our law should elicit from us the best that we have to offer, always appealing to the highest impulses of our nature. Policies that harm people solely because they are winners in life appeal to the lowest impulses in our nature.

It is hard enough for people to come to terms with success, especially in a market setting in which superior traits such as foresight and prudence and good judgment really do lead to profitability. We should learn the virtue of celebrating success or, as the ancient philosophers said, learn to be inspired by the success of others. We should try to emulate success, not punish it. This is the American way and a major reason for the wealth and success of Americans.

It is the same with international politics. We don't have to be number one and we sure don't have to regard every country that does well (think China here) as a threat to be kicked and punched. In a true market economy, gain does not come at anyone's expense. We can all win together, provided we keep the green-eyed monster at bay.

———————

De Jouvenel, Bertrand. 1990. *The Ethics of Redistribution*. Indianapolis: Liberty Fund.

Schoeck, Helmut. 1987. *Envy: A Theory of Social Behavior*. Indianapolis: Liberty Fund.

EVOLUTION VERSUS CREATION

No one person has perfect knowledge as to man's emergence on this earth. Yet almost everyone has a strong religious, scientific, or emotional opinion he or she considers gospel. The creationists frown on the evolutionists, and the evolutionists dismiss the creationists as kooky and unscientific. Lost in this struggle are those who look objectively at all the scientific evidence for evolution without feeling any need to reject the notion of an all-powerful, all-knowing Creator. My personal view is that recognizing the validity of an evolutionary process does not support atheism nor should it diminish one's view about God and the universe.

From my viewpoint, this is a debate about science and religion (and I wish it could be more civil!) and should not involve politicians at all. Why can't this remain an academic debate and not be made the political issue it has become?

The answer is simple. Both sides want to use the state to enforce their views on others. One side doesn't mind using force to expose others to prayer and professing their faith. The other side demands that they have the right never to be offended and demands prohibition of any public expression of faith.

Fortunately, in this country, there's no effort to establish any official state religion as has been done elsewhere. In many parts of the world today theocracies are still being imposed on many people. It is not a mythical threat, and I understand the impulse to resist. At the same time, the past hundred years have also seen secular dictatorships that banish religion in the name of shoring up allegiance to the state alone. I also understand the very real threat of that terrible reality.

The real problem comes when government gets involved in this issue, whether the goal is to push theocracy or merely prayer in a public place, or the opposite, to crush all traces of faith expression in public places.

One of the silliest questions posed to the Republican presidential candidates in 2008 dealt with evolution. Why should an individual running for the presidency in the United States be quizzed as to whether or not he or she believes in evolution? The question was designed in an attempt for the supporters of evolution to embarrass a candidate who supports creationism, or, if the candidate backs away, to drive a wedge between the candidate and the religious right.

The way the question was asked made it even sillier. It occurred May 3, 2007, in the first presidential debate in Simi Valley, California. The debate was moderated by Chris Matthews and John Harris. One of the moderators called for all the candidates who believed in evolution to raise their hands. At the time, my first impression was that this sounded like a third-grade class exercise. I interpreted raising one's hand as an all-or-nothing answer and as an insult and didn't bother to answer the question; nor was I called upon to discuss my views.

Most of the conflict between atheists and believers comes up because of public schools. This issue doesn't exist in private settings such as homes, homeschools, private schools, churches, and art studios, to name a few. In the private sector, every point of view can find a place and these ideas are not a threat to others. As Thomas Jefferson said: "It does me no injury for my neighbor to say there are twenty gods, or no God. It neither picks my pocket nor breaks my leg." In a public school setting, however, it's a major hot-button issue because the school curriculum and all standards of behavior are dictated by the federal government, the Department of Education, and the federal courts.

Though the Constitution in no way prohibits religious expression in public places, the modern interpretation of the Constitution, pushed by the evangelical atheists, demands strict prohibition of public expressions of faith. Athletes can't even say a prayer before a sporting event according to current court rulings. It's hard to understand the great danger in a voluntary prayer while it's considered no threat whatsoever for a minority to use a government power to impose its views on others.

A broad-based tolerance in all directions would go a long way toward eliminating many of the problems, but public schools and public places will continue to exist. In a private setting, the "owners" set the rules and participants come with an understanding of the rules regarding prayer and religious expression and what one wants to hear about evolution.

This still leaves some problems with the possibility that

local schools will overstep the bounds of etiquette or will use some textbooks considered to be offensive to one group or another. In this case, the closest one can come to having the "owner" decide would be for the local school board to make the decision and be subject to public challenge at the polls. The Supreme Court handing down edicts that apply to every single circumstance around the country is not a solution.

This will seem to be less than perfect. But it's a far better solution than having the Supreme Court or the Congress dictate proper decorum with regards to religious expression or picking the books our children will be using in the classroom. Universalization of educational standards and curriculum is exactly the goal of those who seek tyranny over liberty. And if they can use an issue such as prayer in the schools or teaching evolution, they'll not hesitate to do it.

There is one argument against evolution that deserves consideration. If man is evolving and progressing, why is man's involvement in mass killings of one another getting worse and the struggle for peace more difficult? Government wars and exterminations in the twentieth century reached 262 million people killed by their own governments and 44 million people killed in wars. I fear that doesn't say much for the evolutionary process.

—————

Larson, Edward J. 2007. *The Creation-Evolution Debate: Historical Perspectives*. Athens: University of Georgia Press.

Executive Power

A dictator enjoys unrestrained power over the people. The legislative and judicial branches voluntarily cede this power or it's taken by force. Most of the time, it's given up easily, out of fear in time of war and civil disturbances, and with support from the people, although the dictator will also accumulate more power with the use of force. Rarely does an elected leader truly resist the temptation to exert power over the people.

History shows the lust for power to be a human trait, and Jefferson's argument for "binding our leaders down with the chains of the Constitution" was his answer to this temptation. The Constitution was an effort to do just that. But when the mood changes and the people become fearful, they allow the eager leaders, tempted by power, to grab as much as they can, seeing themselves as the only ones who can rescue the people.

Because the Founders understood this, they made an earnest attempt to write a constitution in which the various powers were separate and designed to place checks and balances on all the activities of the government in order to strictly limit the powers of the President and the executive branch. They did not want a dictator to evolve out of the constitutional republic they were designing. Article I, Section 8, defines the limited area over which the Congress, and therefore the whole federal government, was granted authority.

Without a clear limitation on the powers of the federal government, the Constitution would never have been ratified. To further emphasize the limits of Article I, Section 8, the Ninth and Tenth Amendments were added. The debates and the language of the Constitution never suggested that "the general welfare" clause and the "interstate commerce clause" could even hint at justifying a federal welfare-warfare state.

Yet over the years, especially since the Great Depression of the 1930s, a "modern" interpretation was forced on us by our courts and taught in our schools. This meant that the Constitution could be changed at will by the three branches and without proper amendments, since anything called interstate commerce could be regulated without limit, and even martial law could be justified according to the demands of the general welfare. George Bush used his power in near dictatorial ways, passing the National Security and Homeland Security Presidential Directive in 2007 that gave him near dictatorial powers in the event of emergency. Obviously, the Constitution is a dead letter under these conditions.

The welfare clause in the Preamble became a license for specific benefits for one group at the expense of another. The interstate commerce clause became a justification for hindering and regulating everything considered interstate commerce. This has been especially the case since the radical ruling in the *National Relations Board v. Jones and Laughlin Steel Corporation* decision in 1937 (concerning the Wagner Act), which permitted the government to regulate every aspect of American labor contracts. Another case, *United States v. Darby Lumber* in 1941, radically undermined the interstate commerce clause with the court justifying their ruling by declaring the Tenth Amendment "is but a truism" and did not limit federal powers.

In the past ten years the separation of powers between the state and the federal government has virtually disappeared and the federal government has won. Today there is a healthy debate and resistance to this takeover, due to the complete failure of everything the federal government touches.

The shift of power away from Congress to the executive branch is every bit as serious a problem as the sovereignty being taken away from the states. Clearly, the Constitution made the Congress the most important of the three branches. Today, it's the weakest. Congress was to decide the issues of war, money, international and domestic trade, laws, spending, taxes, and foreign relations. Today, these issues are the responsibility of the President—essentially without congressional input.

For the most part, Congress gave up its prerogatives without a fight. Too many members of Congress in the past century had been taught that for our survival we had to have a strong executive. This is unfortunate, since it can only be achieved at the expense of the people's liberty. Excessive, dictatorial executive powers are the enemy of the liberties that were to be protected by the Constitution in our republic. Indeed, our system of education has brainwashed generations of Americans that our truly great presidents had to be wartime presidents. George W. Bush understood this and welcomed his role in a war he manufactured.

To get a more sensible and different perspective on what makes a truly great president one ought to read Ivan Eland's book *Recarving Rushmore: Ranking the Presidents on Peace, Prosperity, and Liberty*. He shows why the so-called weak presidents should be considered great and the so-called great ones should be called the enemies of peace, prosperity, and liberty. Since human nature is such, the Founders understood that presidents would tend to accumulate power. Even though the framers provided protection from this by placing maximum authority in the legislative branch, the extent to which Congress has relinquished power to the executive is startling.

We now have an executive that decides on war and the Congress acquiesces. After Vietnam, many people demanded restraint on a president pursuing war without congressional approval and declaration. Passage of the War Powers Resolution of 1972 was intended to help, but as so often occurs, a problem to be solved only offers opportunity to those who created the problem to gain even more power. Instead of restraining the President, the War Powers Resolution actually gave him authority to pursue war for ninety days without congressional approval. The only problem is that a war of ninety days is virtually impossible to stop. The war promoters scream that to do so is unpatriotic, un-American, and not supporting the troops.

Since World War II, all our wars have been fought without a congressional declaration of war. It's the President who decides and the Congress that submits by appropriating the funds demanded. This presidential authority was never intended by the Constitution.

Today, trade policy has been taken over by the executive

branch, and Congress graciously cedes this power. Transferring authority under fast-track legislation defies the intent of the Constitution. Trade treaties are not entered into, since senatorial approval by two-thirds would be required and more difficult to pass. This has led to international trade agreements such as WTO, NAFTA, and CAFTA that sacrifice national sovereignty to international government organizations. These agreements can supersede state laws as well. The Constitution assigns to the Congress the responsibility of regulating foreign trade. If the people and the Congress preferred that the President and international government entities control trade, the Constitution should have been amended. Ignoring the Constitution on these issues or any issue serves to undermine constitutional legitimacy.

The executive branch, whether headed by a Republican or a Democrat, never hesitates to use the various tools granted or allowed by the neglectful Congress. Executive orders today represent far more than the narrow understanding by our early presidents. Writing an executive order to carry out a constitutional duty is a far cry from using executive orders for the sole purpose of writing laws while circumventing the Congress. During the impasse over abortion during the medical care reform debate in 2009, President Obama "solved" the problem by writing an executive order and ignoring Congress.

Paul Begala's cocky statement regarding executive orders says it all: "Stroke of the pen, law of the land, kinda cool." Though executive orders shouldn't be the law of the land, let there be no doubt that law enforcement agencies and the regulating arm of the bureaucracy treat them as such.

Statements signed by presidents clarify, or put all Americans on notice, as to exactly how they intend to carry out Congress's rules. Executive orders have been around for quite a while and used by both Democrats and Republicans. They have been used much more extensively since the George W. Bush administration in the legislation following 9/11.

Agencies under control of the executive branch have been writing regulations for decades. Congress prompts the process and ignores the constitutional directive for its responsibility to write the laws. Not only does the executive usurp this congressional prerogative, the agencies become both the policeman and the judge in a monstrous system of administrative justice. In this system the citizen is considered guilty until proven innocent. Usually the average citizen is unable to afford legal council to defend himself. Citizens just grin and bear it and pay the penalty as the government bureaucrats swell their ranks with constant pay raises and job security.

The war powers assumed by presidents during periods of conflict may well be the most dangerous assumption of power by the executive branch. Once our president gets us into a "war," even those undeclared, the routine expansion of emergency judicial powers follows. Though this has happened in all our wars, for the most part, when declared wars ended with the defeat of the enemy, the violation of civil liberties by overenergetic presidents tended to return to prewar conditions with an improvement in the protection of civil liberties.

Economic controls are much more easily imposed under a declared emergency. Roosevelt, Truman, and Nixon all ordered wage and price controls. Nixon did it by executive order due to price inflation of the 1970s, which was a consequence of the guns-and-butter philosophy of the 1960s.

With aggressive use and a distorted view of wartime presidential powers after 9/11, George W. Bush established a new precedent for arbitrarily increasing presidential powers. Though the war was not a declared war and terrorism is but a tactic used by desperate people for a variety of reasons, it became necessary to talk incessantly about the "war on terror," claiming that the "war" justified the powers he assumed. There's been no sign that the Obama administration is reversing this dangerous trend. And there's no sign that the Congress will restrain this usurpation of powers by our presidents.

The Supreme Court in 1953 set a precedent in the *United States v. Reynolds* case for current presidential abuse of their constitutionally limited powers. This ruling allowed the executive branch to claim "state secret privileges" as a reason for keeping any and all secrets it claimed, even without showing the evidence, would threaten "national security." President Obama now uses this precedent to hold suspects indefinitely and without charges being made.[1] The state's secrecy provision was also used by the Bush administration to massively expand executive powers. The Freedom of Information Act has not limited this court-approved power, and the Foreign Intelligence Surveillance Act has increased the dangers of runaway executive powers in the post–9/11 era.

Today, the executive branch can ignore a civil trial verdict of innocence if the administration still deems the individual

---

1. "Obama Administration Weighs Indefinite Detention," NPR, November 24, 2010. Story by Dina Temple-Raston.

a threat, and the individual can be thrown in prison indefinitely. Thus, the executive branch has encroached on judicial powers as well.

Any individual, including an American citizen, whom the President considers a threat can actually be targeted for assassination, as we discussed earlier. No charges made, no trial held, no rights guaranteed! This is extremely bad news for the future of the American Republic.

But more often, individuals can be arrested and held indefinitely without charges being made. The right of habeas corpus is no longer guaranteed. The reason given is that national security would be endangered if trials were held. What they don't want to consider is that this type of "justice" can endanger the liberties and safety of all Americans.

In times of declared wars and on battlefields, military courts can be justified. However, claiming that in times of peace the President can establish secret military tribunals and ignore due process is a dangerous move toward the totalitarian state. Anytime it's argued that today's conditions are different and sacrificing liberty for security is necessary, one should always consider exactly how he or she would like to be treated by an overly aggressive federal police officer who falsely identified him or her suspect.

Presidents today have huge control over off-budget spending. Money appropriated for Afghanistan was directed early on by Bush to start the war in Iraq before the proper funds were approved.

Presidents can work hand in glove with the Federal Reserve. The Federal Reserve can loan and give money to other central banks and other governments without congressional approval or oversight. Illegal funding of the CIA from private businesses, banks, and illegal drug trade have been documented. Some have called the CIA the President's secret army. This abuse continues to grow.

The President's Working Group on Financial Markets, with their huge influence and authority over financial markets, can manipulate markets and profit from it—all off budget. The Exchange Stabilization Fund, the CFTC, the SEC, and the Treasury, along with the Federal Reserve, can fund almost anything they desire. It was not difficult to fund the secret wars in Afghanistan and Nicaragua in the 1980s. The ominous power of the executive can easily intimidate a reluctant Congress.

But Congress does nothing to reclaim its authority and the responsibility given it under the Constitution. A large group of conservatives make the earmark controversy the litmus test for conservative credentials and astoundingly demand that Congress deliver to the executive branch the power to earmark all spending. This only enhances presidential power. Voting against an earmark doesn't save a dime—it only allows the executive branch to decide how the money will be spent, which is a clear responsibility of the Congress under the Constitution. The solution to the budgetary crisis is to simply get enough people in Congress to refuse to fund all unconstitutional spending by following the directions of Article I, Section 8.

The outstanding expert on the issue of executive power is Louis Fisher, who spent thirty years researching the subject for the Library of Congress and the Congressional Research Service. I've heard him lament on quite a few occasions

Congress's continual, inexplicable surrendering of its prerogatives and delivering them on a platter to the executive branch. The assumption by the authors of the Constitution overestimated the future Congresses' willingness to keep the power of the presidency in check.

Today's events are reminiscent of the Old Testament story of how the Israelites demanded a king over God's objection. They believed that a king would give them peace and security. The results proved otherwise. So too will it be with America: The dictatorial government that is ever approaching will not provide the security the American people are seeking, and the sacrifice of our liberties will have been for naught.

———

Denson, John. 2001. *Reassessing the Presidency: The Rise of the Executive State and the Decline of Freedom.* Auburn, AL: Mises Institute.

Fisher, Louis. 2004. *Presidential War Power.* Lawrence: University Press of Kansas.

Morely, Felix. 1981. *Freedom and Federalism.* Indianapolis: Liberty Fund.

Savage, Charlie. 2008. *Takeover: The Return of the Imperial Presidency and the Subversion of American Democracy.* New York: Back Bay Books.

FOREIGN AID

There was a time when Republicans opposed all foreign aid. That time has passed, and the only debate now is which countries will receive it and how much. There are very few members in Congress who, on principle, oppose all foreign aid.

Believing foreign aid benefits our national security allows for billions of dollars to be wasted, encouraging a foreign policy that inevitably leads to unintended consequences that come back to haunt us.

Foreign aid support comes for various reasons. We must support our allies and keep them strong. We must, for humanitarian reasons, help impoverished nations. It's our duty. Others argue we are obligated to financially support those countries that yield to our demand that we maintain military bases in their country. Oftentimes, corporations and universities will lobby hard for foreign aid expenditures with the hope of getting a research contract or selling certain products to the recipient country.

For certain, all foreign aid is a form of credit allocation.

American citizens are taxed to fund these foreign giveaway programs. That means funds are taken out of the hands of private citizens, who are prevented from deciding how the money should be spent. Allowing government or bureaucratic decisions on spending capital is always inferior to private companies and people deciding how the money should be spent.

But most importantly, foreign aid never works to achieve the stated goal of helping the poor of other nations. The decisions as to who will receive the money are political at both ends. Our politicians make decisions on where the money is to go and the politicians in the other countries are in charge of how it will be spent.

In poor countries food aid becomes a tool for maintaining political power. Frequently, those in the greatest need are involved in civil war. The aid literally becomes a weapon for one faction to use against another. This usually delays the needed peace effort, by subsidizing one side over the other.

Many of the large foreign aid grants are driven strictly by special interest politics and a pretense that it serves our national security interests. Since the Camp David Accords under Jimmy Carter, Israel has received more than $100 billion and Egypt has received more than $50 billion. It is nice that they have quit killing each other, but if the peace depends on these funds flowing into these two countries, it's not a very stable peace. Both countries become more dependent on us and have less incentive to take care of their own needs. Who knows, peace may have come even without our money.

Foreign aid always has some strings attached. Spending on weapons bought in the United States is commonplace, and one of the main reasons conservative Republicans have been champions of foreign aid. It's good for our military-industrial complex and it's justified because the recipients will then be reliable military allies and well armed. Too often, though, countries that we have subsidized and armed become our enemies and the weapons are used against us. There are far too many examples of this.

Not only do countries receive direct unilateral aid from us, hundreds of billions of dollars have been delivered through multilateral organizations such as the World Bank, the International Monetary Fund, and other Agency for International Development entities. Loans and loan guarantees are frequently used.

The Federal Reserve is allowed to make secret agreements with foreign governments, foreign central banks, and international financial institutions. Since an audit of these agreements has never been allowed, there is no way to know with certainty whether the Fed participates in foreign policy strategy. But in November 2010, the Fed was pressured to cough up information about its practices. Many people were shocked to discover that so much of the newly created money went to the biggest players in the banking industry and to foreign institutions; I was not shocked. I read the revelations as confirmation of what I've long suspected.

With its capability of making secret loans to and guarantees with other countries, the Fed may well be much more involved financially than what Congress does under the appropriation process. But just like the Congress demanding "kickbacks" for their taxpayers' financial gifts, I'm sure the Fed can arrange for favors in return for providing funds in the financial community.

There's nothing wrong with foreign aid per se, as when rich countries help others in poorer countries who may be suffering from a natural disaster. But it has to be private. The odds then are much better that the funds will be put to more constructive use than they are when it's a government transfer.

The only long-term benefit that one country can bestow on another suffering deprivation from socialistic government policies is to export ideas of liberty, free markets, sound money, and private property rights. Just as with material assistance, these ideas must be sent in a voluntary fashion, not by government.

Too often our financial aid is given on condition that the recipients spend the money on education. It's not unusual that this effort turns out to be quite negative. We have made efforts to teach developing nations how to set up an IRS-style income tax system, a central bank, and other social welfare programs. The extreme of this is when the neoconservatives dedicate themselves to "spreading America's goodness" with bombs and bullets. They claim we have a moral obligation to spread democracy around the world. This is usually only an excuse to make their violent efforts sound more humanitarian.

International foreign aid is supposed to reflect the right of everyone to live with dignity, a worthy goal but unachievable by the authoritarian approach of wealth distribution through taxation. This method provides no worthwhile benefits. This international right to live with dignity is the extension of the Freedom from Want of FDR's Four Freedoms. The right to life and liberty in no way implies one's right to someone else's property domestically or internationally.

As long as the American people accept the notion that their

money, taken through taxation and given away to strangers in foreign lands by our politicians, is somehow beneficial to our national interest, foreign aid will continue. When the people demand that the process stop by being more selective as to whom they choose to represent them, or when we go broke and can't afford it, this policy will end.

Complacency comes from guilt that government officials instill in the people and that allows the transfer of wealth in this manner. It's easier to achieve the electorate's support when a country is reasonably prosperous. Many are convinced by the argument that U.S. foreign aid is a small amount—now $50 billion per year—and the rich will pay.

The truth is that borrowed money and inflating the currency to pay for the deficit that foreign aid contributes to puts the burden on the poor and the middle class. Tragically, the humanitarian arguments are far removed from reality. Foreign aid can best be described as taking money from the poor in a rich country and giving it to the rich and powerful in a poor country. Unchecked, it assures that both the donor and recipient countries become poorer in the end.

Blanchette, Jude. 2003. "The Futility of Foreign Aid," in *The Free Market*, Vol. 23, No. 7. Mises Institute.

FOUR FREEDOMS

The Progressive Era in the early part of the twentieth century saw a systematic attack on the principles of liberty by both Democrats and Republicans. This involved William McKinley and Theodore Roosevelt as well as the Wilsonian onslaught that gave us the Federal Reserve, the income tax, the Seventeenth Amendment, and an interventionist foreign policy with World War I. On September 30, 2010, Germany finally paid the last of its war debt from World War I, but the legacy of this ghastly period of history lives on. The sharp attack on our liberties was institutionalized by Franklin Delano Roosevelt in the 1930s.

FDR, in a well-known speech on January 6, 1941, put words to the process in his odious Four Freedoms Speech. His first two freedoms restated the First Amendment: freedom of speech and expression and freedom of religion. The Constitution was clear, however, that the First Amendment, as the others, was originally intended to apply to the Congress and the federal government. The First Amendment opens with an emphatic: "Congress shall write no law." And if Congress cannot write a law restricting our freedom of expression, certainly the judiciary or the executive branch could not either.

Roosevelt changed this. The Founders assured that the individual states would be responsible for protection of their own citizens and their goal was strictly to restrain the federal government in any abuse of our liberties. FDR not only implied that enforcement was a federal matter but emphasized that he was issuing a world mandate, applying the phrase "everywhere in the world" to each of his listed "freedoms."

Fine: It would be nice if all individual rights would be honored around the world, just as President Wilson pushed his high-minded foreign policy of aggressively "making the world safe for democracy." But Roosevelt was making a commitment for worldwide enforcement of his guarantees, and this was quite a change in our responsibilities.

His last two freedoms are the ones that radically institutionalized the concept of rights in the United States. These rights also would apply to the entire world, according to Roosevelt, implying that world government would be a natural consequence of these efforts for enforcement purposes.

FDR's third freedom was "Freedom from Want—Everywhere in the World." This means he believed he could legislate or dictate economic prosperity and security for the world's populations. He claimed these goals were the answer to dictatorships but never gave an answer as to where the authority came from to assure government distribution of the necessities of life or how it could be accomplished without violence or violation of the rights of the individuals who paid the taxes to accomplish this. He referred to this as a "moral order."

Pursuing a policy of "freedom from want" is nothing more

than a license to steal. Such a program guarantees poverty for the masses and power to the government elite. To describe an "absence of want" as a right for every individual mocks the notion that every individual has a right to his or her life and a responsibility for it. To describe the redistribution of wealth by an authoritarian government as "freedom" can only lead to socialist or fascistic schemes—of which we have seen many.

Roosevelt's fourth freedom was "Freedom from Fear"—as if it was only so easy! Hardly does any government, whose goal it is to expand its authority over the people, sincerely want to eliminate fear. It is fear, pumped up by those in authority, that frightens the people into begging for the government to protect them from the perceived ravages of the free market economy and the infidels about to attack us. Roosevelt claimed this would be achieved by worldwide reduction of armaments to prevent aggression.

Roosevelt's motivation and intent are unknown to me, but the results of his effort did not serve the cause of freedom in the United States. Within seven months of this speech, Roosevelt stopped all oil shipments to Japan which helped lead to the bombing of Pearl Harbor. All the while, Roosevelt preached a distorted view of freedom; he was maneuvering us into war. The result has been that the United States is the largest producer and distributor of weapons in all of history.

Eleanor Roosevelt saw to it that this concept of the four freedoms was incorporated in the United Nation's Declaration of Human Rights. In its Preamble that document states: "Freedom from fear and want has been proclaimed the highest aspiration of the common people." It's more accurate to say it's the highest aspiration of promoters of world government to accept this understanding of rights and this method of achieving peace.

Any effort to mandate or enforce the goal of making everyone free from want and fear through government action will guarantee the destruction of the concept of personal liberty. Whether it's local government or world government, and no matter the motivation, this effort can only destroy one's right to life, liberty, and property. But we have been living with this effort, made popular by FDR, for seventy years, and results should be self-evident. Our country and the world are more fearful and in greater need than ever, facing a financial crisis of epic proportions.

Roosevelt no doubt would claim his Four Freedoms were based on a moral imperative. Yet everything he believed in and promoted was based on an immoral principle of government force, whether it was the promotion of the use of force in the economy or his militarism abroad—all financed by historic deficits and with great hostility toward sound money. Stealing the gold from American citizens hardly fell into the category of protecting freedom. If the goal is to guarantee to the people freedom from want, the only option is to strive for a free society with free markets.

A free society is based on a simple moral imperative. Everyone's life is his own, and the fruits of his labor should be his as well. No part of it belongs to the government as a matter of right. This right to life comes naturally to everyone, with the gift of liberty and the right to keep the fruits of one's labor. The most that should ever be expected of government is to protect that liberty. That authority, gained by the explicit consent of the people, should be strictly limited. Consenting to a greater role for government violates the moral defense of freedom.

Though this imperative is based on a moral premise, the free society requires legal tolerance toward personal moral behavior or habits of others insofar as they are peaceful and do not engage in aggressive force. This leaves all personal decisions relating to personal moral behavior to each individual. It needs a tolerance that is frequently not practiced. That's not to say that freedom is a free-for-all and that we can behave in any manner we want. A free people do not use force to mold personal moral behavior, but a free people do entrust the management of social norms to the courts of taste and manners that arise spontaneously within civilization.

Powers that the government holds should arrive through the consent of the governed. One should never be permitted to assume this arbitrary power over others, nor can a majority of the people consent to giving away the liberty of others. If this is allowed, it shatters the notion that a truly free society and a limited government are designed to protect the minority and prevent the majority from becoming the dictator by winning elections through majority vote.

This impossible notion that government can guarantee freedom from want and fear destroys the concept of liberty. Instead, it is the exact opposite. It claims that all individuals and groups—limited to those who know how to influence or take over government—have a right to whatever they want or need and it can be obtained by robbing from those who produce. Government and its agents become armed bandits marauding the country, robbing and threatening for the benefit of the special interests.

The idea of freedom from want and fear as a mandate of government opens up Pandora's box. "Fear" is a nebulous term that can be subjectively defined and artificially created. Wants are endless and are unrelated to the definition of freedom. Under these conditions government is expected to provide for any need or desire. And since government never produces anything, its only option is to steal from one group and pass what it has stolen on to the next. One would expect that such a system would breed a corrupt political system of big money and lobbyists.

It is absurd to assume that government can legislate and devise a system where prosperity and all wants are fulfilled by destroying the basic premise underpinning a free society. The defense of private property, free choices, contracts, and sound money is impossible once the notion of rights is undermined.

Most people believe the people have a "right" to food, shelter, clothing, medical care, education, and jobs. This misguided school of thought has been around a long time and is responsible for the poverty and economic suffering and wars that we are forced to live with. All this because of a confused concept of what freedom is all about. It is due to this misunderstanding that liberty and prosperity must suffer. Any attempt to achieve the goal of "freedom from want" can only be done by the use of government force and at the sacrifice of personal liberty.

The Founders of our country rejected this goal, knowing it was an impossible task for government and would only bring us hardship. Instead of freedom meaning that the government is responsible for redistributing wealth to make sure all have "freedom from want," it should instead be understood that true freedom is based on the moral principle that each of us has a right to our life and liberty and the fruits of our labor. These are two completely opposite views on freedom. They cannot exist side by side, nor can the principle of one's right to his or her life be watered down.

Many believe that politics is the art of compromise. Certain political goals may be served in this manner, but compromising this basic moral principle serves the pragmatist-utilitarian belief that government planning is superior to individual decision making. Those who claim that a little compromise is crucial to silence the demands of the authoritarians, the free-loaders, and the powerful few who end up controlling the government are always willing to give up some fraction of their liberties and property in the hope that the demand for more benefits or privilege will be satiated. But it never happens. The more they get the more they demand. They never become free from want.

Legislators who do not hold firm convictions or understand the nature of freedom, but generally recognize the danger of the welfare system, easily succumb to a proposal to grant just a little bit of wealth transfer by government force, hoping it will always remain minimal. Granting food stamps benefits to 2 percent of the population in need seems like a reasonable thing to do. But what is not realized is that though only 2 percent get undeserved benefits from the 98 percent, 100 percent of the principle of individual liberty has been sacrificed. That's not a compromise; that's called selling out one's core beliefs.

It was only to be expected that the dependency of 2 percent would grow and spread. This process started decades before

FDR's Four Freedoms speech and originally was for helping corporate, business, and banking interests. The twentieth
century saw this principle of special interest government taking care of people's needs spread to the common man out of
"fairness" and political pressure, especially since the Depression of the 1930s.

Here is a good example of how a compromise can lead to
chaos. The personal income tax began at 1 percent and applied
only to the rich. Just look at the size of the tax code today.
Those 20,000 pages are total Greek to all members of Congress, and even the IRS agents cannot agree on the code's
interpretation. A 1 percent concession on the principle of
taxing income has brought us to where we are today in this
horrendous, impossibly complex tax system. Even those who
don't technically pay a tax on their income suffer as well. Indirectly, there are costs passed on to other workers and consumers. Payroll taxes are a huge burden to the poor. They are
looting everyone, crushing us all under the financial strain.

All political energy for greater than 100 years has been
directed toward increasing government power to determine
who will receive the benefits. The result has been crumbs to
the poor and an attack on the middle class, while Wall Street
and the banks continue to benefit from the bailouts. Only a
clear understanding and protection of individual liberty can
rescue us from the pending economic and political disaster.

It's such an irony that so many expect that government
can protect us from fear. Depending on government protection from all potential outside threats and domestic violence
requires a great deal of sacrifice of our freedom and especially
our privacy. The irony is that those who hunger for power

over others—for their own good—know that the people will welcome government's promises of security when fear is prevalent. But it is commonplace for the would-be tyrants to create fear or exaggerate it on purpose so that people will actually rush to the government saviors, demanding safety with a willingness to sacrifice liberty.

Nevertheless, fear is constantly being manufactured by our leaders, Republicans and Democrats, by invoking a current "Hitler" about to attack us: Saddam Hussein, Ahmadinejad, the Taliban, the communists, al Qaeda, or whomever. This fear is required to get the people's support for fighting unnecessary wars and supporting the military industrial complex. The fear is concocted. The war is very clearly not necessary. The results are devastating to our security and our prosperity. The real fear ought to be directed toward our own leaders and instigators of our policies.

It's pretty sad when President Obama can justify massively expanding the war in Afghanistan and Pakistan and justify his actions by referencing Christian just-war theory, the greatness of Gandhi, and the nonviolent approach of Martin Luther King, Jr. Fear, war, lies, all melted into a policy that expands the state while destroying our economy and liberties.

President George W. Bush constantly preached war while couching all his speeches in freedom-loving language. It was always because we were free and prosperous that Muslim radicals wanted to kill us. The real reason was never hinted at: that it was a reflection of our failed foreign policy. According to President Bush, everything that he did was to protect freedom. Yet he was selling everything through fear. Those who disagreed were immediately labeled enemies of freedom and friends of the radicals. We were either with him or against him. This is nothing new.

His conclusion was exactly the opposite of that of James Madison, who said correctly that "war was the most dreaded enemy of liberty." The President would have us believe that preventive war was the best friend of freedom. For him and his successor, war is peace. It is disgraceful that President Obama, whom many believed to be the candidate of peace, could be handed the Nobel Peace Prize while carrying on senseless wars based on lies and continually expanding the war machine. It's almost hard to believe.

The American people seem overly willing to accept war, economic sacrifice, and loss of liberty as long as the President, whether FDR, Bush, or Obama, claims his actions are well intentioned and are done to protect our freedoms. Any disagreement means that one does not share a love of freedom. And that is exactly how fear works.

Flynn, John T. 1944. *As We Go Marching.* New York: Doubleday.

Flynn, John T. [1955] 2008. *The Roosevelt Myth.* Auburn, AL: Mises Institute.

GLOBAL WARMING

You can count me among the global-warming skeptics. I gather that my ranks have grown enough so that the fear of global warming is now replaced with a more generalized fear of "climate change," covering all empirical contingencies.

But regardless of whether one believes global warming is real, I seriously doubt the capacity of a global body made up of bureaucrats and scientists on the public payroll, when given the power to attempt a global climate manipulation, to cook up a workable plan with effects that cannot be discerned for twenty or more years. I've seen how government programs work. They aren't designed to last more than a single election cycle. The idea that government can plan weather patterns for decades strikes me as the height of absurdity.

Crucial to this whole scheme has been the voice of radical environmentalism. Many of the people in this movement simply do not desire economic progress. They loathe the internal combustion engine. They are against pesticides, asphalt, oil, cars, meat, and modernity in all its forms. They long for a simpler time when there were only 500 million people living on earth because that is all that the food supply would sustain. This attitude is creepy and dangerous, an unserious, intellectual luxury that, in fact, if taken to its logical conclusion, could unravel economic progress and lead to suffering and death.

Building up fear and manipulating people into demanding that government save us is how radical environmentalists operate. Artificial fear not only generates support but demands that we pursue war policies, no matter how dangerous and ill-advised they may be. We saw how fear worked to build the state in 2008 and the following years. Bailouts for huge banks and corporations were rushed through Congress and assisted by the Federal Reserve after the people, and even members of Congress, become convinced that an economic Armageddon was at our doorstep.

The same type of fear propaganda has been raised to the extreme by the environmental movement determined to socialize our nation and deindustrialize it, seemingly on purpose.

Radical environmentalism has systematically undermined the defense of free markets for decades, but especially in the past twenty years. Everything from early public school indoctrination to our media and Hollywood have created such a poisoned atmosphere of political correctness that any questioning or dissent on the science used to support the radical environmentalist position is ridiculed and written off as crazy talk. Even reputable scientists who question the assumption and data used are not afforded the slightest respect regardless of the authenticity of their challenges.

The whole movement is energized by pumping up fear and nonverifiable propaganda. This radical environmental movement evolved from the antinuclear hysteria that stopped all nuclear plant development for the past thirty years, causing a severe price to be paid by our economic system. Some have estimated that the loss of efficiency resulting from this policy of obstructing development of nuclear power has cost us an estimated ten trillion dollars. Hysterical resistance to nuclear power also forced an increase in the rise of less environmentally friendly alternatives.

Instead, these same individual groups promote government-subsidized wind power. I'm sympathetic to the idea of wind power, and in the right circumstances, it's quite practical. I happen to own a windmill attached to a well pump. It may cut my electric bill a couple of dollars, but the truth is, wind power is not competitive, nor is it a good environmental alternative. To replace one nuclear power generator you need windmills to cover an area the size of Connecticut. Sensible green environmentalists are becoming aware of this and are taking a second look at nuclear power.

The other incentive for the extremists to propagandize against technology and free markets has been the obvious failure of socialism in the twentieth century after the collapse of the Soviet Union. Yet that is when the world recognized the total failure of socialism. It had been predicted many years before by Ludwig von Mises. Tactics changed and great emphasis was placed on "saving the planet" as the excuse needed for government take-over of economic activity. Defending socialism openly was no longer good political strategy, but its failure in the twentieth century did not diminish the desire of many to pursue the same goals but with a varied strategy and different terminology.

Actually, the precise type of socialism changed as well. The Soviet and Chinese communist type of socialism is no longer the ideal they strive for. Government intervention that works with corporations—a form of corporatism—is now an acceptable form of socialism, sometimes referred to as fascism. Unfortunately, if left unchecked it leads to outright military fascism of the worst kind. The medical care takeover by government demonstrates this. Even with the massive government takeover of health care by the Obama administration, the drug companies, insurance companies, health management companies, large hospitals, and even the American Medical Association are all bidding for a piece of the pie. Corporations thrive, the patients suffer, and the free market deteriorates further.

The radicalization of the country by the environmentalists pursues the same strategy. Cap and trade legislation will introduce a whole new product of CO_2 permits that will be created and traded by the big financial interests bailed out after the crash, such as Goldman Sachs. Control over industrial production will be achieved, which is the socialist goal, and the corporations and certain Wall Street financial firms will be big players and beneficiaries in the process.

How does all this come about? Why do so many fall for propaganda and the pseudoscience that this whole movement spews out? It's out of fear. It took quite a few years to convince the majority of Americans to accept the idea that CO_2 was a poison whose production caused global warming of crisis proportion. Public school indoctrination cannot be dismissed as being a major contributor to this gross misunderstanding.

The real message that underlies the goal of the radical

environmentalists is to blame modern man for every change in nature. They *have* avoided blaming volcanic eruptions as man caused—so far. Nature itself is a cause of atmospheric pollution, and this source is gigantic and comparable to all the man-made ills one can name. Calling attention to the comparison is something the CO_2 police are not interested in.

As one sided as the debate over global warming has been for decades, common sense and true science have begun to have an impact. Not only have the scientific arguments against global warming alarmists been challenged, but evidence now points to ulterior motivations and manipulation of pseudoscience as proof of global warming being a consequence of industrial manufacturing.[1] The availability of e-mails written by promoters of global warming documented much of what many suspected. Statistics were biased, and evidence was destroyed. The environmental globalists lost a lot of credibility, but the debate is far from over. Washington, DC, and our major universities and media all pump up the fear that an environmental catastrophe awaits us. To challenge this in public is equivalent to being the archenemy of the people, un-American, and unpatriotic.

Most Americans have been bamboozled into believing that all reputable scientists believe in global warming and that CO_2 emissions are a major problem. The truth is there are just as many and even more qualified scientists refuting the sketchy and questionable evidence regarding global warming.

---

1. The evidence of manipulation here is overwhelming. But consider Ralph Alexander, *Global Warming False Alarm* (Royal Oak, Michigan: Canterbury, 2009).

The evidence presented was chosen to support a predetermined conclusion.

Supporters of global warming theories vary. Some truly believe, some are brainwashed, some join to keep an academic career going, others know it is politically correct, but the real philosophic motivation came from the authoritarians who sought more power and resented progress. Some are also neo-Malthusians who see a grave danger in an unwanted pregnancy and population growth that compounds the threat to the environment. They do not understand how industrial growth in a free market is the only solution to poverty and hunger. There was a time when I did not choose to take on the radical environmentalists, giving them the benefit of the doubt for their good intentions. And there are many who have been influenced by the false science. Only good science can refute this. In the past, I stuck with some neutralizing advice since so few extreme environmentalists are open minded, pleading with them that they at least study both sides of the argument. This is still good advice for some, but beware, the Al Gores of the world won't be yielding to this advice anytime soon.

The greatest challenge to those who believe man is not guilty could be the charge that they don't care about the environment. The truth is that if the CO_2 hysteria is a hoax, new regulations not only will hurt the environment but will massively increase poverty and hunger in the world. Evidence is strong that cap and trade type legislation not only undermines productivity and wealth, many believe it increases CO_2 emissions. This results from factories leaving more efficient conditions and being pushed into third world countries where the cheapest form of fossil fuel is used.

The charge that defenders of the free market don't care about the environment is obviously false. Polluting one's neighbor's property, air, or water is contrary to market ethics and law. Trading permits to pollute would not be considered. Only central economic planners come up with schemes like this.

If this were just an academic discussion it wouldn't matter that much, but it has major ramifications; if the extremists are not refuted we will pay dearly for it and compound the economic crisis that we've already brought on ourselves.

Once the radicals realized that the decades-old rant on global warming was losing credibility because evidence was showing that temperatures may well be falling, they shifted their propaganda language to "climate change." Climate change has been going on for millions of years, but now it's all the fault of man's operating in a free market economy. And it's become just another excuse for more government—global in scope—to deal with the "impending disaster."

Man, over the centuries, became more civilized and, with technology, advanced and learned how to harness energy to protect us from the elements and at the same time raised our standard of living. By using energy placed on the earth for a purpose, we overcame the deadly natural elements of weather—heat and cold, wind and rain, floods and droughts. People conquered the difficulties of persistent and unpredictable climate change, and now we're told that we caused the very problem we have so successfully been able to overcome to a large degree.

Dr. Arthur B. Robinson, publisher and editor of the newsletter *Access to Energy*, and other scientists confirmed that climate change and temperature variations are related to sunspot activity and water vapor. "A sixfold increase in hydrocarbon use since 1940 has had no noticeable effect on atmospheric temperature or on the trend of glacial length," according to Dr. Robinson. The CO_2 in the atmosphere has increased by 2 percent in the past fifty years but is unrelated to temperature changes. It has been shown that higher CO_2 levels will cause plants to grow faster and larger with less water.

It took a lot of years of concerted effort to scare the people into believing that grave danger lies ahead unless we institute radical new laws worldwide limiting growth and taxing energy. Though the tide is turning, it will require many more years and hard evidence to come back to sanity with regards to CO_2 emissions and the use of hydrocarbons for energy. Truth, though inconvenient at times, will win out in the end. Al Gore is already on the defensive. His Nobel Peace Prize is hardly evidence of his credibility. Don't forget that Barack Obama got the Nobel Prize for peace while massively expanding the war in south-central Asia. War is peace; superstition is science. All with a straight face!

The green movement has brought about all kinds of changes in the way we live. Some of the changes are not necessarily bad, but the good changes and conservation could have come without all the programs that actually have a negative economic and environmental impact. Certainly, recycling for the most part consumes more energy than it saves.[2] Recycling aluminum makes economic sense, but that would happen even without the demand to recycle everything from paper to glass and plastic.

---

2. Daniel K. Benjamin, "Eight Great Myths of Recycling," Jane S. Shaw, ed., PERC Policy Series, number PS-28 (September 2003) http://www.perc .org/pdf/ps28.pdf.

The same people who demand that we quit using hydro-carbon fuels usually hate the cleanest and cheapest source of energy—nuclear. That's the reason we have not had a new nuclear plant built in thirty years. (Hopefully, this will change. A license has finally been granted for two new nuclear reactors in my district in Bay City, even though all hurdles have, as of yet, not been overcome.)

And to top it off, they also express great fear that we are now at "peak oil," and for that reason too, we are told, we must conserve (and suffer a bit if necessary) for the benefit of future generations.

If the extremists had not gained the upper hand there would still be plenty of fretting about "peak oil," and they would still be wringing their hands and demanding a federal government policy that will guarantee energy independence. Don't use oil or coal, avoid nuclear, and stay energy independent at low cost. Taxes constantly rising, regulations increasing, inflation increasing, and obstacles placed in the way of developing new fuel, and the planners decide that national economic planning is not enough—to regulate energy, we are told, there must be a globalized solution.

Authoritarians are obsessed with planning and despise free market policies. They have no interest in an objective analysis of the peak oil theory that argues the world will soon be out of oil. Peak oil is a nonproblem for a couple of reasons. Trillions of dollars are being misallocated into seeking "green" replace-ments at very high costs and a detriment to our environment. Windmills and solar panels to replace hydrocarbon with-out using nuclear would destroy unbelievable acreage in the United States and around the world and would never come close to providing the energy needed to sustain a decent standard of living for the people of the world.

Whether or not we have reached "peak oil" would be of little relevance if the market were allowed to solve the problem of providing the cheapest and cleanest energy needed. We may well be at that point where we will no longer see an increase in available oil for drilling. My guess is that fear tactics and pessimism have influenced this consensus. The fear is driven by those who don't want hydrocarbons to ever be used. Some are too pessimistic, because over the past decades new discoveries have constantly surprised the economic planners.

Besides, technology is quite capable of obtaining clean liquefied coal—something the United States has in abundant supply—as well as providing a safe and clean and cheaper way of using oil from sand or shale. The truth is, I don't know nor does any other human being know how much hydrocarbon energy is available worldwide. Not even Al Gore! And whether or not it can be used in an environmentally approved manner, my guess is that there's a lot more oil and gas yet to be discovered.

This whole scandalous debate is misleading. The only thing that counts is whether the free market or government planners are in charge of providing energy to the people. "Energy independence" shouldn't be the goal with the government in charge. That's a sure way to create an unwanted foreign dependence and for shortages to develop.

A free market would allow alternate fuels to develop more efficiently than large central economic planners dictating a program. Nuclear energy is safe and clean and cheap. If we were forced to rely on nuclear power we could easily adapt. Other countries already have.

A national energy policy, a Department of Energy, an energy czar, thousands of regulations and multiple taxes and subsidies are totally unnecessary. A national policy of freedom would ask for no more government planning for energy needs than a cell phone planning program is necessary to make sure all poor people can afford a government-approved cell phone distributed by a department of mass communications run by the government. The organic progress of markets is the source of economic development.

It's a loss of both confidence and understanding of how markets work that causes so many people to accept the need for government to provide us with goods and services. There should be no difference between the distribution of cell phones, computers, TVs, medical care, or energy. It's amazing that people don't understand that the more the market is involved and the smaller the government, the lower the price, the better the distribution, and the higher the quality. The authoritarian approach too often wins the propaganda war, using fear as its weapon in gaining public acceptance of flawed economic thinking. If the economic arguments are too complex to understand, simply defending liberty as a moral right should suffice.

Anderson, Terry. 2001. *Free Market Environmentalism*. New York: Palgrave Macmillan.

Horner, Christopher. 2007. *The Politically Incorrect Guide to Global Warming*. Washington, DC: Regnery Publishing.

GUN CONTROL

The gun control movement has lost momentum in recent years. The Democratic Party has been conspicuously silent on the issue in recent elections because they know it's a political loser. In the midst of declining public support for new gun laws, more and more states have adopted concealed-carry programs.[1] The 9/11 terrorist attacks and rising fears about security only made matters worse for gun-control proponents, as millions of Americans were starkly reminded that we should not rely on government to protect us from criminals.

Gun-control advocates tell us that removing guns from

---

1. The National Rifle Association writes: "Since 1991, when violent crime peaked in the U.S., 24 states have adopted "shall issue" laws, replacing laws that prohibited carrying or that issued carry permits on a very restrictive basis; many other federal, state, and local gun control laws have been eliminated or made less restrictive; and the number of privately-owned guns has risen by about 90 million. The numbers of gun owners and firearms, RTC states, and people carrying firearms for protection, have risen to all-time highs, and through 2008 the nation's murder rate has decreased 46 percent to a 43-year low, and the total violent crime rate has decreased 41 percent to a 35-year low. Preliminary data reported by the FBI indicate that violent crime decreased further in the first half of 2009." http://www.nraila.org.

society makes us safer. But that is simply an impossibility. The fact is that firearm technology exists. It cannot be uninvented. As long as there is metalworking and welding capability, it matters not what gun laws are imposed upon law-abiding people. Those who wish to have guns, and disregard the law, will have guns. Paradoxically, gun control clears a path for violence and makes aggression more likely, whether the aggressor is a terrorist or a government.

I don't really believe "gun-free" zones make any difference. If they did, why would the worst shootings consistently happen in gun-free zones such as schools? And while accidents do happen, aggressive, terroristic shootings like this are unheard of at gun and knife shows, the antithesis of a gun-free zone. It bears repeating that an armed society truly is a polite society. Even if you don't like guns and don't want to own them, you benefit from those who do. It is better that criminals imagine they face an armed rather than an unarmed population.

History shows us that another tragedy of gun laws is genocide. Hitler, for example, knew well that in order to enact his "final solution," disarmament was a necessary precursor. While it is an extreme case that an unarmed populace was killed by their government, if a government is going to kill its own people, it will in fact have to disarm them first so they cannot fight back. Disarmament must happen at a time when overall trust in government is high, and under the guise of safety for the people, or perhaps the children. Knowing that any government, no matter how idealistically started, can become despotic, the Founders enabled the future freedom of Americans by enacting the Second Amendment.

In our own country, we should be ever vigilant against

any attempts to disarm the people, especially in an economic downturn. I worry that violent crime will rise sharply in the coming days, and as states and municipalities grow even more financially strained, the police will be less able or willing to respond to crime.

In many areas, local police could become more and more absorbed with revenue-generating activities, like minor traffic violations and the asset forfeiture opportunities of nonviolent drug offenses. Your safety has always, ultimately, been your own responsibility, but never more so than now. People have a natural right to defend themselves. Governments that take that away from their people are highly suspect.

Tyrants from Hitler to Mao to Stalin have sought to disarm their own citizens, for the simple reason that unarmed people are easier to control. Our Founders, having just expelled the British army, knew that the right to bear arms served as the guardian of every other right. This is the principle so often ignored by both sides in the gun control debate. Only armed citizens can ultimately resist tyrannical government.

Halbrook, Stephen. "Were the Founding Fathers in Favor of Gun Ownership?" *Washington Times*, November 5, 2000. http://www.independent.org.

Lott, John. 2010. *More Guns, Less Crime*. Chicago: University of Chicago Press.

HATE CRIMES

Passing legislation concerning crimes against minorities is supposed to show compassion and prove that our society does not discriminate. In fact, these laws do the opposite. Confidence that such efforts will help protect minorities causes a gross misunderstanding of individual rights. If all individuals should be treated the same under the law, providing greater penalties to those who commit crimes against certain racial or sexual orientation groups nullifies this effort. It means that the law provides lesser penalties to those individuals committing crimes against people without that favored orientation.

A power given to government to place a greater penalty on someone, assuming they understand the motivation for the crime—always a subjective conclusion—is a consequence of the victims belonging to a certain group. If this can be done, the power is exactly the same power that once was used to *excuse* violence if it was against a black or gay person. The only solution is to insist that all rights are individual and unrelated to belonging to a particular group.

The fallacy of this type of legislation has led to the routine understanding of groups having rights rather than all individuals having equal rights. Too often, we hear reference to gay rights, minority rights, and women's rights, etc., which undermines the concept of individual liberty.

The idea that a crime can be judged as to whether it was motivated by hate for certain groups introduces the notion of a thought police. If someone is robbed, beaten, or killed, the penalty should be unrelated to what the perpetrator was thinking at the time. It hardly matters. The actions are the actions. Imposing preferential penalties endorses the concept of relative rights, which is of course a very dangerous, slippery slope. It implies that some victims have greater worth than others. The extra and arbitrary enforcement power mocks the principle of equal justice before the law. Why should the penalty for assault be different depending on race, sexual orientation, or membership in a particular group?

Because some criminals have in the past been punished *less* harshly due to their victims' belonging to a particular group is hardly a justification for a criminal to be punished *more* harshly for the same reason. It's best we drop the whole concept of hyphenated rights and refer only to individual rights.

If we continue to arbitrarily punish someone more severely for committing a "hate" crime, we must make an assessment of the thoughts and speech of the perpetrator. It won't take a giant leap for Congress to punish bigoted speech even without an act of violence. Political correctness has already gone too far, with great social penalties for people who inadvertently and without malice or in jest offend certain ethnic, racial, or sexual groups. The mischief makers believe certain groups deserve protection from the slightest insult from rude people.

This ironically bestows less respect to groups that "need" special protection due to a perceived weakness.

Most of the effort to punish "hate crimes" and restrict speech is driven by political concerns. If it comes to speech restrictions imposed by government, patriotism will be the preferred excuse.

When hate crime legislation is written or proposed it comes up short in promoting justice.

When hate crime legislation is not driven by political concerns, it relates more to social order than anything else. The perceived goal is to address certain crimes and for emotional reasons exact greater penalties for certain individuals. Most people think of this in a one-sided manner. Included are crimes that involve white on black or other minorities, straight on gay, Christian on Muslim, Muslim on Jew, yet the reverse of these generally is not labeled a hate crime.

Extending this to international events, it's not a hate crime for American bombers to kill innocent Muslims. That's only collateral damage. Retaliation against Americans occupying a foreign country 7,000 miles from our homeland is called terrorism, supposedly motivated only by ingrained and irrational hate.

Hate crime legislation and the obsession with political correctness seem to satisfy the urge to condemn thoughtless people by misusing the law. This misuse then accomplishes nothing in solving the problems, while it promotes a perverted view of equal justice—a result that was never intended.

IMMIGRATION

There seem to be two extreme positions on immigration: completely closed borders and totally open borders. The Constitution, common sense, and the philosophy of freedom offer a principled alternative to these two rash options.

It's best to try to understand why immigration is such a hot-button issue for most Americans. There are many reasons why the politics of immigration are so emotionally charged. The most telling reason is related to economic concerns and violence; immigrants, it is said, take jobs from American working people; federal mandates require states to provide free medical and educational benefits to illegals; a weak economy exaggerates the economic consequences of legal and illegal immigration.

The political motivations are important contributing factors as well and are the concerns of many Americans. It is assumed that all immigrants, including illegals, will benefit liberals and Democrats at the voting booth. Evidence exists that some illegals do vote and they don't vote for Republicans.

Illegals are counted in the census, creating a situation where they can statistically add up to several congressional districts. Texas, for instance, gained four new seats after the 2010 census was completed and this was, to a large degree, a reflection of our immigration policies.

Due to the immensity of this emotionally charged problem, a simple answer under current conditions will not be easily found. In the ideal libertarian world, borders would be blurred and open. It would be something similar to what the Constitution did with the borders between the various states. Civilization has not yet come even close to being capable of such a policy, though it engages some in a theoretical discussion.

The libertarians who argue for completely open borders for the free flow of goods and people fail to realize that a truly libertarian society would not necessarily be that open. The land and property would be privately owned and controlled by the owners, who would have the right to prevent newcomers from entering without their permission. There would be no government havens or welfare benefits and new immigrants would come only after a sponsor's permission.

Under today's circumstances, with a government-precipitated recession (a depression for those who earn under $30,000 a year) and promises of welfare, obviously some rules are required.

It's important to note that the greatest resentment comes from government-mandated free services and a government-created unemployment crisis. Fix these two problems and finding a scapegoat for our economic crisis wouldn't be necessary.

A free and prosperous economy always looks for labor; immigrant workers would be needed and welcomed. This need could be managed by a generous guest worker program, not by illegal immigrants receiving benefits for the family and securing an easy route to permanent citizenship and thus becoming pawns of partisan political interests.

Since Washington will not soon come to its senses and allow for the needed economic corrections to restore a healthy free market economy, we are forced to deal with current conditions, which are rapidly deteriorating.

Even today with all our government excesses we have millions of people and businesses protected by private security. Dow Chemical has fences and private security guards, as do most of the chemical plants located a few miles from where I live. There are no trespassers and if a problem occurs, the police or sheriff is called.

But if a rancher on our border wants to stop trespassers on his land, he is forbidden to do so. The Feds don't even allow the state law enforcement officers to interfere! This, they argue, could lead to violence if an appropriate use of force is not used. Shooting suspected illegal aliens on sight would be a horrendous error and serious people are concerned about it happening.

At the federal government–maintained borders, where a war is going on, the violence is already out of control and growing. The conditions we have created with illegal trafficking in immigrants is serious, but the recent escalation has involved the drug cartels and border guards, the military, and the police, a consequence of the ridiculous notion that drug prohibition is a sensible social policy.

Everyone by now should know that our current war on drugs makes no more sense than alcohol prohibition did in the 1920s. One only needs to study the drug trade and corruption ongoing in Afghanistan to see the danger of the war on drugs. The huge profits that can be made are a significant incentive for corruption across the board.

Even with a healthy economy and stricter border controls, the issue of what to do with twelve-million-plus illegals already here would persist. One side says use the U.S. Army, round them up, and ship them home. The other side says give them amnesty, make them full-fledged citizens, and reward the lawbreakers, thus insulting and unfairly penalizing those who have patiently waited and obeyed our immigration laws.

The first choice—sending twelve to fifteen million illegals home—isn't going to happen and should not happen. Neither the determination or the ability to accomplish it exists. Besides, if each case is looked at separately, we would find ourselves splitting up families and deporting some who have lived here for decades, if not their entire life, and who never lived for any length of time in Mexico. This would hardly be a Good Samaritan approach to the problem. It would be incompatible with human rights.

The toughest part of showing any compassion or tolerance to the illegal immigrants who are very much Americanized is the tremendous encouragement it gives for more immigrants to come illegally and avoid the wait and bureaucracy. Considering what they face at home, they see the risk of sneaking in as being minor compared to the risk of dying in poverty in Central America.

Some of the resentment by Americans is that many immigrants are "Americanized" rather quickly.

Most immigrants do not come for handouts; rather, they

come for survival reasons and have a work ethic superior to many of our own citizens who have grown dependent on welfare and unemployment benefits. This anger may reflect embarrassment as much as anything.

Many claim that illegal immigrants take American jobs. This is true, but most of the jobs they "take" are the ones unemployed Americans refuse at the wage offered. Rarely is this even minimum wage; it's usually higher. It's hard to hide the fact that resentment toward a Hispanic immigrant is more common than that toward a European illegal immigrant.

Immigration laws, out of practicality, can never be equally enforced on those who have been assimilated for five to ten or even twenty years as compared to those caught currently coming through our border states in the Southwest. On the immigration issue I have found no one with the wisdom of Solomon. My humble suggestions on what to do follow.

- Restore our economy to a healthy free market with sound money and eliminate deficit-financed government. A vibrant economy will minimize the problems and produce a high demand for both domestic and immigrant labor.
- Abolish the welfare state. The incentive to always take a job—at whatever wage available—must prevail. A healthy economy, absent Federal Reserve–induced recession or depression and inflation, will keep real wages high.
- With free markets and private property, a need for immigrant labor becomes obvious. Make it legal and easy with a generous visitor work program.

- Enforce the laws now on the books with more border guards; permit states to enforce the law; allow landowners to provide private property security assistance, just as we do every day throughout the United States, and to work with Federal Border Control authorities. Private landowners have a right to post No Trespassing signs on their property to achieve this.

- Do not grant automatic citizenship to children of illegal immigrants born in the United States, deliberately or accidentally.

- Stop all federal mandates on the states to provide free education and medical care for illegal immigrants. The absurdity that South Texas schools are overburdened with Mexican children going back and forth over the border each day to our public school systems is resented by cash-strapped school districts.

- Bilingualism should always be voluntary and not compelled by law.

- Don't punish third parties for not being keen to act as law enforcement agents in regard to illegal immigration. Blaming American employers and fining them for hiring an individual, directly or indirectly, possibly with a counterfeit identification, strikes me as a compulsory servitude not permitted under the Constitution. Determining who is legal or not is a police and court function, not a responsibility of private business.

- Same goes for the Catholic Church. When those who suffer the chaos of immigration and drug wars on the border are helped by the Church, the Church should never be seen as an accomplice to a crime. Let the Church show the compassion that's required to pick up the pieces of a government-created mess.

- End the drug war. The deteriorating economic conditions and the mess with immigration invite the violence of the drug lords and corrupt officials on both sides. It's time to break up the coalition of the religious drug warriors and the drug dealers who fight any effort to decriminalize drugs. It's time to treat all drugs the way we treat alcohol and cigarettes, substances that kill millions more than hard drugs do. The drug war is deadly and allows drug lords to make a lot more money than legalized drugs ever would. The drug war and the illegal immigration across our southern borders cannot be separated.

- Immigrants who can't be sent back due to the magnitude of the problem should not be given citizenship—no amnesty should be granted. Maybe a "green card" with an asterisk could be issued. This in-between status, keeping illegal immigrants in limbo, will be condemned by the welfare left as being too harsh and condemned by the confused right as being too generous. It will be said that it will create a class of second-class citizens. Yet it could be argued that it may well allow some immigrants who come here illegally a beneficial status without automatic citizenship or tax-supported benefits—a much better option than deportation.

- Those immigrants, legal or illegal, who incite violence or commit crimes of violence should be prosecuted under the law and lose their right to stay in this country.

- The police should not be prohibited from determining an individual's citizenship if the person is caught participating in a crime. This is far different from stopping anyone anytime and demanding the individual present documentation of a legal status. That invokes the principle of "reasonable cause," not reasonable suspicion.

This solution is far from perfect, but solutions to government-induced problems are never easy. Since our economic problems have been the major contributing factor, all other solutions come up short. Maximum freedom for everyone is the best way to go in solving any of our problems.

Another concern I have with the immigration issue is that the strong border protection proponents are as interested in regulating *our* right to freely *exit* the country as they are in preventing illegal entry. No longer can we travel even to Canada or Mexico without a U.S. passport. Our government keeps tabs on our every move, which involves a lot more than looking for drug dealers, illegal immigrants, or stopping a potential terrorist.

Financial controls have been growing since the 1970s, and as the financial crisis worsens, not only will our coming and going be closely monitored, so will all our financial transactions.

Taking your money out of the country physically or electronically is strictly regulated by the eagle eyes of the FBI, the CIA, the Department of Homeland Security, and, you would never guess, the IRS as well. Violations of currency transaction laws, even when not associated with any criminal activity, are severely punished. Expatriation is frowned upon. Currency controls—limits on all overseas transactions and purchases—are commonplace in a faltering economy with a falling currency, which we will have to deal with one day.

A tight border policy to keep certain people out is one thing, but tight border control to limit our ability to leave when we please is something else. America is already working on an electronic financial curtain, which I predict will steadily get worse. The leaders of neither the Republican nor the Democratic party can expect to protect our civil liberties when times get tough: Both support illegal wars; both support Patriot Act suppression of our privacy; both strongly endorse the multi-trillion dollar bailout of Wall Street. Neither party will protect our right to vote with our feet and take our money with us. The right of a citizen to leave the country anytime with his wealth and without government interference is a sharp dividing line between a free society and a dictatorship.

We must be vigilant when the cry is for closed borders, since such a policy may turn out to be more harmful to us than those who come here illegally. The Patriot Act did great harm to the liberties of the American people, and that sacrifice has not made us safer. Arizona-type immigration legislation can turn out to be harmful. Being able to stop any American citizen under the vague charge of "suspicion" is dangerous, even more so in the age of secret prisons and a stated position of assassinating American citizens if deemed a "threat," without charges ever being made. The Real ID, supported by those demanding stricter control of our borders, was rejected by many because it was eventually seen as a step toward a national ID card.

There's no reason to assume that any single group of hardworking Americans won't accept the principles of a free society. That's what most immigrants seek regardless of the color of their skin. Why shouldn't they be open to the arguments of defending private property, free markets, sound money, right to life, low taxes, less war, protection of civil liberties, and especially a foreign policy designed for peace rather than perpetual war?

Some conservatives and Republicans, in my view, insult many minorities by appealing for their votes only by trying to outdo the Democrats with giveaway programs. Why shouldn't a strong message of personal liberty, self-reliance, and economic opportunity be appealing to immigrants as well as lifelong citizens? With the total failure of the welfare state and our foreign policy, it will become more evident that the door is wide open for the solutions that a free society provides.

INSURANCE

O ne of the most serious misconceptions in public affairs today is related to an erroneous understanding of government insurance. Once government gets involved in providing insurance for any economic purpose, it no longer qualifies as insurance.

Insurance is about measuring risk and finding market opportunities to reduce the consequences associated with inescapable risk that exists as part of our lives. The market provides insurance against untimely death, against automotive accidents, against fire in our homes, against burglary, and the like. The market does not provide insurance against risk that we create on our own. For example, you cannot buy insurance against losing the lottery, against business failure, against losing a sports match. This is because those are risks we create on our own. Market-based insurance is about cushioning the results of inadvertent events that negatively affect our lives.

Insurance is only profitable for both the insurer and the insured if risk is properly measured and priced. Only the competitive market can measure risk and find a price for the insurance. In the same way that the failure of socialism is inevitable due to the absence of free market pricing, government subsidized or regulated insurance will always fail in the same fashion, because there is a moral hazard embedded as part of its underlying structure: It is not properly priced according to the level of risk. Regardless of how we behave or what we do, our premiums do not change and the payout does not change. Moral hazard, that is, the tendency to adopt the very behaviors against which we are being insured, is all but guaranteed.

The government's definition of insurance is grossly misleading. Social Security is not, properly considered, insurance. Government-provided health benefits are not insurance either. And even such institutions as tax-funded flood insurance are not really insurance. All these programs are more accurately considered transfer payments. They redistribute wealth from one group to another. The rhetoric about insurance is just a cover to give these institutions legitimacy, effectively fooling people as to their true nature.

In fact, the term "government insurance" is an oxymoron—a total contradiction. And this applies to all government "insurance" programs. It comes from the deliberate twisting of language by those who know better, and economic ignorance on the part of others. Many believe—at least they want to believe—the government is quite capable of "insuring" all of us against risks: economic, personal, and foreign.

When government provides "free" benefits or services, people prefer not to admit they are actually receiving a subsidy or welfare. People feel good that they can "pay their own way," not realizing that the program or assistance would cost a lot more or wouldn't be available without government. The future harm done and the penalty that inevitably is paid far surpass facing up to the truth that government has nothing to give to some, other than that which they steal from others.

One approach is accomplished by voluntary choices; the other depends on an authoritarian approach to managing society. If we ever expect to make progress in solving our problems while preserving liberty, the term "government insurance" must be removed from our lexicon.

In the past hundred years, too many, and especially those in public educational institutions, have been taught that government supervision is efficient and proper. The trend toward dependence on government solutions violates the restraints in the Constitution and ignores history's explicit record of authoritarian government's failure.

If we follow the rules of limited government and personal responsibility, the issue of moral hazard would be dramatically reduced to those who commit fraud against insurance companies instead of endorsing an entire political and economic system based on immoral behavior that has given us our economic crisis and a foreign policy of perpetual war.

The authoritarian approach of government has appeal despite its history of devastating failure. Trust in authoritarianism is the foundation on which modern-day moral hazard rests. Those who promote the virtues of government interference in our lives and economy do it with a proud arrogance, convinced that average people can't and won't do what's in their best interest.

The planners are not bashful in saying that average people aren't smart enough to take care of themselves. They deny they seek power over others just for the sake of power—heaven forbid. Whether they seek power for their own sake or they are truly motivated to make a better world, most authoritarians pursue government and domination over others by espousing humanitarian causes passed off as virtues. And for a long time, too many citizens have accepted the rationale that we need government to bring about a fair, moral, peaceful, and prosperous society. This deception persists as we witness the perpetration of failed policies even though we're in an economic crisis brought on by these false premises.

What we really need is a generous dose of reality. If this understanding is not challenged and refuted, the moral hazard that will result will guarantee an end to the grand American experiment in personal liberty and self-reliance. H. L. Mencken said, "The urge to save humanity is almost always a false front for the urge to rule."

But it also requires the people's complacency to buy into the free lunch argument. Not everyone wants their freedom and accepts responsibility for their own well-being. The problem is, there are always individuals who want to control others and a significant number of people who believe they will benefit forever from the gravy train. This allows the erosion of liberty to progress.

And then both groups come to believe their own lies. The authoritarian is convinced he is needed to take care of the stupid and inept of society, otherwise they will suffer. Though authoritarians reek with arrogance and the power serves as an aphrodisiac for them, they convince themselves they are truly serving humanity.

The recipients of the humanitarian efforts never see themselves as participating in an immoral process, nor do they see the ultimate failure of the collectivist approach to improving mankind, whether socially or economically.

Almost all tyrannies are achieved with public acceptance, as a result of successful humanitarian propaganda that guarantees fairly distributed prosperity and personal and national security. Those who do not accept these premises are deemed unpatriotic and uncaring of their fellow man. Government propaganda is a powerful weapon used to instill fear into the hearts and minds of the citizens. Once this is done, it's easy to get the people to accept government authority they otherwise would have rejected.

C. S. Lewis warned of the great danger of this "worst" tyranny. "Of all tyrannies a tyranny sincerely executed for the good of its victims may be the most oppressive. It may be better to live under robber barons than under omnipotent moral busybodies. The robber baron's cruelty may sometimes sleep, his cupidity may at some point be satiated, but those who torment us for our own good will torment us without end for they do so with the approval of their own conscience."

The danger of using humanitarian arguments is well known. Henry David Thoreau said in *Walden* that if he saw such an individual coming at him he would run for his life. Bastiat detested the do-gooders' attitude as "philanthropic despotism." Isabel Paterson recognized it as "the humanitarian with the guillotine."

The saying that the road to hell is paved with good intentions dates in various forms back to as early as the twelfth century. Today we see that the road to tyranny is paved with delusions of grandeur. One would think that after so many warnings over the centuries we would be more alert to the danger of deceitful humanitarianism gone amok. But I suppose wielding power by some combined with a desire for a free lunch by others makes it difficult to overcome these human traits. A "winning the lottery" attitude prevails.

Yet that's what a free society attempts to do—properly understand "humanitarianism." And for a while in this country, we did emphasize the value of liberty over security and authority. The question is, Will we ever again get our priorities straight? Let's hope so, since all human progress depends on it.

———•———

Paterson, Isabel. 1993. *The God of the Machine*. New Brunswick, NJ: Transaction Publishers.

KEYNESIANISM

Modern-day economic policies throughout the world have been greatly influenced by J. M. Keynes's *The General Theory of Employment, Interest and Money*, published in 1936. Many believe that Keynes was the originator of this theory of massive government intervention to keep an economy strong. Ludwig von Mises made the point that Keynes was not actually presenting any new ideas. Keynes's prescription for getting out of the Depression of the 1930s had been around for a very long time, and it was those ideas that actually got us into the Depression. By 1936, they had already done great harm to the United States and the world economy.

But something did change with the publication of *The General Theory*. Keynes gave the governments of the world a seemingly scientific rationale for doing what governments wanted to do anyway. Government intervention gained further acceptance as the world's official economic theory—except for the more radical interventionists who advocated outright socialism, communism, or fascism. Inflation, price controls, and government controls have actually been known for literally thousands of years.

Mises's explanation for Keynes's notoriety was that those who already practiced interventionist economics believed that Keynes provided them with a "scientific" explanation for doing the things that they were already doing.

Our economic and political leaders were anxious to remove the restraints on government growth that free markets and the gold standard had placed on them. Having "scientific" justification for their plan to have government manage all parts of the economy emboldened them in their efforts. The disastrous shape of the economy in the 1930s provided the fear that intimidated people into accepting the promises of the New Dealers while ignoring their loss of liberty.

FDR actually, with reverse psychology, taught Americans to fear "fear" itself and worked to generate more of it. The fact that the Austrian free market economists had already explained the boom-bust cycle and predicted the onset of the Depression meant that they had to be discredited in order to expand the age of welfarism, inflationism, and warfarism.

The sad part is that the Keynesians won the intellectual and political arguments, even though the system they devised was destined to fail and had been tried many times before.

The good news is that all the shortcomings and errors of a centrally managed economy are now becoming readily apparent, though it has taken a remarkably painful correction for them to do so. Though Washington has yet to grasp the reality of the failure of our economic policies of the past eighty years, the American grassroots have a different opinion. Many had hoped that the failure in 1989–1990 of radical economic interventionism, as practiced by the Chinese and Soviet communists, would usher in an age of free markets and individual liberty. It didn't happen, and instead we got greater worldwide support for Keynesian policies that perpetuated the theory that central economic planning was necessary to sustain economic growth. Dropping the militarism of communism and National Socialism (fascism) was thought to be enough to make economic planning palatable to the people.

The failure to recognize the shortcomings of regulated trade, inflationism, and macroeconomic management, and the danger of the government being the protector of last resort for all economic activities has allowed a much larger economic bubble to develop. That worldwide bubble economy which is on its last legs must be understood in order to refute the false notions that created the bubble.

Government and private sector spending borrowed money is not a panacea as Keynesians claim. Spending money on bailouts, propping up malinvestments, borrowing, and inflating the currency cannot produce sound economic growth. Debt finally consumes the fictitious wealth built on sand that deceived the politicians, Main Street, and Wall Street into believing real economic growth was occurring. Government borrowing and spending is not the solution; it's the problem. Producing and saving is the source of sound economic growth, a policy Keynesians readily decry.

Emphasizing spending and borrowing means that the problems relating to borrowing, inflation, and the cause of the business cycle need not be addressed. Federal Reserve Board Chairman Ben Bernanke, as all Federal Reserve Board chairmen tend to do, frequently chides the U.S. Congress for deficit spending, but at the same time Bernanke argues that deficits are justified during recessions and war, both of which are perpetual.

All this clamor and grandstanding against deficits divert the people's attention from the question of whether the Fed has any knowledge whatsoever concerning what the proper interest rates and the money supply are supposed to be in order to generate sound economic growth. The fact is that without a Federal Reserve to accommodate deficit spending through monetary inflation, huge deficits would be virtually impossible. Though many mainstream economists now admit that interest rates were held too low for too long between 2000 and 2008, they nevertheless believed that even lower interest rates, indefinitely, is the Keynesian answer to a Keynesian-created recession.

For a while, the policy of inflating the currency during a recession can keep the bubble temporarily inflated. From 1971 to 2000 it worked at various times to some degree, but for the past ten years, spending and money creation have not reenergized a slumping economy. The idea that wealth without productive effort is possible is a Keynesian myth. It is this myth that deceives the Fed into believing it can create capital with the click of a computer and reject the notion that true capital can only come from production and savings.

This myth perpetuates the notion that a government and its citizens can live beyond their means and never be forced to live beneath their means. Depending on government stimulus programs, paid for with deficits and money creation, becomes an economic narcotic addiction. The longer the dependency lasts, the greater the dosage required to alleviate temporarily the unwelcome symptoms of the necessary correction.

Politicians are unable to tolerate any symptoms coming from stopping or even slowing the policies that require excess spending, borrowing, and monetary inflation. The message that the markets are sending today is that the age of Keynesian central economic planning is over.

The meltdown of 2008 and its aftermath was a global event resulting from the fact that the world has accepted the dollar as the reserve standard and that all economies are linked to its value and therefore to the status of our economy; the maintaining of a global empire also amounts to a subsidy for the dollar. The failure of Keynesianism is the belief that central economic planning is workable, that spending is a panacea, that borrowing is unlimited, that deficits don't matter, and that governments can solve all our problems. All one has to do is listen to the Paul Krugmans of the world. It's amazing to me, but it seems he actually believes what he espouses. He has swallowed the bait hook, line, and sinker.

To reject the pie-in-the-sky promises of Keynesianism, one would have to reject the authoritarian goals of welfarism and warfarism on the cheap. But that's too much to expect at present. It won't occur deliberately by the Keynesians, but eventually an economic collapse will end it. Ultimately, the only alternative is to outright reject all Keynesian economic theory and replace it with the more modern understanding that the role of government should be based on honest money.

The end stages of the current monetary and economic system—based on a pure fiat dollar—that started in 1971 are growing more apparent every day. Grassroots Americans are well ahead of the political leaders in Washington. Average Americans are very much aware of how serious our problems are and literally laugh at the old clichés regarding increased government spending, more government programs, and the importance of our representatives bringing home the pork. Something big is now ongoing in our political system.

Still, there are plenty of disagreements as to exactly what should be done. Agreeing on the solution to each problem we face is secondary to agreeing to the moral principle that defines the role of government in a free society. There remains a significant number of people in Washington whose goal it is to nationalize our whole economy. The angry Americans now gathering in larger numbers and affecting political races are certainly not crying out for socialism.

Accepting the principle of free markets, sound money, and private property and recognizing that the welfare-warfare state is incompatible with our Constitution would go a long way to solving our economic crisis. This would require debunking all Keynesian economic false assumptions and understanding how significant a role the central bank plays in facilitating the authoritarian approach of government.

The grand safety net that many believe the government can provide is a policy failure that has caused millions to believe they would be taken care of no matter the circumstances. It is now evident that all government promises are suspect, and millions of Americans realize that they better take charge of their future and not blindly depend on federal government promises.

We have for years papered over the many mistakes made by false promises and an economy manipulated by spending and artificially low interest rates. Sadly, the reality of our shrinking wealth is becoming more and more evident by the day.

Here are some of those misconceptions that are now causing a great deal of hardship to the average American citizen.

- Everyone can own their own house with the help of a subprime mortgage and assistance from a government housing program.
- Unemployment insurance can provide income indefinitely for those out of work.
- Education is free.
- Medical care is a right.
- Bank deposits are safe (but what about the value of the money?) because the FDIC and the insured loans will always be there to protect the depositors.
- "Capital" is unlimited because it's provided by the Federal Reserve, and it does not require savings.
- Insurance—flood, mortgage, medical—can be provided by government at lower than market rates while forgetting that once the government provides this service, it's no longer insurance but rather a welfare benefit.
- The GDP can be increased by government spending with borrowed or newly created money.
- Deficits are good—no need to worry.
- The Plunge Protection Team—the President's Working Group on Financial Markets—can prevent a stock market crash. It is designed to keep Wall Street going and keep the investments going. (The President's Working Group was established by Ronald Reagan in 1987 by executive order to stop rapid market corrections.)
- Government regulations make markets safe—SEC, Sarbanes-Oxley, new reforms (Dodd-Frank reform

legislation)—even though they only add more moral hazard and increased costs with higher consumer prices.

- Oil well drilling and coal mining are safe because government grants licenses and leases and inspects operations while removing this responsibility from business and labor.
- Governments are capable of managing public land and natural resources.
- OSHA can provide worker safety, and EPA protects our environment with no need to be concerned about cost.
- Welfare programs help the poor, yet corporate welfare and foreign welfare get far greater benefits.
- The fact that the poor suffer first with an economic downturn, with loss of homes, jobs, and standard of living, is ignored.
- Social Security will always be there (until the baby boomers retire and the dollar loses its value).
- Taxes are okay if they are made to be "fair."
- DEA, FDA, and the Consumer Protection Agency keep citizens safe.
- Licensing guarantees quality and protects consumers and patients.
- Only government can manage the highway "industry," yet more than 3,000 individuals die every month in accidents.

The dedication of the Washington political class to government management is not isolated to one party alone. Most conservatives in Congress don't think of themselves as supporters of Keynesian economics. But in truth, most are strong advocates of a special kind of "military" Keynesianism while being critical of liberal Keynesian politics of taxing, spending, and regulating the domestic economy. This involves another kind of stimulus of spending money on the military-industrial complex rather than purely domestic sectors like schools and infrastructure.

Most conservatives, along with many liberal and moderates, support militarism and world occupation, which makes it convenient to believe that military spending is a "patriotic" jobs program. They want to protect freedom and create jobs—great politics, especially if the jobs end up in certain members' districts.

Think of the clichés that conservatives use to push their own form of big government. They say that want to protect our oil, remake the Middle East, make the world safe for democracy, get rid of the bad guys, fight cold wars and hot wars, fight the global war on terrorism, stop radical Islam, arrest the supposed danger of North Korea, all while condemning big government. Incidentally, these programs are all about providing jobs for one's congressional district.

I constantly heard the jobs argument to get support for military spending. Major weapons systems are built in many different states, and congressional districts garner the votes required to build even those weapons that serve no benefit to our security. Instead, military buildup contributes to our economic insecurity.

Military Keynesianism supported by both conservatives and liberals has led to an obscene amount of taxpayer dollars being spent, now surpassing the military spending of all other nations combined. And the politicians feel good about it. They can tout their "conservativism" even while spending as never before. We face zero threat from any country invading the United States, yet we never stop the massive spending on weapons. The military culture has made us the largest arms merchant of the world, and of all history.

Having so many weapons, especially those offensive in nature, only encourages the deeply flawed and immoral policy of "preventive war," which is really just another phrase for aggression. Since World War II, in many of the conflicts around the world, U.S. weapons have been used on both sides, and not infrequently, against us.

Military Keynesianism is every bit as harmful as domestic Keynesianism. Yes, some jobs are created to build bombs and missiles, but only at the expense of other jobs that would make more productive use of capital. Manufacturing and blowing up missiles and bombs cannot raise the standard of living of American citizens—it's an economic negative: more debt and no benefits to American citizens.

The destruction that our weapons causes always requires that American taxpayers pay for rebuilding the infrastructure we destroyed in the land we occupied. We cannot become wealthier with this system—only poorer, which we're now discovering.

Military Keynesianism invites mercantilist policies. Frequently, our armies follow corporate investments around the world, and have for more than a hundred years. General Smedley Butler dramatically explained in "War Is a Racket" how for thirty-three years he was deceived into serving American corporate interests. It's no secret that many believe we're in the Middle East to protect "our" oil. When the Gulf War broke out, President Bush stated that our need to rout the Iraqis out of Kuwait was to protect "our" oil and protect American jobs.

There's something about military Keynesianism that I dislike even more than domestic economic Keynesianism. Too many times, I've seen how the conservative agenda of cutting government gets overtaken by this ideological attachment to unlimited military spending. It's been happening for decades. It was precisely this uncritical attitude that conservatives have toward military spending that diverted the so-called Reagan revolution. Even under Democratic administrations, the Republicans fear pushing too hard for domestic spending cuts; they worry about political retaliation that would also gut military spending, and they cannot stand for that.

Military Keynesianism is justified by our foreign policy of occupation and nation building and preventive war. Innocent people die, property is destroyed, and the world is made a more dangerous place. Running up the deficits with welfare spending at home certainly does not make our economy stronger, nor do the poor benefit in the long run, but at least it's not based on promoting violence for various and sundry reasons and risking escalation of the small wars for which the authorities are always planning.

Higgs, Robert. 2006. *Depression, War, and Cold War: Studies in Political Economy.* New York: Oxford University Press.

Mises, Ludwig von. [1919] 2009. *Nation, State, and Economy.* Indianapolis: Liberty Fund.

Woods, Thomas. 2009. *Meltdown: A Free-Market Look at Why the Stock Market Collapsed, the Economy Tanked, and Government Bailouts Will Make Things Worse.* Washington, DC: Regnery Publishing.

LOBBYING

I have on frequent occasions heard it expressed by both friends and foes that we must crack down on the lobbyists who "run the country." Sounds like a reasonable suggestion, but how we deal with this problem is crucial. The power that lobbyists have is a reflection of the system that has evolved in both local and national governments. It's a significant symptom, but it's not a disease in itself.

Lobbying is protected by the First Amendment's admonition that "the Congress shall make no laws respecting... the right of the people... to petition the government." "Petitioning" is a legitimate right and should be used in a positive way. Certainly, proponents of gun ownership, right to life, low taxes, and sound money—any cause, really—deserve the right to petition the Congress at will.

But what about the hundreds of millions of dollars being spent to control the government's handouts and privileges granted to the special interests? Drug companies, organized medicine, insurance companies, the military-industrial complex, foreign lobbyists, and on and on have a vital stake in their lobbying efforts and their money does indeed influence votes in Congress. The question, then, is if they have a right to petition, how can the abuse be eliminated?

The ideal answer is that if we had a Congress dedicated to influencing only those things explicitly authorized in the Constitution, there would be very little up for auction by the politicians, thus there would be little incentive to spend big lobbying bucks to gain special benefits. It should be no more complicated that the enforcement of any law.

But human nature being as it is, the day that a republic is born is the first day nibbling away at the law of the Constitution and the law of morality begins. Certainly, the railroads and public works proponents were aggressive lobbyists well before the twentieth century. A properly sized government would solve most of the problems dealing with immoral and outrageous lobbyists' power. There would be less on the table to purchase.

Yet what are the odds that the federal government is about to shrink to its proper size and not be overwhelmingly involved in every domestic and international economic transaction? That's not going to happen anytime soon. This fact puts pressure on many well-meaning citizens and congressmen who would like to curtail the power of government and regulate the buying and selling of votes to satisfy the powerful at the expense of the weak and unrepresented.

Some argue that this is a reason for term limits. Though I have voted for and supported term limits, I have never held the belief that they would solve much of anything. Besides, strict term limits would require an amendment to the Constitution, and that's not going to happen. Term limits, whether voluntary or mandated, provide no guarantee that the replacements will do a better job. In fact, it could go the other way and create incentives for new politicians to take as much as they can, hand out as much as they can, while they are able.

With voluntary term limits now less popular than ever, the principled members stick to their promises and those less principled ignore their pledges to serve a certain length of time. The few I saw leave after their self-imposed limits were not replaced with anyone dedicated to reform and to strictly following the Constitution. Nothing of substance was achieved and something was lost by these voluntary term limits.

The only option we have under today's conditions of runaway government is to send to Washington only representatives who will have the character to resist the temptation to blend in with the crowd. There is tremendous pressure on new members on their arrival to be "team players," with the promise of committee assignments and rewards for their districts, and to accept the well-entrenched notion that idealism is not well received in Washington, especially by one's party's leadership. This is especially true if the President and the congressional leadership are members of your party.

After all, we are told, they were voted in to "do a job." And what is that job? It is not to refuse favors, reject vote trading, turn down government money, and make government leaner. On the contrary, the ethos of Washington is that the job of the elected politician is to serve the company that employs them, and that company is government. They are told that they should serve the system or get another job. Very few new politicians can reject this logic and rationale. They want to be successful and earn the respect of their new colleagues. This means playing along and doing an ever better job of this as time goes on.

If members ignored these pressures and stood firm, the lobbyists' money would buy nothing and be wasted. This would kill the incentive to buy favoritism. One would think that it should not be that difficult to find men and women willing to resist the pressure of their peers. But it is. No one likes to experience the derision of their colleagues. No one wants to be thought of as a person doing a "bad job" at the only thing that Washington does well, which is redistributing wealth and accumulating power unto itself.

In placing in office individuals favorable to their cause, those who have so much to gain materially are too often more aggressive than those more complacent individuals content to be left alone.

The only solution for this is for the disenfranchised to awaken and fight the good fight to send better people to Washington. This requires a heroic political effort but must be accompanied with an educational revolution that convinces the masses that their interests are best served by providing liberty and sound economic policies rather than largesse.

Quite possibly the revolt as expressed in the Tea Party movement is a sign that the disenfranchised are angry enough over the bailouts that their political action will bring about changes in Washington, with better people and placing proper pressure on those already there to break the grip that the special interests lobbyists have over the system.

The imminent bankruptcy will, in a positive manner, assist in this effort to reform the system. Once it's recognized that demanding more from a government that is failing to fulfill its promises is futile, the process unwinds and the people will be forced to become more self-reliant.

Under those conditions, we have an opportunity to emphasize that protection of liberty is our most important goal. Flowing from this will be a greater prosperity more fairly distributed than the unfair system we now have that rewards the rich who buy power in Washington at the expense of the middle class. Legislating control over those who petition Congress, that is, the lobbyists, serves no benefit and would undermine the rights of those individuals who want to lobby the government for a proper redress of grievances.

MARRIAGE

M ost Americans do not question the requirement to obtain a license to get married. As in just about everything else, this requirement generates unnecessary problems and heated disagreements. If the government was not involved there would be no discussion or controversy over the definition of marriage. Why should the government give permission to two individuals for them to call themselves married? In a free society, something that we do not truly enjoy, all voluntary and consensual agreements would be recognized. If disputes arose, the courts could be involved as in any other civil dispute.

But look at where we are today, constantly fighting over the definition and legality of marriage. Under our system, the federal government was granted no authority over this issue. Many Americans would even amend the Constitution to deal with the argument by defining marriage. This attempt only exacerbates the emotionally charged debate on both sides.

I'd like to settle the debate by turning it into a First Amendment issue: the right of free speech. Everyone can have his or her own definition of what marriage means, and if an agreement or contract is reached by the participants, it will qualify as a civil contract if desired.

The supercharged emotions are on both extremes of the issue, because neither extreme accepts the principles of a free society. One side is all too willing to have the state use the law to force a narrow definition of marriage on everyone without a hint of tolerance. The other side—a minority opinion—wants the law to help them gain social acceptance even though this is impossible for law to achieve. Those who seek social acceptance of gay marriage are also motivated by the desire to force government and private entities to provide spousal benefits. When dealing with government benefits, this becomes an economic redistribution issue—a problem that would not be found in a truly free society.

When it comes to forcing "equal" treatment in hiring or receiving insurance benefits, that problem should be solved by voluntary agreement—just as voluntary agreement provides the tolerance and understanding for those who chose lifestyles and alternative definitions of marriage. You can't accept one without the other.

Even without a truly free society—since I don't see it on the horizon soon—if what government provided had real Social Security accounts that could be passed on to family survivors, individuals could name whomever they wanted to be their beneficiary, just as with private insurance. It seems, though, that the Social Security system will never be a sound government-run insurance program, so choice in designating beneficiaries under today's circumstances is nothing more than expanding a welfare program.

The definition of marriage is what divides so many. Why not tolerate everybody's definition as long as neither side uses force to impose its views on the other? Problem solved! It doesn't happen because of the lack of tolerance on both sides. One side wants a narrow definition for all, and the other side wants a broad definition that demands full acceptance by those who choose not to subsidize or socialize with people with whom they are uncomfortable.

I personally identify with the dictionary definition of marriage: "The social institution under which a man and woman establish their decision to live together as husband and wife by legal commitments or religious ceremony." If others who choose a different definition do not impose their standards on anyone else, they have a First Amendment right to their own definition and access to the courts to arbitrate any civil disputes.

There should essentially be no limits to the voluntary definition of marriage. "Voluntary" should be slightly qualified. Since a child cannot make adult decisions, and though a twelve-year-old may agree to marriage, it can hardly be justified as an uncoerced arrangement. Mental handicap may also be an exception. If any rules need to apply in our system of government, they would fall to the states and not the federal government. The mentally handicapped should be protected and decisions made for them by their guardians and rarely the state. Currently, there are twelve states that recognize common-law marriage. There's no license required, and it is recognized as a legal entity.

This issue hardly justifies an amendment to the Constitution; passage or even a heated debate only serves to divide us

and achieves nothing. It is typical of how government intervention in social issues serves no useful purpose. With a bit
more tolerance and a lot less government involvement in our
lives, this needless problem and emotionally charged debate
could be easily avoided. The best approach is to make marriage a private matter. Though there may be a traditional dictionary definition of marriage, the First Amendment should
include allowing people to use whatever definition they like as
long as force and fraud are excluded.

When we no longer believe that civilization is dependent on
government expansion, regulating excesses, and a license for
everything we do, we will know that civilization and the ideas
of liberty are advancing. In economics, licensing is designed
by the special interests to suppress competition. Licensing for
social reasons reflects the intolerant person's desire to mold
other people's behavior to their standard. Both depend on the
use of illegitimate government force.

MEDICAL CARE

The prevailing attitude of the American people is that everyone has a right to medical care. This is an intellectual error that will lead us down the path toward destroying what is good in the current system and replacing it with a system that will be terrible for everyone. The supposed right to medical care can only be guaranteed at others' expense. The transfer can only be arranged by force. This creates oppressive bureaucracies, encourages overutilization of resources, and leads to technological stagnation and inevitably to rationing and deprivation.

It's true that everyone has a right to *pursue* medical care without being hindered by government policies. But that is not the system we have today. Today's messed-up medical system is a result of forty years of government interference in the process. Regulations, inflation, tax laws, and federal mandates to provide care through corporate-run HMOs, interference in providing insurance, massive subsidies, and licensing have all played a negative role in the delivery of medical care in the United States.

The zealots now demanding even more government involvement do not realize that those in need and the people who
require better care are victims of previous misdirected policies. All the well-intentioned humanitarian programs are of
no benefit if they are based on false premises.

Can one imagine what it would be like if, thirty years
ago, for national security reasons, the U.S. government took
responsibility for guaranteeing that every man, woman, and
child had a cell phone, called it a right, and justified it for
national defense purposes? It would have been a nightmare.
Quality would have never improved, prices would be sky high,
and distribution lousy. But we now have affordable cell phones
and the prices will continue to drop as more and more competition is encouraged by the market.

It's only through government interference that a hospital
can charge $1,000 for a toothbrush and get paid for it. In the
same way, it's only the Department of Defense that pays $700
for a $5 hammer. It's the nature of government to produce
low-quality products and services at extremely high prices.
Socialist, bureaucratic, and interventionist economic systems
inevitably injure most of the people who are supposed to be
helped, and at a very high cost.

Modern technology has been with us for several decades. It
has been a real asset to all industries and has helped to keep
prices in check as quality improved. This has been especially
true in electronics like cell phones, TVs, and computers. Though
medicine has greatly benefited from new technology, the cost
of medicine, instead of dropping, has significantly increased.

There's a reason for this. Managed care and government

interference for the past forty-five years, with huge amounts of government money injected into the system, achieved only higher prices and poorer distribution of all medical services. The system of government-managed care has caused doctors, medical insurance companies, managed care companies, hospitals, and especially patients to be unhappy with the system. Very few are satisfied. Even those with Medicaid or Medicare realize that both programs are bankrupt and are unsustainable under current conditions.

Important in this debate over medical care is a proper understanding of what insurance is and is not (see the section on Insurance for a more in-depth discussion). True insurance measures risk and is an important tool for free markets to function. The current use of the word "insurance" in dealing with government-managed health care has been deliberately substituted for government social welfare schemes. Since the majority of Americans see medical care as a right, the assumption is that "insurance" is a right and thereby qualifies for total government control.

Authentic price competition exists in providing car insurance for all Americans. It's sold across state borders, and different policies are available. Owners of older cars frequently drop collision insurance, and the amount of coverage varies. Though auto insurance is required by the states, it's a far cry from required health insurance. Since government has placed so many mandates on the health insurance companies and doesn't permit market-based pricing in either premiums or service delivery, the services they offer can no longer qualify as insurance.

It's obvious to me what would happen if similar rules were placed on the purchase of car insurance. Suppose the benevolent planners decided that a car was crucial to hold a job, and so the job provided car insurance, which was, in turn, declared a right. It would then be quite logical to say that that person couldn't get to work unless the insurance companies paid for all services, gasoline, and all repairs. Older cars that went ten miles to the gallon and needed constant repairs would not be charged more, or it would be claimed the insurance companies were discriminating against a "precondition" and the poor.

Once the "insurance" was provided—with government subsidies—every little problem would be taken care of, whether it was critical or not. It would invite abuse of the system. Excess fuel usage, repairs, and even fraud would prompt a need for thousands of bureaucrats to monitor the whole program, and people would be required to get prior approval. But then again, it is claimed that by rooting out waste and fraud, the government could save enough money to pay for the program and have enough money left over to reduce the national debt. Suddenly, all the problems are miraculously solved!

Obviously, car insurance companies could not survive if they were forced to repair every car that was damaged or nonfunctional prior to the purchase of insurance. How efficient would it be for government-mandated food insurance, including first-dollar purchases, to assure good eating habits to provide good health? It would be argued that it would "save" billions by promoting good health and eliminating obesity. Reasonable people would laugh at such a proposal, and yet that's parallel to what is being proposed for the medical care system.

Once insurance companies are required by the government to insure against preconditions, it's no longer insurance—it's a social welfare mandate and will result in bankrupting the insurance companies, or they will be bailed out by a government subsidy, further bankrupting the government. So far no one has mandated insurance companies sell fire insurance to a person whose house is on fire, or insurance on a beach house once the hurricane is a few miles offshore. Most people understand this, but for some reason they refuse to draw the analogy to medical insurance.

True deregulation of the insurance industry would legalize various options that would appeal to individuals who don't want to pay for care they do not need. Instead of making all preconditions insurable, adjusting coverage to the wishes of the individuals would drive costs down. Rating smokers and motorcyclists and overweight hypertensives makes economic sense. Why should those who have better health habits pay more to take care of those who don't?

When buying home insurance the customer picks exactly what he wants covered and fits it to his budgetary needs. This discretion for productive purposes must be allowed in buying medical insurance. The interstate commerce clause was designed to allow all goods and services and people to be able to cross state lines and not be hindered, as current laws have done for the sale of medical insurance.

Mandating first-dollar expenditures to be covered by medical insurance, something that has been going on for years, can't work. It only raises the cost of insurance. Coverage for office visits and prescription drugs are thought to be wonderful cure-alls, but they aren't. They have to be paid for by higher insurance premiums. Medical insurance has turned into a system of prepaid services dictated by government rules, dominated by a convoluted system of HMOs and PPOs, and has its roots in the Nixon administration of the early 1970s.

I entered the medical field when government involvement was low and third-party payments were mostly for hospital care and emergencies, not for first-dollar expenses. For the most part charges were always the minimum. With managed care and the first-dollar payment, the charges are always the maximum because there is no incentive for either the patients or the providers to keep charges down. Third-party payments encourage abuse, which prompts price controls. All price controls lead to shortages. Today, we have high costs, controls, and a lot of unhappy people. More government only means the problems will get worse.

Someone might say that medical insurance can't be compared to car insurance since medical care is vital, a car isn't. In fact, the greater the importance of anything, the stronger the reason not to depend on a government redistributionist system. A government system of anything has a nearly perfect record of failure—whether it's stopping war, preserving liberty, guaranteeing sound money, or generating economic prosperity.

I grant you, the emotional argument for government intrusion in medical care is different from that for car insurance, but the two sectors are operating under the same set of economic laws. Those economic laws give us cheap cell phones, TVs, and computers with constant improvement in quality in every sector that is more or less free of direct government management. That same system could give us quality health care at decreasing costs. Congress, the President, and the courts may tamper constantly with the laws of the land to favor the special interests. They also try to interfere with the laws of economics, but those laws can't be repealed, and since that is not understood we all suffer the consequences.

Politicians and their constituents are always trying to circumvent the annoying rules of the market, but that only brings about the opposite of the results they seek. Instead, worse conditions result for the very people they're trying to provide services for without requiring that they pay for them.

The misunderstanding about the notion of individual rights and insurance contributes significantly to the medical care crisis and the economy in general. Most Americans know there are ongoing economic crises, but some people suffer much more than others. Those who have not been hit hard and those who are quite happy with their medical care whether it's coming from Medicaid, Medicare, the VA, or active military or private insurance should be concerned as well because government distortion of distribution and costs is ingrained in the system. The system is fragile as is the economy, and a lot more people are going to become unhappy with their current coverage. One main reason is that inflation is alive and well in this country.

Patients' most common complaint is that medical care costs too much. We hear about this more often than we hear complaints about the quality of care. Mismanagement by government surely does push costs up, as do AMA and government restrictions on competition, and old-fashioned inflation is a major contributor as well.

Inflating the money supply never pushes all prices and

wages up equally. If it did, there would be a lot less complaining about it. Of course, the malinvestment would still be a serious concern. Some prices go up and others can actually drop. Those areas that governments "stimulate" by additional legislation will cause greater inflationary pressures in those areas, such as housing, education, and medical care. The escalating cost of medical care cannot be completely solved unless the source of inflation and excessive government mandates are addressed.

Even with all of these changes, there must still be some attention given to reforming tort law. Defensive medicine is epidemic and is unbelievably expensive. Tort law today benefits most the trial lawyers and only helps injured patients modestly or not at all. Doctors' additional expenses and pressure to run every test conceivable contribute much to medical care cost increases, especially amplified with third-party payers.

Too often doctors and hospitals are successfully sued for injuries when no one with certainty knows who is to blame. Conservatives react by hastily endorsing national tort reform with restrictions on awards. Constitutionally, this is the wrong approach. Morally, injured patients deserve compensation. Only a free market approach can solve this dilemma.

Legalizing contracts could go a long way to solving this problem. Today, an agreement between patients and doctors on limiting liability and establishing third-party arbitration does not hold up in court. Antitrust laws prohibit doctors from working together to devise contracts for a no-fault type of insurance that would exclude the trial lawyers from ripping off the system.

Unfair arbitration and settlements would prompt patients

to look for only those who offer fair settlements. When we buy a car, most purchasers know exactly what the warranty promises and how long it lasts and how much an extended warranty costs. With no lawyer fees, cases would be settled quickly and patients would receive benefits. Criminal acts obviously would not be protected, only bad outcomes.

In obstetrics, the doctor is blamed for all bad outcomes regardless of fault and held responsible for any problem developing for twenty-one years. A policy for nine months and delivery paid for by doctor and patient to compensate for any bad outcome is a policy that could probably evolve. Trial lawyers would be hysterical if this free market solution ever became legal.

Tax credits should be offered for all medical care costs, including insurance for care as well as for problems of shared liability. What if every fender-bender car accident required a trial to determine the degree of injury and benefits and faults? Car insurance companies work out the details rather quickly without trial lawyers receiving the greatest benefit.

There must be more competition for individuals entering into the medical field. Licensing strictly limits the number of individuals who can provide patient care. Many of these problems trace to the Flexner Report of 1910, which was financed by the Carnegie Foundation and strongly supported by the AMA. Many medical schools were closed and the number of doctors was drastically reduced. The motivation was to close down medical schools that catered to women, minorities, and especially homeopathy. We continue to suffer from these changes, which were designed to protect physicians' income and promote allopathic medicine over the more natural cures and prevention of homeopathic medicine.

The point is not to endorse one or another theory of medicine. The point is that we need consumer choice and the process of market-based improvements to take over. To this end, we need to remove any obstacles for people seeking holistic and nutritional alternatives to current medical care. We must remove the threat of further regulations pushed by the drug companies now working worldwide to limit these alternatives. True competition in the delivery of medical care is what is needed, not more government meddling.

Obama has been accused of pushing for socialized medicine. This is not exactly true. Maybe in time it will become a total government program. But actually his reforms are very similar to reforms pushed by the Republicans over the decades. The Republican Party under Eisenhower established the Department of Health, Education, and Welfare in the 1950s. Nixon pushed through managed care ERISA laws in the early 1970s after a decade of Democrats implementing their Medicare and Medicaid programs with strong Republican support. The Reagan administration expanded medical transfer payments. Prescription drug programs were passed by the George Bush administration and a Republican Congress.

And now it's the Democrats' turn once again. Republicans shout "socialized medicine" as they become the nominal opponents of Obama Care.

A better description of what has helped over the past forty to fifty years is the takeover of medical care by the corporations. We now have a form of corporatism veering toward fascism. We all know about the military-industrial complex; few understand the danger of the medical-industrial complex. Though we hear rhetoric condemning the drug and insurance companies, you can be sure that no changes will be made in the system without the prior approval of the biggest players in the industry. Regardless of party, corporate special interests are protected. This involves medical management companies, hospitals, organized medicine like the AMA, drug companies, and insurance companies. It is these corporate entities that must come to Washington, spending millions on lobbying efforts to protect their financial interests; concern for the patient is a smokescreen.

Corporations, unions, and governments stand between the patients and their doctors regardless of motivation. The quality and cost of medical care can never be improved by forcing on the American people greater debt-financed involvement in medical care. Medicare and Medicaid are already bankrupt. Creating a new trillion-dollar system will only hasten the day of reckoning.

MONETARY POLICY

I have written in great detail about the shortcomings and grave danger of an unchecked central bank—the Federal Reserve—but the argument needs to be repeated in every discussion of public policy.[1] All talk about the dangers of big government and loss of liberty is inadequate if the negative impact of the money managers is not addressed. Avoiding the subject, deliberately or not, serves the interest of those who support expanding government welfare and promotes an indirect way to pay for unpopular and unjust wars.

The problem is easily summarized. Money was once rooted in a scarce commodity like gold or silver. It could not be manufactured by governments. In the late eighteenth and in the nineteenth centuries, there were many debates about the first and second Bank of the United States. In 1913, Congress created the Federal Reserve with the power to print new money.

---

1. See, for example, *End the Fed* (New York: Grand Central Publishing, 2010); *The Case for Gold* (Washington, DC: Government Printing Office, 1982; Auburn, AL: Mises Institute, 2007).

This allowed government to pay for wars and welfare, but it also generated economic instability with booms and busts. Each time we've gone through this, the government and the Fed removed more of money's commodity backing. Since 1971, the dollar is not redeemable in anything but itself. It is nothing but a symbol, and there are no limits on the number of dollars government and the Fed can create. The result has been an unchecked expansion of the state and a brutal and long inflation that has reduced our living standards in deceptive ways.

Until just a few years ago, the number of Americans who understood the dangers of this policy of monetary destruction was quite small. Most Americans, because of what they had been taught for decades, believe the Federal Reserve provides the ultimate safety net for everyone concerned: bankers, Wall Street, investors, businesses, employees, consumers, et al. Most believe that the Fed gets us out of jams such as too much inflation, recessions, or too high interest rates.

Alan Greenspan was called the Maestro and was heralded as the genius who had a magic touch and could fine-tune the economy in a new economic era. The fact that the Fed was set up to be the lender of last resort, along with easy credit granted by the Fed, encouraged huge malinvestment and excessive debt. The gargantuan size of the derivatives market—a crisis not yet resolved—could not have occurred without a Federal Reserve and the moral hazard its policies generate. The Fed should have been blamed for most of our economic problems rather than credited with providing solutions to them.

Legislation and regulations added fuel to the fires of speculative excesses, especially in home mortgage derivatives.

Keynesians encouraged everyone to trust the safety net of government spending and Federal Reserve easy credit. This misplaced trust, based on false assumptions, has generated, in my estimation, the largest financial bubble in all of history.

The Fed has, in the past, been able to take credit for the good times and for pulling us out of the bad times. But no longer will it remain exempt from blame. The monetary system guarantees that investors and banks will push the envelope and make careless speculative decisions that generate a bubble economy waiting to burst.

I'm sure the historians one day will express great amazement as to some of the silly notions that were accepted as being sound for so many years, before the current collapse occurred. What sane person would advise a family member or a friend who was in over his head financially, in debt, and about to lose his home that the solution was to borrow more money and spend it and sign up for as many new credit cards as possible? It is ludicrous. In addition, he is told that it is not necessary to work overtime or take a second job to reduce his debt.

And yet that's exactly what our nation has been doing—in spades—since the crisis hit in 2008. And the Keynesians are still surprised and annoyed that the economy has not recovered. Their answer continues to be spend more, borrow more, and increase the debt even faster. It's hard to believe that reasonable people believe this. An individual is not better off by assuming more debt and spending more, so how can a nation expect to be?

Keynesians have lost the intellectual debate. After the total failure of the most militant forms of economic planning—fascism and communism—the worldwide failure of Keynesian-type central economic planning is staring us in the face. They have but one card left to play: the argument that anyone who doesn't go along with their bailout programs, which are nothing more than rehashes of the programs that created the crisis, doesn't care about people and is devoid of all compassion. Instead of debating the underlying economic policies, they resort to demagoguing the issue with innuendoes and false charges regarding compassion.

Keynesians and their political cronies in Washington are quick to accuse anyone who opposes unlimited unemployment benefits as heartless. The question they won't even consider is what would they do if it were shown that extracting funds from the productive economy to subsidize unemployment results in prolonging the unemployment and actually increases the number of jobs lost? As funds are drained away from those who are barely hanging on and trying to expand their businesses, the economy is made weaker.

Those who refuse to engage in the intellectual debate and look at the consequences of ideas and policies resort to politicizing the issue with offers of transfer programs based on increased taxation and inflation in order to maintain power. If a reversal of this process is not achieved, total bankruptcy will force us to consider an entirely new system.

I would like to see a dollar as good as gold. I would like to see the banking system operating as it would under free enterprise, meaning no central bank. I would like to see competitive currencies emerge on the market and be permitted to thrive. I've been pushing for these solutions for decades. The problem of the transition is not technical. It can happen. The problem is political. Paper money is a drug and Washington is addicted. What, then, is a realistic solution? As Hayek used to say, we need choice in currency. Washington should get out of the way and let another system built on human choice emerge spontaneously. That would require an end to the crackdown on competitive currencies. I'm fully confident that we would see the dollar outcompeted in time.

———•———

Hayek, F. A. 2009. *Choice in Currency: A Way to Stop Inflation.* Auburn, AL: Mises Institute.

Paul, Ron. [1982] 2008. *The Case for Gold.* Auburn, AL: Mises Institute.

Rothbard, Murray. [1963] 2008. *What Has Government Done to Our Money?* Auburn, AL: Mises Institute.

MORAL HAZARD

The expression "moral hazard" is frequently used today to describe economic decisions that have been influenced by government programs. It's generally recognized that with a government policy that insulates against risk, individuals might react differently than they otherwise would have. These changes in behavior are sometimes subconscious and seem natural, yet the consequence turns out to be hazardous to all parties involved.

Our society and economic system is now engulfed with moral hazard and its many serious unintended economic consequences. The term "moral hazard" originated in the sixteenth century. It was initially used to describe behavioral changes as a consequence of owning insurance. English insurance companies, in the late nineteenth century, became especially aware of this phenomenon.

They came to understand that individuals who had property insurance were more inclined to engage in risky behavior knowing that compensation was guaranteed if the property was lost or damaged by fire, carelessness, or theft. It was recognized that insurance may well be, under certain circumstances, an incentive for arson and other forms of fraud meant to cheat the insurance companies. This early use of the term was associated with explicitly immoral behavior.

The modern use of the term started in the 1960s and was applied to government economic policies. This more recent meaning dropped the emphasis on immoral or fraudulent behavior and concentrated on inadvertent economic consequences of government policies that interfered in the free market economy. The past fifty years have given us an epidemic of government intrusions in all economic decisions, and the results have been an exponential growth of consequences that represent moral hazard.

Moral hazard in economics is not too far removed from the concept of unintended consequences brought about by all government policies. Government actions, regardless of motives, are promoted with promises that the people will be insured or protected against every risk conceivable, from natural disasters, health problems, and economic needs to foreign threats. We live in an age when the majority believes the government is the ultimate protector, not only from all outside risks but also from our own unwise behavior.

The government now is expected to protect us from ourselves. This should be offensive to anyone who loves liberty. We are not expected to make any decisions for ourselves. Governments make sure everything we use or take into our bodies will be safe and beneficial. If we need an immunization, no need to think, the government will pay and provide it for us without question. No personal responsibility is required in making the decision; no market-directed consumer groups can be expected to supersede bureaucratic decisions that involve everyone. When mistakes are made with central economic planning, the consequences are horrendous and magnified.

The moral hazard of accepting assurance from our government that we will be taken care of with only a modicum of loss of freedom is unlimited and is a significant reason why we are facing an economic and political crisis today.

Contrary to the current conventional wisdom that uses the term "moral hazard" while avoiding the implications that this process doesn't imply immoral behavior, this book emphasizes the immorality associated with the term. Though private insurance is discussed, I'm more interested in discussing the concept of moral hazard as it relates more broadly to government policies, assurances, insurance, myths, guarantees, clichés, false notions, lies, emotional arguments, and economic planning.

Using this broad definition of moral hazard, it can apply as well to policies designed to regulate personal habits and to the fallacies associated with foreign affairs. It includes all the unintended consequences of government actions and programs.

Instead of using moral hazard as a benign, nonjudgmental economic term, I emphasize how most government action is hazardous to morality. Government assumption of illicit power starts the process and it spreads to the special interests, which use these powers to serve their own interest. Though they may do this consciously for gain, the ultimate hazard later on cancels out the "benefits" they may have gained.

Home-building and mortgage companies benefit from easy credit in the short run and promote policies that artificially stimulate home building, but later on suffer consequences beyond their expectations. The participants are not innocent of wrongdoing. The government acts immorally by illegally assuming its powers, and the business interests yield to the offer and act immorally by participating in the political process. Those who argue that moral hazard is strictly an economic phenomenon disagree and want to characterize this participation as merely an intended consequence of no moral significance.

The new Percora Investigation, the Financial Crisis Inquiry Commission established by Congress, started public hearings in January 2010. But we cannot expect that this government inquiry will be any more helpful than the first one was in 1932, and for very similar reasons. All the members of the commission and most likely all who testify are totally oblivious to free market Austrian economics and have no understanding of how artificially low interest rates and Federal Reserve policy are the culprits. In many ways, it's just another cover-up permitting the Fed to escape blame and gain a massive new expansion of regulatory power. The new commission will once again blame free markets, sound money, and lack of regulation for the crisis, unless the right ideas are presented and accepted.

We cannot depend on any government commission to be objective enough to sort out the issues. Their job is to defend the need for government and ignore or downplay its errors. A solution can't possibly be found by talking only to the people whose policies caused the disaster and who never anticipated the crisis.

The establishment economists' first awareness came after the collapse of the financial markets; yet there were many free market economists who were well aware of the pending crisis, the financial bubble, and how it came about. If it ignores those individuals who correctly expected the bubble to burst, there is not much hope for this commission to return us to a sound economy.

Even the end beneficiaries of a government housing program of easy credit and congressional affirmative action programs are participating in the immoral process. One group steals, another becomes the "fence," and the recipient doesn't complain; that is, until the magic wears off, the system unravels, and only the very well-connected continue to salvage benefits in the bailouts.

Moral hazard should be considered an immoral process in today's usage. It's a hazard to morality to devise grandiose schemes that promise so much, and when the scheme fails or has bad consequences, they write it off as simply people who believe they are protected from risk acting in unpredictable ways. It is argued that it's a mere consequence that we should be aware of and guard against without condemning the whole process.

Justifying moral hazard as a benign economic reaction should be seen as part of the grand scheme of central economic planning, including regulating personal habits and enforcing foreign policy and the harm that results. The economic planners argue that the problems can be solved merely with more regulations and more promises.

———•———

Grant, James. 1994. *Money of the Mind*. New York: Farrar, Straus and Giroux.

MORALITY IN GOVERNMENT

The U.S. government has been operating without a moral compass for decades, and without a moral compass, the rule of law is meaningless. Neoconservatism, which follows the philosophy of Leo Strauss and Irving Kristol, along with the modern-day liberals who accept the principle of authoritarianism, provides no moral leadership. And most people in Washington, though influenced by both ideologies in various forms, may not be devout followers or even aware of their influence.

There are no neat categories in which members of Congress can be placed. The Obama administration, though continuing many of the policies of the neoconservatives of the previous administration, is not as visibly run by the neocons at the American Enterprise Institute. But it makes little difference.

The prevailing attitude in Washington has evolved because there has been no moral compass or respect for the rule of law or individual liberty. Regardless of what party is in power, social welfarism, government regulation of personal nonviolent habits, and foreign military entanglements never change, despite the campaign promises regarding the Constitution or freedom. Policies are dictated by prevailing attitudes and influenced by the ideology of the establishment that supports unlimited government. So-called conservatives' support for preventive wars and so-called liberals' support for social welfare policies always prevail in the moral vacuum that exists. Everything that happens in Washington is done in defiance of the moral precepts that undermine individual liberty.

Without a moral foundation to government policies, the purpose of government no longer has any resemblance to the intent of those who settled our country and rebelled against the tyranny of King George.

The majority of Americans today expect to be taken care of by the government. They care little about where the government will get the resources to satisfy all the needs that might arise. Certainly there's little concern expressed about the morality of a welfare state associated with massive economic intervention. Those who are on the receiving end of the government transfer system, whether it's the wealthy, the poor, or the middle class, don't want to be bothered with the question of whether or not the whole system is based on a moral principle. It would never occur to them that theft and violence are used to carry out these policies.

The transition away from the original notion upon which we were founded, that government was to be strictly limited to the protection of individuals from out-of-control government authoritarians, has been going on a long time. Washington responds to the noise that the voters make, and the demand for ultimate security and an economic safety net for all has overwhelmed the cries by some who ask only for their liberty.

The time when government was held in check by the limitations placed in the Constitution has long been forgotten.

The erosion started early, and it could be argued that even the Constitution itself weakened this principle that was embedded in the Articles of Confederation. In spite of the early erosion of personal liberty, it was in the twentieth century that the moral compass guarding our liberties was completely cast aside.

What moral system should government follow? The same one individuals follow. Do not steal. Do not murder. Do not bear false witness. Do not covet. Do not foster vice. If governments would merely follow the moral law that all religions recognize, we would live in a world of peace, prosperity, and freedom. The system is called classical liberalism. Liberty is not complicated.

NOBLE LIE

The noble lie is anything but noble. The idea is mostly associated with government, for good reason. Government lies to us to manipulate public opinion to bring about certain results, like war and wealth redistribution. But because the noble lie persists and too many people over the centuries have lived by it, it has created an environment in which moral hazard thrives. Lies perpetuate themselves even though most people know two lies don't equal the truth.

Plato may have given birth to the noble lie concept in *The Republic* in 380 BC, but it has survived the centuries. Machiavelli in *The Prince* (1513) glorified government lying and argued that it was good for both parties, the government and the people. Religious reinforcement of the noble lie has been commonly used throughout history. Plato argued that its benefits are a moral good, while in the twentieth century it has been argued that modern-day rulers have license to lie because of their natural intellectual superiority.

Present-day champions of the noble lie are the neoconservatives, and their influence is strongly bipartisan. The principle of lying and deception for the people's "benefit" is endorsed by each administration regardless of party. The lies are considered noble since a cohesive society is sought. Modern-day neoconservatives have been largely influenced by Leo Strauss, who studied and was influenced by Plato and especially by Machiavelli. According to the neoconservatives, lying is reserved for the nobility; it's not for the common person who may lie on an IRS form. Lying is reserved for the powerful and those who claim they are the only ones who can take care of the ignorant and disillusioned masses.

Adolph Hitler took the concept of the noble lie into something even worse. In *Mein Kampf*, he argued that if governments made their lies "colossal," nobody would challenge the notion that anybody could deliberately make up something so far from the truth.

Hermann Goering, second in charge to Hitler, had an even more cynical understanding of how to use lying and patriotism. Goering said from his prison cell in Nuremberg in 1946, as recorded by G. M. Gilbert in his *Nuremberg Diary*:

Why would some poor slob on a farm want to risk his life in a war when the best that he can get out of it is to come back to his farm in one piece? But, after all, it is the leaders of the country who determine the policy and it's always a simple matter to drag the people along, whether it is a democracy or a fascist dictatorship or a communist dictatorship . . . that is easy. All you have to do is to tell them they are being attacked and denounce the pacifist for lack of patriotism and exposing the country to danger. It works the same way in any country.

Leo Strauss came to the United States in 1938 at the age of thirty-nine and built a reputation at the University of Chicago, where he influenced a lot of future advisers and appointees of the George W. Bush administration.

Some of the well-known neoconservatives who influenced our foreign policy over the past decade include Paul Wolfowitz, Abram Shulsky, William Kristol, Irving Kristol, John Podhoretz, Michael Ledeen, Stephen Cambone, and Richard Perle. There are many others. Each has had some connection to Strauss and has been influenced by him directly or indirectly.

The ideas that stem from Strauss are quite frightening and when accepted can only lead to consequences that are hazardous to morality and political stability. These views are based on absolute rejection of trust in a free society. Unless they are refuted, only tyranny can result.

Here are some of the ideas that permeate the neoconservative philosophy.

- The elite have a responsibility to deceive the masses.
- Rulers are superior and have a right and obligation over those who are inferior.
- A cynical use of religion is important for delivering the message to a compliant society, arguing that this prevents individuals from independent thinking.
- External threats unite the people; fear is a necessary ingredient for success. According to Machiavelli, if an external threat does not exist, the leaders must create one.
- This unites the people and they become more obedient to the state. Neoconservatives argue that this is in the best interest of the people since individualism is basically

evil and the elite must meet their obligation to rule the incompetent.

- Religion, lies, and war are the tools used by the neoconservatives to suppress individualism and fortify a ruling elite. These views in various degrees and on certain issues are endorsed by the leaders of both political parties. This is why individualism is under constant attack and why the philosophy of the Founders has been so severely undermined. Neoconservatives will always deny they believe in these principles (part of their noble lying) since it would blow their cover.

- They actually do the opposite, claiming title to superpatriotism, and anyone who disagrees with their wars and welfare schemes is un-American, unpatriotic, nonhumanitarian, against the troops, and on and on.

Revitalizing the spirit of liberty could be achieved if the people demanded to hear the truth; that is exactly what the neoconservatives dread. Today, most government lying, in cooperation with the main street media, is propaganda and spin. This is recognized and accepted by those who are seeking truth. War propaganda is a well-known phenomenon and even though many are aware of it, its incessant use by government officials and media works rather well in pushing people into a pro-war frenzy.

In Congress, I do not attend the top secret briefings for any updates on a current crisis. I'm convinced I'll only hear propaganda (lies) and spin (for political cover). Truth can be found elsewhere. It is much more likely to pop up on the Internet than in one of our so-called top secret briefings.

Fortunately, we still get whistle blowers coming forth and revealing the truth. The availability of the Internet has provided a great alternative to the major media, but it continues to struggle to compete with or refute the political bully pulpit and the progovernment bias of the major networks and well-covered political speeches. Nowadays, you can be pretty sure that if there is some important revelation about the workings of government, it comes not from major networks but from independent website operators. These are the people who are willing to take the risks and release the truth regardless of the fallout.

WikiLeaks is the most recent example. It has been charged that Julian Assange, the Internet publisher of the information he has gained access to, has committed a heinous crime deserving prosecution for treason and execution or even assassination. But should we not at least ask how the U.S. government can charge an Australian citizen with treason for publishing U.S. secret information that he himself did not steal?

It's safe to assume that if the elites who want to run our lives justify lying, they obviously have something to hide and are doing things they ought not to be doing. Liars hide the people from the truth. Government secrecy becomes necessary to protect the facade that allows domination over the people. The citizens' privacy must not be allowed or else the people will plot against the government and expose its corruption.

Irving Kristol actually argued that there should be different sets of truth for different categories of people. He believed that the idea of one set of truths for everyone is a modern-day fallacy. Communism was based on the belief that only the party established the truth, and it was not rigid; it changed according to political priorities. Without a belief that truth exists apart from what government says it is, peace, prosperity, and progress are impossible.

———

Thompson, C. Bradley. 2010. *Neoconservatism: An Obituary for an Idea*. New York: Paradigm Publishers.

PATRIOTISM

To be an American patriot means to love liberty. That's not the definition used today however. It's amazing and discouraging to see what is argued for in the name of patriotism. If you do not support funding for undeclared and illegal wars, you're frequently called unpatriotic. If you do not support a flag-burning amendment to the Constitution, you're said to be unpatriotic. Not being blindly obedient to the state or simply to challenge the power of the state is considered unpatriotic. It is readily assumed that unquestioned loyalty to government is synonymous with patriotism. Others, though, believe that a good patriot is one who is willing to stand up to his or her government when the rights of the people are being abused and when the government pursues bad policies. True patriotism requires supporting the people even under dire circumstances and threat of government punishment. Great danger is imminent when any criticism of the government is considered unpatriotic. Patriotism never demands obedience to the state but rather obedience to the principles of liberty.

Quite often when I listen to demagogues in Washington

stating their views on patriotism to garner support for more and more government meddling, I'm reminded of the 1775 quote of Samuel Johnson regarding patriotism. Patriotism, according to Johnson, "is the last refuge of a scoundrel," and there are quite a few of those in Washington. The arrogance and manipulation of naming a piece of legislation that severely undermines the Fourth Amendment and calling it the Patriot Act says it all.

Call it patriotism and opposition disappears. It's easier to go along than do the work to explain the hypocrisy of the process. Politically, it's always tempting to take the easy way out and appear to be doing the right thing and do it with "patriotic" enthusiasm—even if the opposite is being accomplished.

Just think about how many lies U.S. citizens have been told over the years to rally their support for lost causes once military hostilities start. The propaganda and lies accelerate to prevent the people from failing to support the effort, even with great economic pain. Logic does not work; false patriotism does.

Patriotism to me is to always support the cause of liberty, and it turns out that governments over the ages have notoriously been the chief abusers of liberty. The original American patriots declared independence from an abusive government.

The aphrodisiac of power overwhelms many well-intentioned individuals who go into government with high ideals. Championing change as an outsider is easily morphed into a patriotic fervor to protect the state once the politicians become part of what they previously argued was the enemy. It's a powerful argument for not giving power to elected or unelected officials, since so few remain diligent defenders of individual rights.

Blindly accepting the false patriotism that permeates our political system has significantly altered behavior, and always in a negative way. Loyalty to bad policy for patriotic reasons, no matter how harmful it's been to us, is always folly. Patriotism always demands victory and success no matter how foolish and harmful. No one is permitted to acknowledge a mistake in policy. Bad policies are continued for "patriotic" reasons, even when seeking a victory or success that's elusive.

Because admitting mistakes—since policy mistakes are so egregious and indefensible by logic—is impossible, an emotional appeal is required to keep the people engaged and supportive. This obsession of never being willing to admit grave errors applies to both domestic and foreign policy errors. Patriotism evokes a support comparable to the divine right of kings. It was once heretical to challenge "God's will." Today, if one demands a true change in policy and by doing so admits to our egregious past errors, charges of disloyalty and lack of patriotism are loudly heard. Today's heresy is to challenge the state, something not tolerated by the elites in charge of our government. This obedience in the name of patriotism provides the support from the masses that is required to keep the current system going. There's great moral hazard to this evil and deceptive use of patriotism.

This requires an ever-watchful eye, with true patriots insisting that governments cannot act in secrecy. Government transparency is the credo of a patriot. Loyalty to the people should not be confused with loyalty to the government. If one is forced to make a choice between the two, it's evident that the government has excessive power. When the two are in conflict, it's the responsibility of the patriot to expose the danger and work on behalf of the people, even if doing so requires opposition to the government.

Some say that defending government actions—right or wrong—is required of a patriot. Yet it is better said that a patriot's responsibility is to condemn the evil actions of government rather than endorsing them by either supporting them or ignoring them in the name of patriotism.

Too many believe that not supporting a military effort, no matter how wrongheaded it may be, is a sign of weakness and unmanliness. The noble warrior image that has survived since primitive times forces many to persist in foolish policies. Look at how long LBJ and Nixon refused to admit the truth even at the cost of tens of thousands of American and Vietnamese casualties. Even today, walking away from a useless and stupid, senseless war in Central Asia is impossible because the American majority are still—in spite of recent and ancient history—demanding a macho victory regardless of cost and with nothing to be gained and lives to be lost.

It seems that if we want strong leaders, we should have leaders with enough self-confidence and strength of character to defy conventional wisdom and the chants of false patriotism and pride. The glory of victory in senseless war should never replace the dignity of peace in a sane world. Rarely is there enough victory to be found to enjoy the glory in a hollow victory. And there certainly is no glory in the outright defeat that can come from a useless war.

POLITICAL CORRECTNESS

The obsession with political correctness is epidemic. Many public figures are persecuted for speaking incorrectly according to the PC police. The worst part is that definitions of the violations are constantly changing. Some people are exempt from an infraction while others may lose their job or even an elected position. Candidates have been destroyed by a media intent on enforcing the code of political correctness according to their own unwritten rules.

But politicians have learned to be the aggressors. They mock their opponents for politically incorrect use of words, and the media are quick to join in the condemnation. It's not officially an infringement of freedom of speech, but it's very close. Though the punishment is not by legal sanction, it nevertheless can be quite damaging.

It's all about control and power over others. There's no decent motivation by those who play the game of political correctness. Sometimes people can be excused for making mistakes by saying, "Well, at least he has good intentions." Not so for the ones who jump at the chance of scoring points at the expense of others or exerting arbitrary power over them or promoting a political agenda.

PC is never designed to protect the dignity of individuals or groups who might be insulted or maligned. It's driven by cynicism, scoring political points, or trying to prove that the challengers to incorrect speech are morally superior. More likely, they are driven by a feeling of inferiority and are trying to prove to themselves with a pretense of moral outrage that they themselves deserve respect, not the "victims" of insensitive language. The whole process is a reflection of an authoritarian society.

By the dictates of the never-named supervisor or administrator of political correctness, there are now quite a few words we must be careful never to use. The original intent to stop outright racist, sexist, or homophobic language does nothing to change people's attitudes and language. The silliness has made fools of those who get carried away with enforcing the extremes. People who are overly sensitive in a serious way and want political correctness enforced have to be insecure and easily intimidated.

The results of the equal rights feminist movement were not all beneficial. Sometimes it meant that women would be subjected to coercive and grueling conditions just as happened to men—like being placed in harm's way in no-win undeclared wars. Most likely, when the draft becomes necessary and is reinstituted, the rules will dictate that women as well as men will be drafted. This is not an idle threat. All women should remember that if there were no plans for the draft, registration for the draft would have been eliminated a long time ago.

Political correctness has been used in the military to regulate

language used by "tough marines." Women demand inclusive-
ness, and yet when offensive language or jokes are told, many
will rush to the authorities complaining that they are offended
and the "guilty" parties must be reprimanded or punished.

This whole process of political correctness is a danger over
and above the social stigma and penalties placed on the "guilty"
parties. But it can get worse. Already there have been attempts
at banning books and songs that contain words deemed offensive to particular groups. It will not take much for the political correctness movement to target the correctness of political
ideas. All totalitarian societies seek to control thoughts and
ideas. I have been excluded from certain events because of my
"controversial" political views.

We already have laws on the books that require lesser penalties for those who commit crimes against "straight" people
because those crimes were not motivated by politically incorrect thinking. The hate police, or the thought police, are
entrenched in our legislative and judicial process, and political
correctness, though at times it seems silly and frivolous, might
well evolve into a federal police effort to maintain order when
society becomes unruly in difficult economic times. Maintaining order and safety is the goal at all costs in a totalitarian
system. Under those conditions, liberty becomes the enemy.

PROHIBITION

Prohibition is not compatible with a free society. Prohibiting acts of violence is one thing, but laws that prohibit the use of certain substances—food, drugs, or alcohol—by adults is a dangerous intrusion on personal liberty. Prohibition is motivated by busybodies who have a gross misunderstanding of the unintended consequences of attempts to improve other people's habits and character through government force. Time and time again, we are shown that it simply does not work. If there are to be any regulations on the use of certain substances in the United States, it was intended that this should be done by the individual states, not by the federal government.

The experiment with outright prohibition of all alcoholic beverages in the United States started with the passage of the Eighteenth Amendment on January 29, 1919. This climaxed a temperance movement that started well before the Civil War. The motivation was to stop drunkenness and the consequences of excessive drinking. Those who promoted prohibition showed no concern for the large majority who drank alcohol responsibly for enjoyment and whose rights would be violated by prohibition.

To stop the excesses of a few, the many were required to give up their freedom of choice to enjoy a glass of wine or beer. It was rationalized that this sacrifice was legitimate and worthy of government enforcement to improve society as a whole as long as it was endorsed by the majority. Here let us offer some praise for Franklin D. Roosevelt: He ushered in the repeal of Prohibition, an action that won him vast affection from the American people, a true liberalization effort that made the country freer. It is a striking irony that this great day in American history bought him the political capital to bring about the unworkable New Deal, which fastened government control on the country in other ways.

The only good thing about the process was that, in 1919, the American people and the U.S. Congress had enough respect and understanding of the Constitution to know that an amendment was required to authorize Prohibition. This realization prompted the passage of the ill-fated Eighteenth Amendment. Today, the federal government hands down a myriad of "prohibitions" and mandates without the slightest concern about their constitutionality. The entire drug war is an arbitrary prohibition that violates the Constitution, a process that has been going on for nearly seventy-five years. Great harm has occurred since the drug war was accelerated by the Nixon administration in the early 1970s.

Alcohol prohibition was destined to wreak havoc on the American people. It bred lawlessness and underworld criminal syndicates, which made huge profits. Prohibiting any desired substance inevitably leads to a black market, as history has shown countless times, and never achieves its goal of eliminating the use. Since ingredients were no longer readily available, the quality of the alcohol produced by bootleggers led to blindness and death. That was in addition to the many who lost their lives in the violence that occurred in its delivery, just as is happening today in the war on drugs. The appetite for alcohol remained strong despite the effort of the government to enforce its prohibition.

It is quite true that alcohol is a deadly drug when abused. Accidents and illnesses are definitely related to its misuse. Those responsible for the accidents must be held accountable. Those who abuse alcohol and suffer disease or addiction, not the government or the taxpayers, are responsible for their own actions. Furthermore, in the age of growing government medicine, the government (i.e., someone else) must pay the medical bills, so we can be assured that governments local and national will dictate our eating, smoking, drinking, and exercise habits to keep health-care costs down. Give up liberty, and the government will give us good health! Hardly! It never works out that way.

The total failure of alcohol prohibition was an important lesson for many, but there are still too many who do not realize that the harm done by alcohol prohibition was not nearly as bad as what we suffer today with the ill-advised modern war on drugs.

I know a lot of politicians who agree with this position but are convinced that the political risk involved prevents them from trying to change the laws regarding illegal drug use.

My position on the drug war has been known for years, and in spite of my opponents using it against me, it has seemingly never hurt me in my reelection efforts. And my district is a Bible Belt conservative district. My assessment is that the people are a lot more sophisticated about the issue than the politicians give them credit for. Though they aren't demanding a total repeal of drug prohibition, they are informed enough not to punish a politician willing to take a forthright position on changing the laws regarding illegal drugs.

In Texas, it's common knowledge that the current wars on the Mexico-Texas border are, to a large extent, about drugs. Ironically, the two strongest groups that want to maintain the status quo of prohibition are the drug dealers and many Christian conservatives—two groups with opposite motivations but who share a common interest in keeping the drug war going.

At the federal level, the cost to pursue the drug war in the past forty years runs into hundreds of billions of dollars. The social cost, including the loss of civil liberties, is incalculable. Crime relating to the drug laws far surpasses the crime related to the fifteen years of alcohol prohibition. I expect that someday the country will wake up and suddenly decide, as we did in 1933, that prohibition to improve personal behavior is a lost cause, and the second repeal of prohibition will occur. This is more likely now than ever before because of the growing perception that the federal government is inept and that individual states must reassert themselves in order to provide more sensible government to their citizens. The Tenth Amendment is in the process of being reborn.

But even with signs that more Americans are becoming aware of the senselessness of the war on drugs, we have local and national politicians demanding even more control, and over much more benign substances such as fatty foods, raw milk, and salt. The idea that in a free society each individual decides for himself what is good or bad and what is risky is completely foreign to the patronizing moralizers who are now in control. But because most of them are users of alcohol, they never bring up the subject of alcohol prohibition anymore. I was rather shocked, after working with a progressive on lightening penalties for marijuana use, that I was met with great resistance to my suggestion that we permit raw milk to be sold without government restrictions. He was convinced that the people would need government protection from this "danger."

That's why the basic principle of freedom of choice with responsibility for one's actions solves a lot of dilemmas when it comes to the proper role of government in our lives.

Most Americans fail to recognize that throughout most of our history drug laws didn't exist. There's reliable evidence that the laws have done nothing to decrease drug usage while contributing significantly to street crime. Responsibility for teaching about the dangers of drugs falls principally on parents. Parents teach children about the dangers of highways, high places, stoves, household poisons, swimming pools, etc. It's their responsibility to warn about all dangers, including alcohol, cigarettes, drugs, and bad diets.

Government should not compel or prohibit any personal activity when that activity poses danger to that individual alone. Drinking and smoking marijuana is one thing, but driving recklessly under the influence is quite another. When an individual threatens the lives of others, there is a role for government to restrain that violence.

The government today is involved in compulsion or prohibition of just about everything in our daily activities. Many times these efforts are well intentioned. Other times they result from a philosophic belief that average people need smart humanitarian politicians and bureaucrats to take care of them. The people, they claim, are not smart enough to make their own decisions. And unfortunately, many citizens go along, believing the government will provide perfect safety for them in everything they do. Since governments can't deliver, this assumption provides a grand moral hazard of complacency and will only be reversed with either a dictatorship or a national bankruptcy that awakens the people and forces positive changes.

Thornton, Mark. 1991. *The Economics of Prohibition*. Salt Lake City: University of Utah Press.

PUBLIC LAND

I n a free society, the land is owned by the people, not the government. We started out rather well in our early history, and a reasonable precedent was set for the land east of the Mississippi. Even today, federal ownership of the land in the eastern third of the United States is minimal, but there's a steady effort by the authoritarians in Congress to continually increase federal ownership of land across the entire country.

The development of the West was quite different. After annexation, federal government policy was always to retain ownership of most of the land even after statehood was granted. Government management of land is atrocious. Management of the commons, whether it's grazing or mining, proves to be bureaucratic, inefficient, and serving the special interests. Usually the choice is between picking beneficiaries of government policy or prohibiting any development. Rarely is it considered to turn the land over to the states for the purpose of its being sold. Since we didn't need the federal government to manage or own the lands east of the Mississippi for worthwhile development, why should it be necessary for the government to own the land west of the Mississippi and stifle progress?

Total federal ownership is more than one third of the land mass of the fifty states. But that's not the only problem for those who believe in private ownership of land. Taxation and regulations are so cumbersome that landowners are essentially renters with no rights to the land. If taxes are not paid, the land is quickly taken by the state. School taxes are especially onerous throughout the country—with little to show for them. Regulations governing land use, from local to federal governments, makes developing land horribly difficult. Cities and their surrounding jurisdictions, counties, and states, all must give their approval before an owner can proceed to make use of his land. This is so even if there is no threat to a neighbor's property. Each jurisdiction has many overlapping regulations.

The federal government uses an iron fist to show that it is the real "owner" by overriding all state and local laws. Many times these rules and regulations are driven by radical environmentalists. The Environmental Protection Agency, Fish and Wildlife, the Department of Homeland Security, Federal Emergency Management Agency, the Corps of Engineers, all must be satisfied. There are strong hints that the United Nations will be involved in land management in the United States as well.

Many people believe that the federal government is needed for national parks and therefore they never ask questions about how much land the federal government owns outside of the park system. The truth is that most federally owned land is not part of a national park. The states in the east certainly have adequate parks without the federal ownership. Who knows, private entities such as Ducks Unlimited or The Nature Conservancy may be the types of organizations that would provide "national" parks in a free society. Fees from the people who use the parks would be a fairer way to finance parks than by taxing the 90 or so percent of citizens who never get to enjoy them.

Over the years I have heard numerous stories about how the wealthy, and yes, even politicians, will purchase their hideaway in a remote area and then subsequently see to it that thousands of acres around them are purchased by the federal government to guarantee their privacy at the expense of the taxpayers. Many private estates are adjacent to government-owned lands and that's not just a coincidence.

Some argue that in the West, the land has to be managed by the federal government due to the natural resources available. They argue that these resources belong to the people and shouldn't fall into the hands of a few rich individuals. They, of course, prefer the benevolence of a few wise politicians. Never would they admit that special interests will benefit from bureaucratic and political schemes.

Texas is a good example of how private ownership of land facilitated the development and use of its natural resources—especially oil, gas, and coal. In the beginning, the Spanish land grants allowed large blocks of land to fall into the hands of a few. But over time, for economic reasons, this land was broken up into smaller and smaller pieces. Ownership of the oil was divided according to private property rights, which allowed many less wealthy people to benefit. The risks were taken by the entrepreneurs and the benefits were spread generously to small landowners with mineral rights and to the workers who labored in the industry. Before joining the union—probably a mistake—the Republic of Texas owned very little land. Texas never needed the federal government to manage its progress, whether it concerned natural resources, agriculture, or ranching.

The rest of the West could be developed the same way as Texas by turning the federal land over to the state to be sold. The natural monuments issue would present the greatest resistance. By making this an exception, a lot could still be accomplished by turning millions of acres over to the states. As the land is sold, a portion of the funds could be used to lower the national debt.

Unfortunately, we're not moving in that direction. But it's more likely to happen as a result of the breakdown of the federal government with the states picking up the pieces than by Congress and the President doing it in a deliberate, intelligent fashion.

Our biggest current battle is to restrain the eminent domain enthusiasts at all levels of government. The Fifth Amendment was written more to assure that land taken by the government was adequately paid for than it was to give the right to government to confiscate property at will. This assumption was based on the fact that it was known that governments traditionally do take land at will from private owners. But too often governments didn't pay fair value for it. It's actually impossible to precisely define "just compensation" as the Constitution requires.

Values are established subjectively, not by some estimate made by a government agent based on recent sales in the area or some other scheme. Land or a home may have a special value to its owner. It might have been in the family for a long time. The owners may be emotionally attached to the homes or property for sentimental reasons, and to them it has value far above what the government decides. Pure and simple, eminent domain is government force used to empower the state or help communities as a whole at the expense of individuals. Motivations are generally well intentioned to provide road easements, utility easements, or parks. Requests for government to pay fair value for land taken date back to early Roman law and were recognized in the Magna Carta in 1215.

Recently, though, this device has become an instrument not to serve the "public" but to serve the special interests. The Fifth Amendment was written assuming the government would take property only for "public use"—never for someone else's private benefit.

Today's corporations and private businesses ask local governments to condemn land in order to resell it to them. The promise is that the land value will go up, the business will pay more taxes, the municipality will benefit, and the new business will earn more money with its new, preferable location. Sounds like a good deal, except for the individual who was forced to sell the land and lose his or her right of property ownership.

This is a modern distortion and abuse of the principle of eminent domain. If anything, we should be moving in the opposite direction which makes it more difficult to impose eminent domain for the purpose of "public" use. We should not be allowing it for the benefit of some special interest.

A clear understanding of the right to own private property

is crucial in maintaining a free society. Without this, a free society cannot exist.

Epstein, Richard. 1985. *Takings: Private Property and the Power of Eminent Domain*. Boston: Harvard University Press.

Racism

The term "racism" is thrown around loosely these days. Sometimes it applies, and sometimes it does not. I define the term as (1) the defining and disparaging of a whole people due primarily to its racial, ethnic, or religious makeup, which leads to (2) the desire to deny an individual or group full rights in the civic community, and (3) the related impulse to see some harm come to an individual or group through private or public means. The terms "racism" or "racist" could apply to one or all of the above.

With this definition in mind, it should be clear that racism is a problem that begins with a denial of individualism. A racist believes that some group trait always trumps all individual traits. This is the first error, and it stems from a desire to simplify the reality of group heterogeneity (people really are different) for the sake of convenience or quick thinking.

I'm not talking about the universal tendency to generalize based on particular circumstances of time and place. This is part of the expectations that we develop based on observed behavior of group solidarity. And of course people act with group solidarity. If you doubt it, watch any sports match and see the way many thousands can simultaneously cheer for a team. It is not racism, of course, to expect the fans of one team to cheer if their team makes a point. But if you believe that this shared interest of a group obliterates individual differences, or that individual differences do not matter at all by comparison to the group trait, we see the beginnings of a racist cast of mind.

When people cannot let go of generalizations to face the reality of counterexamples, there is a problem. A white person who sees no good in any action or words of a black person provides the most obvious example of racism. Another example of such thinking comes from dismissing the views of, for example, a black economist who disagrees with the socialist bias of the.NAACP. The assumption is made that the economist is not somehow "thinking like a black." The same dismissals can be made by or toward any group. Black leaders can caricature whites and whites can caricature blacks based on group prejudice. This is different from regular prejudices, which one might say are a normal part of life and constantly being formed and corrected based on real-world experience.

The problem of personal attitudes is, however, not the crucial issue. The problem is how these attitudes come to have a political expression. During the great wave of European immigration to the United States in the late nineteenth century, the anti-Italian and anti-Irish feelings on the part of the majority might have been understandable from historical context, but they led to real effects in the form of political disabilities being imposed on these groups. It was the same with the Jim Crow laws that followed Reconstruction in the South.

Such laws not only violated human rights; they led to long-simmering resentments that had terrible human and political consequences.

Wartime is an environment that breeds wicked forms of racism. This is because governments love to turn existing prejudices into hate in order to mobilize the masses. In the First World War, the anti-German hysteria led to suppression of German cultural forms and widespread suspicion toward German Americans. In the Second World War, Germans suffered again, but Japanese even more so. It is incredible to imagine the horrible truth that all Americans of Japanese descent were rounded up and put into concentration ("internment") camps. During the Cold War, Russians in the United States were suspected of being communists until they openly and aggressively proclaimed their hatred for the rules of their homeland.

If we hate racism, we must also hate war since it is war that has bred all these malignant types of racism. In our time, we observe the same happening to those of the Islamic faith. Members of both parties are demonizing these people and encouraging an anti-Islamic feeling across the broad population. Christians are being told, as in George Orwell, that "we've always been at war with Islam," that Islam is an inherently warlike religion, that "they" are taking over America with their mosques, clothing, and law. This whole campaign has the earmarks of a new Cold War, and perhaps hot war, in which Islam replaces atheistic communism as the enemy of choice.

What is striking about this form of racism is how little it has to do with reality. The 9/11 hijackers were not devout Muslims, but we are often led to believe that they were. The government of Saddam Hussein was secular, not an Islamic state, though the U.S. attack and decadelong sanctions against Iraq were sold to Americans as a part of a "clash of civilizations" and the beginning of a long struggle against Islam. There can be no question that government elites are leading Christians and Jews to believe that the struggle against Islam is our most important foreign policy priority.

What none of this mentions is that Islam, Christianity, and Judaism lived in peace, sometimes in the same regions of Europe, for some 700 years between the eighth and fifteenth centuries. This period in Spanish history is known as the Convivencia, or coexistence. It is widely credited with having brought the wisdom of Greek philosophy to Europe. How did this happen? Through trade, cultural exchange, and liberal institutions of law. This is possible. It is possible now if we would stop this endless circle of attack and reprisal, from which only the governments of the world benefit. Peace can happen again, but only if the United States stops occupying Arab countries, supporting governments that are not supported by their people, funding occupations in the Middle East, imposing sanctions against Islamic countries, and inspiring anti-Islamic tirades within the U.S. population.

I can well remember propaganda from the 1980s under the Reagan administration, when conservative leaders claimed that it was crucial for the anti-Soviet cause that Americans embrace Islam. And why? Because Islam was against secular liberalism, for the family, and, most importantly, against Soviet rule in Afghanistan. The "freedom fighters" might be violent and hold to a different religion, but that didn't matter because they opposed the Soviet occupation, which was all that mattered given the political priority at the time. Never mind that these very people later morphed into the hated Taliban that we overthrew and who now constitute the core of al Qaeda!

Government-backed racism is designed to shore up government power. The idea is to steer popular opinion that should be directed against one's own government toward some evil foreign enemy. This is the essence of the propaganda that has accompanied every U.S. war effort—and probably every war effort by every government. Racism thrives on dehumanizing people, encouraging people to believe that the object of their hated is not deserving of human rights. It is even more despicable when governments do these things even as they claim to be protecting the rest of us against racism at home.

I really don't know what is worse: the false claims of racism or the harboring of prejudice; the actual sponsorship of racism by the government itself in wartime or the support of "affirmative action" and "quotas" in the name of ending racism. All these actions are contrary to the individualism that a free society should uphold without compromise.

———

Mann, Vivian (ed.). 2007. *Convivencia: Jews, Muslims, and Christians in Medieval Spain*. New York: George Braziller.

Mises, Ludwig von. [1956] 1983. *Theory and History*. Auburn, AL: Mises Institute.

Rand, Ayn. "Racism," *The Objectivist Newsletter*, September 1963.

Religion and Liberty

A theists are fond of saying that radical religious beliefs and doctrines are the source of all that is wrong with the world. They argue that wars result from strong religious beliefs and that the various religions have never succeeded in caring for the poor and the sick, thus justifying the call for authoritarian government to forcibly redistribute wealth and provide care for the needy. They resort to socialism, not free markets, in their attempt to accomplish these goals.

They cite the Christian Crusades and abuses of the church-driven Spanish Empire as an example. The Old Testament is filled with stories of Jewish violence, and to this day the violence in the Middle East is associated with various biblical interpretations that stir conflict among the thousands who hold current deeds to land and homes taken from them. Blaming the wars waged by kings who claimed their title by divine right is not unusual.

Yet if one looks at the history of the twentieth century, the mass killings carried out by the fascist and communist atheists reveal a slaughter impossible to conceive of. Estimates are that the godless dictators of these countries killed 262 million of their own people, far surpassing the estimated 44 million military personnel killed in war. Clearly, secularism is not always about peace.

Though it is true that throughout history much harm and killing was carried out in the name of religion, this has always reflected a distorted understanding of official religious beliefs. Within nearly all the great religions, we find extremists who promote violence in the name of God. All Christians are not Christian imperialists who endorse preventive war in the Middle East. All Jews do not endorse the violence used to displace the Arabs and Muslims and steal their land in the Middle East. All Muslims do not endorse senseless killing by suicide terrorists.

It appears that when killing and war are carried out in the name of a particular religion, they are done by distorting the religion and following a false doctrine. It should not be assumed that it was the religion itself that prompted the violence.

Instead of religious beliefs being the cause of war, it is more likely that those who want war co-opt religion and falsely claim the enemy is attacking their religious values. How many times have we heard neoconservatives repeat the mantra that religious fanatics attack us for our freedoms and prosperity? Neoconservatives deliberately use religion to stir up hatred toward the enemy.

Not only do some distort religious orthodoxy to gain support for war, reaction to aggressive secular attacks serves as an incentive for religious extremists to recruit defenders to fight off the invaders. The Soviet occupation spurred the growth of the religion-driven mujahedeen (later to become the Taliban). The United States financed and encouraged the teaching of radical Islam to fight the Soviets. What we didn't understand was that this radicalization of religious beliefs would one day be directed toward us—as it was on 9/11. Islam does not teach that the mass killing of innocent civilians is moral, yet foreign occupation can serve as a tremendous incentive to radicalize religious beliefs.

Christian imperialism that endorses preventive war in the Middle East should not be allowed to destroy the message delivered by the Prince of Peace. It's a far stretch and a great distortion to use Christianity in any way to justify aggression and violence.

Christianity, instead (from my point of view), emphasizes the importance of the dignity of the individual and how the lowliest in all of society are equal to those who rule over us regardless of the overwhelming force and power they wield. The Christian message is that no tyrant can destroy the dignity and self-worth of any individual, regardless of circumstances.

Christ dealt with spiritual matters, not temporal or political. Salvation for believers was the message, not drawing future geographic boundaries in a small portion of the world.

Just think of the energy spent and fighting that has gone on over a relatively small piece of land in the Holy Land compared to the amount spent dwelling on the message of love and peace. The temporal world must have rules that protect private property ownership and allow for the eternal disagreements regarding religion. These can be contemplated intellectually without the use of force to impose one person's views on another.

The Founders were right to reject the notion that the federal government be permitted to establish an official religion, without being hostile to those who express their spiritual views in private or public places. Neither evangelical atheists whose goal it is to abolish any public expression of religious belief nor promoters of a theocracy should be able to force their views on others. A free society with freedom of expression protects the rights of both.

Some believe that the Golden Rule should bring all factions together. This means all religions and nonbelievers. Violence indeed has been sanctioned by the great religions, but without theological justification. The principle of the Golden Rule has been endorsed by all the great religions. This was known as early as the time of Confucius. Calls for love, forgiveness, and the Golden Rule have been expressed in some form since ancient times.

Following is a list that comes from RaceMatters.org.

Love . . . in the World's Great Religions

- Christianity: "Beloved, let us love one another, for love is of God; and everyone that loveth is born of God, and knoweth God. He that loveth not, knoweth not God, for God is Love."
- Confuciansim: "To love all men is the greatest benevolence."
- Buddhism: "Let a man cultivate towards the whole world a heart of love."
- Hinduism: "One can best worship the Lord through Love."

- Islam: "Love is this, that thou shouldst account thyself very little and God very great."
- Sikhism: "God will regenerate those in whose hearts there is love."
- Judaism: "Thou shalt love the Lord thy God with all thy heart, and thy neighbor as thyself."
- Jainism: "The days are of most profit to him who acts in love."
- Zoroastrianism: "Man is the beloved of the Lord, and should love him in return."
- Baha'i: "Love Me that I may love thee. If thou lovest Me not, My love can no wise reach thee."
- Shinto: "Love is the representative of the Lord."

The Golden Rule…According to the World's Great Religions

- Christianity: "All things whatsoever ye would that men should do to you, do ye even so to them." (Matthew 7:12)
- Confucianism: "Do not unto others what you would not have them do unto you."
- Buddhism: "Hurt not others in ways that you yourself would find hurtful." (Udana-Varga, 5:18)
- Baha'i: "Blessed is he who preferred his brother before himself." (Baha'u'llah, Tablets of Baha'u'llah, 71)
- Islam: "Hurt no one that no one may hurt you." (Muhammad, "The Farewell Sermon")
- Judaism: "That which is hateful to you do not do to your fellow."
- Humanists and atheists do not condemn the Golden Rule.

Peace in the World's Great Religions

- Christianity: Blessed are the peacemakers, for they shall be called the children of God.
- Judaism: When a man's ways please the Lord, he maketh even his enemies to be at peace with him.
- Buddhism: There is no happiness greater than peace.
- Hinduism: Without meditation, where is peace? Without peace, where is happiness?
- Islam: God will guide men to peace. If they will heed him, He will lead them from the darkness of war to the light of peace.
- Shinto: Let the Earth be free from trouble and men live at peace under the protection of the Divine.
- Baha'i: War is death while peace is life.
- Sikhism: Only in the Name of the Lord do we find our peace.
- Confucianism: Seek to be in harmony with all your neighbors...live in peace with your brethren.
- Mahatma Gandhi's opinion on this issue: "Like the bee gathering honey from different flowers, the wise person accepts the essence of different scriptures and sees only the good in all religions."

The Ten Commandments

- The Ten Commandments are traditionally known to be part of the foundation of Christianity and Judaism.
- The Qur'an in different places essentially repeats the Ten Commandments, indicating that Muslims do not believe

that this message has been corrupted from their divine origin as other provisions of the Torah and the Gospels have. The Qur'an endorses the following: One God; No idol worship; Do not take God's name in vain; One day a week for special prayers; Honor our parents; Do not murder; Do not commit adultery; Do not steal; Do not withhold testimony; Do not covet what others have.

These great religions represent billions of people who agree on love, the Golden Rule, and the Ten Commandments. We are brought together by believing in one God, supposedly the same one, yet we fight and hate and lack tolerance and understanding. The positive truth is perverted and replaced by arrogant enforcers willing to initiate war and aggression for selfish interests while distorting religious belief.

Modern Machiavellians, the neocons, admit they diligently use extreme religious beliefs not to promote love and peace, but to galvanize people to fight and supposedly to preserve the true religion. It is this influence by antireligious nonbelievers that incites hatred between the different religions and that leads to so much violence and hatred. A better understanding and greater tolerance would provide the courage for believers of different faiths to resist the political demagogues who for their own selfish reasons use violence as the tool for managing their tyrannical governments.

Too many wars are fought claiming God's blessing—on both sides. It's "your God against our God, yet the same." For wars to be diminished, this attitude must change.

The mass slaughter of the twentieth century was not a result of religious conflicts. Even today, the hostility in the Middle East, though seen by many Muslims as a modern Christian Crusade against Islam, religion is used by some to justify geopolitical goals, such as control over the world's oil supply. This, in turn, motivates others to radicalize those injured by such a policy in the name of Allah. Bad foreign policy is more the culprit than radical religious views. Bad policy invites extremism in religious activities—on both sides.

Though most religions and most people accept the basic premise of the Golden Rule—Do unto others as you would have them do unto you—there are some who could not care less. There are those who have no self-esteem and are self-haters and naturally self-destructive. Why would they care about treating others better than they treat themselves when they don't place any value on their own lives? Put a person like this in charge of other people and trouble results. It's not too infrequent that individuals like this find a way to the top of the political heap. Being insecure and hateful, participating in violence to bring about good things to compensate for a sense of inferiority is not unusual. A guilt complex in proponents of big governments has been recognized for some time.

The masochist gets pleasure in dominating others and doesn't care about the Golden Rule. The more power, the greater the sense of superiority that nourishes the masochist's ego.

Ignorance of how humanitarian government programs do harm rather than good fuels the efforts of do-gooders to justify and relish the power that they use over others. I have been told, in serious discussions with other members of Congress, that the people are too "stupid" to care for themselves and need smart, generous, and caring public servants to take care of them. These individuals actually believe they are not violating the Golden Rule but rather serving God's purpose.

It's not unheard of for "intellectuals" to claim that free markets are destructive and the Golden Rule mandates an authoritarian state to right the wrongs of uneven distribution of wealth. One would not think that a "rule" asking all to treat others as they would like to be treated could be used to condemn free markets—the only system ever to alleviate famine and subsistence living. Yet this is what has been done.

Even something as concise and clearly understood for centuries as the Golden Rule can be twisted by human beings to serve the opposite goals. War becomes peace, love becomes violence, and the Golden Rule is used to destroy the wealth of the world and thus impoverish the masses.

If we conclude that the age-old Golden Rule is of value in how we should treat others (and other countries as well), it cannot be left standing that free market capitalism is its greatest enemy. A Golden Rule attitude merely facilitates a market economy. Even if the Golden Rule is not named as a guiding policy, free markets, private property, contracts, sound money, and self-interest would always promote the system that is sought by Golden Rule proponents.

It is the moral principle of individual liberty that is vitally needed to achieve the fairest and most prosperous society. As precious as religious values are when properly applied, a society that agrees on the principle of liberty makes personal religious and social beliefs less threatening.

Atheists, believers, the selfish individuals—even when annoying—can all interact with and not threaten those with whom they disagree. All benefit by practicing a tolerance that they would choose for themselves.

The basic moral principle of individualism emphasizes not only an absolute right to one's own life but the opposite as well: that no one has a right to another person's life or liberty or property. This principle clearly states no one has a right to initiate violence against another. There can be no individual aggression and no national aggression either. This is what the Golden Rule should mean. It's a basic political position that has been endorsed by all the great religions of the world as well as most moral secularists.

It's crucial to grasp that a flawed misunderstanding of what the Golden Rule means can be used to justify violent redistribution of wealth and wars of aggression and must not go unchallenged. It's bad enough that history has been filled with thousands who find themselves in positions of power and don't even pretend to endorse this basic Golden Rule principle.

There are too many—and I have met quite a few of them from across the political spectrum—whose working premise is that the masses don't deserve the right to their life or property and must be cared for by their benevolent masters. This rationalization is used so the authoritarians can enjoy exerting power over others just for the sake of power.

Because we no longer have a moral compass to guide our political system, we now face the prospect of economic and social upheaval. Without a moral foundation to our political system it's a free-for-all, and those who understand how to use government power benefit the most. Government is driven by envy and avarice, not the self-interest that drives free markets and is condemned as selfish by the enemies of liberty.

A system of government without limit, if unchecked, will destroy production and impoverish the nation. The only answer is to better understand economics and monetary systems, as well as social and foreign policies, with the hope that they will change once it becomes clear that government policies are a threat to all of us.

SECURITY

M any Americans believe that it is necessary to sacrifice
some freedom for security in order to preserve freedom
in the greater sense. Others believe that if some freedom is
sacrificed for security, neither can be achieved. This question
has been around for a long time: Must we sacrifice some freedom to provide the security needed to enjoy our freedom? We
have heard a positive answer to this question by too many
Americans, especially since 9/11.

More than 200 years ago, Ben Franklin warned us about it.
His often-quoted warning seems to have been totally ignored
in modern America. Succinctly put, Franklin warned: "They
that can give up essential liberty to obtain a little tempo-
rary safety deserve neither liberty nor safety." And, I might
add, they will get neither. The tragedy is that the would-be
tyrants, in collaboration with the victims of government fearmongering, who demand ultimate safety destroy the liberties
of those who are convinced that there is no need ever to sacrifice any liberty in the belief that the government will protect
us from all harm.

George W. Bush was totally confused on this issue. Deliberate or not, I don't know, but he claimed his prime responsibility was to keep all Americans safe, not obeying the Constitution. This was a bad set of priorities. His legal adviser John Yoo gave Bush strong support for this belief and argued that the President could ignore laws and the Constitution when they interfered with his goal of striving for safety. The presidential oath of office specifically says the President's obligation is to "preserve, protect, and defend the Constitution."

As we've seen throughout history, fear drives the growth of government. If there's no natural or inadvertent crisis, one is easily created or imagined by those who agitate for the authoritarian state. Fear will ignite a demand to be taken care of. In a free society, where depending on government is minimal or absent, any real crisis serves to motivate individuals, families, churches, and communities to come together and work to offset the crisis, whether it comes from natural causes such as floods, droughts, fire, illness, or predators or is man-made. Once dependency on government for both rich and poor is ingrained in society, any perceived, actual, or created crisis will prompt a demand for a rescue at any cost.

And usually the costs are to be borne by others—so it is hoped. Any benefits are short-lived. They are never fairly distributed, and all benefits are achieved through theft. The assumption that government can rescue us from all problems, and it's not the individual's responsibility to plan for unforeseen circumstances, causes behavior changes that magnify all crises through a constant erosion of liberty.

We might reflect on how we achieve security in our everyday lives. We have locks on our doors, provided by private manufacturers. We use privately provided alarm systems. We depend on the idea that others are going to drive safely, and the incentive to do so comes from a private system of insurance. Some people own and carry guns for security. Their efforts help everyone by deterring criminality. Commercial establishments such as banks and jewelry stores hire private security guards. Malls and subdivisions have their own security apparatus.

If we reflect on how security works in the real world, we discover a huge and important role for private enterprise, and we find that the vast government apparatus of "national security" does not keep us safe so much as threaten our liberties by regarding the entire citizenry as a threat. Private security does not threaten our civil liberties, but government-provided security does.

And yet to oppose attacks on our civil liberties for the good of the state is considered unpatriotic and un-American. The advice we get from the authoritarians is, "Don't ever let a crisis go to waste" (as Rahm Emanuel put it). It was a mere thirty-four days after the 9/11 attacks on the Twin Towers that the Patriot Act was passed by Congress. It was more than 300 pages in length and was available to us on the House floor only one hour before the short debate started. Much of what was included in the bill actually had been proposed off and on for years before the attack. The impact and fear generated by the attacks on the Towers offered the opportunity that many of the neoconservatives were anxiously waiting for.

The Patriot Act represented a radical departure from the protections of the Fourth Amendment. It authorized self-written search warrants (FBI and other agents) and national security letters and essentially undermined the privacy of all Americans protected by our Constitution. No records are now safe from the government. All Americans are potential terrorists and subject to unrestrained searches by our government "protectors."

The Patriot Act passed easily in both Houses. The fact that an extremely unpatriotic piece of legislation was called the Patriot Act tells you about the arrogance and cynicism that exists in Washington, DC. Congress and the people went along due to the heightened fear and the public pressure to do something. A steady stream of similar legislation over the past decade has decimated the liberties of the American people. Most are still unaware of the significance of the loss of constitutional restraints on our government officials.

This is no small issue. Our liberties have been seriously eroded. Before 9/11 we were spending approximately $40 billion annually on intelligence gathering. A strong argument could be made that this spending was a total waste, having failed to warn us of the impending disaster even with evidence we now know was available. Today, agencies dedicated to gathering intelligence spend $80 billion per year. Who in America can say they feel safer because of this secret spending and interference in other countries? The truth is we're less safe because of it and certainly poorer. But in addition, we cannot assume the spying is only on our enemies.

The surveillance now includes e-mail, telephone, mail, and all activities of American citizens. There is no privacy left. This all results from the false assumption that sacrificing a little freedom for safety is acceptable.

Most Americans continue to believe that the government

is spending about the right amount on the military, which many people equate with security. But how many people know how ridiculously high U.S. military spending is compared with that of other countries? In 2009, world military expenditures were $1.531 trillion, according to the *Stockholm International Peace Research Institute Yearbook* of 2010. Fully 46.5 percent of that was spent by the United States! The next highest expense was by China, which comprised only 6.6 percent of the total. After that came France with 4.2 percent, the United Kingdom with 3.8 percent, and Russia with 3.5 percent. And how much of the rest of the world's spending is due to nations protecting themselves against the United States as the perceived threat?

Now, most Americans can't even conceive of other countries believing the United States to be a threat. And yet, ours is the only government that will travel to far distant lands to overthrow governments, station troops, and drop bombs on people. The United States is the only country to have ever used nuclear weapons against people. And we are surprised that many people in the world regard the United States as a threat?

Though many had hopes that the Obama administration would change direction and soften the aggression and abuse of the Patriot Act, it has supported its extension. This includes access to library and bookstore records, a broader definition of the "lone wolf" provisions, and roving wiretaps. There was no resistance by the Republican Party or the Democratic leadership in the Congress.

President Obama continues the attitude of generally using executive orders to write law. Signing statements to qualify any legislation he signs is still used. Protecting the principle of "state secrets" without concern for citizens' privacy is being continued by the current administration. There will be no repeal of the Military Commissions Act, and secret renditions continue, no changes in the Patriot Act, and no increase in transparency of the federal government. We're still locked into sacrificing liberty for illusory promises of security. The National Security Agency continues to get more power while the government gets more secrecy and the people's privacy is destroyed.

Although the abuses are always directed toward "terrorists" or enemy combatants, it's a precedent that could easily open the door for denying due process to any American citizen. Already American citizens have been victims of the new system that denies ordinary rights guaranteed in the Constitution.

Because we are not in a declared war, military justice is not supposed to be used. That is what the Constitution says. Suspects now held in our many secret prisons are neither protected by the Geneva Convention nor the Constitution, and yet suspects can be held indefinitely without charges being made or individuals given the right of habeas corpus. This process has been endorsed by both the Bush and Obama administrations. The current rules for arresting individuals in countries that we have invaded and occupied have been established by executive order at the expense of the Constitution.

Indefinite detention without charges or access to counsel, no matter what the authorities think the prisoners did, is a grave danger to all of us. If the executive order that permitted such detention is allowed to stand, it won't take too many years or too many emergencies to totally destroy freedom as we have known it. Conditions are ripe for some form of dictatorship to emerge. Dependency on government to care for us in all ways has caused the majority of the people and their congressional representatives to act in a way that guarantees our problems will get worse.

We are witnessing the destruction of the liberties that took centuries to establish in order to rein in the kings of old.

SLAVERY

John Quincy Adams was not an abolitionist, but he wanted the slavery issue debated. After serving four years as President, he was elected to the U.S. Congress, where he served for seventeen years. Hardly would any ex-President consider that today. During his congressional career, he tried to bring the slave issue discussion to the House floor. However, the gag laws forbade it. But after a long struggle, in 1844 he successfully got rid of those laws and the matter could be discussed.

This is sometimes the fate of crucial issues such as slavery. Discussion of them is banned. Those who spoke out strongly against slavery were frowned upon and suffered for it socially and politically. But they persisted in any case. Though there were some who resorted to violence to force release of slaves, many others helped protect runaway slaves to keep them from being forced to return to their owners as mandated by federal fugitive slave laws.

Still, the fundamental issue did not go away. You can

silence debate but you can't sweep fundamental moral issues such as slavery under the carpet. And what is slavery? It is the presumption that one human being can literally own and control another human being, such that the slave can be worked, bought, and sold without the free exercise of individual volition. Extrapolating that idea in the macro sense, isn't that also the case with a whole society ruled by a vast leviathan state? We got rid of the individual form of slavery and replaced it with a growing problem of another kind of slavery. Think of the draft, confiscatory taxation, laws and mandates against home schooling, speech controls, or any number of impositions of life and property, and regulations designed to control our social and business associations. There is a sense in which these can all be considered forms of slavery.

The issue of government ownership and control of society is also a moral issue. And no matter how much the elites try to shut down debate, the issue is not going away.

William Lloyd Garrison and Wendell Phillips stand out as champion opponents of no compromise on slavery, part of the more radical abolitionist movement. Their efforts were heroic examples of perseverance as they pursued their convictions for decades.

Wendell Phillips became known as the voice of the abolitionist movement while Garrison was known as the backbone. Phillips's efforts consumed him for twenty-five years. He eventually achieved his victory, but tragically it was accomplished only with a ghastly and probably needless Civil War that took greater than six hundred thousand American lives. It was tragic that the abolishment of slavery was not achieved as it had been in all other Western nations, peacefully. More attention should have been paid to John Quincy Adams's tenacity to do it with a change in the Constitution.

Generally speaking, the abolitionists were supporters of secession. They wanted to separate themselves in the northeast from the slave owners of the South and let them deal with the issue. As Garrison said:

By the dissolution of the Union we shall give the finishing blow to the slave system; and then God will make it possible for us to form a true, vital, enduring, all-embracing Union, from the Atlantic to the Pacific—one God to be worshipped, one Savior to be revered, one policy to be carried out—freedom everywhere to all the people, without regard to complexion or race—and the blessing of God resting upon us all! I want to see that glorious day!

In this effort, the question was never raised that the states didn't have a right to secede. Many people who favored secession also believed, and rightly, that the modern industrial state would eventually work to eliminate slavery.

Phillips paid a high price for his long effort to rid the country of the scourge of slavery. Throughout all of early America he was scorned and ridiculed. He never wavered in his convictions and saw himself as an agitator and reformer whose goal was to force the American people to face the issue of slavery as a moral imperative.

Though others supported this cause, Wendell Phillips

demonstrated how one individual with determination and truth on his side can influence an entire nation. His unyielding efforts based on strong beliefs in pursuing justice are an example of character rarely found in today's society.

Wendell Phillips, though not frequently recognized as an important figure in our history, should inspire anyone who seeks the plain truth about a proper political system. Garrison is much better known for his antislave efforts than is Wendell Phillips, and he served a great role, but Phillips delivered the message and inspired the masses.

Most importantly, Wendell Phillips knew the importance of the agitator. The agitator proselytizes; he does not write the laws. The purpose of the agitator is to change people's opinion so that great and significant social change can be achieved. Elimination of slavery from this continent, after more than 200 years, was a goal he clearly understood and sought.

The role of the strategic planner for change in the social order is completely different from the chicanery of the politician forced to accommodate both sides, speak in double-talk, and move ever so slowly in one direction or another. The politician tinkers around the edges while the revolutionaries—either good or evil—work to change the fundamentals of the political structure once the agitators have prepared the way.

Those who agitate for change deal with precise ideas, not fuzzy compromise. This appeals to common sense, personal conscience, and fairness. This approach is ignored when conditions seem to be stable, but when a crisis hits, the views of those who argued for change are suddenly listened to. Quiescent years can go by, requiring great patience and determination and education.

Phillips, interestingly enough, in talking about this subject, used as an example reformer and agitator Richard Cobden, who sought free trade as a tool of peace and worked a long time for the repeal of the corn laws and the promotion of free trade. Success came when Prime Minister Robert Peel succeeded in passing the laws necessary to do exactly this.

Ludwig von Mises qualifies for similar praise. He never yielded to the establishment that scorned him and punished him for his views. Yet today, he is a hero to millions for his willingness to stand firm on his principled defense of the free market and explain how it benefits the masses.

We now live in an age where the current system is being challenged for philosophic and practical reasons. Its failure is becoming more evident every day. There have been plenty of agitators and reformers for decades expecting and warning of lowering living standards brought on by regimentation of the social and economic order. They have offered the practical alternative of freedom. Fortunately, their voices are growing louder and there's reason to be hopeful that our times will prompt a sea change in Americans' understanding of what the role of government ought to be.

I certainly agree that every so often, after long periods of apathy, when the people, driven by the architects of fear, have plunged into dependency, agitators have their day. That which had been ignored and scorned bursts forward with sudden credibility and offers an alternative to the failed ideas that bred and nourished tyrannical government.

Though great agitators for liberty in past centuries have struggled to keep the spirit alive, the climate looks quite healthy for significant and fruitful social and political changes to come out of hibernation. We all need to become agitators for liberty, else we end up in a permanent state of slavery.

STATES' RIGHTS

Technically, states don't have "rights"—only individuals do. But states are legal entities that are very important in the governmental structure of the United States, of course. They serve as a kind of bulwark against an overweening federal government. The Constitution was written with an intent to protect the independence of each state by establishing for the states a very limited relationship to the federal government. States do have a "right" under the Tenth Amendment to retain all powers not explicitly delegated to the federal government by the Constitution. Systematically over the years, this understanding has been destroyed.

A defense of a "states' rights" today generally elicits the charge that this is nothing more than a plot to restore some kind of ancient servitude. This claim really is preposterous. Jefferson believed in states' rights. Even Hamilton had to pay lip service to the idea. An attack on the very notion of states' rights is ultimately an attack on the form of government that the Founders established.

Though the Constitution made an effort to protect the

sovereignty of the states with the Ninth and Tenth Amendments, its effort obviously failed. This is more a reflection of the stewards of liberty's efforts over the course of our history than because of a poorly written Constitution. No words on paper can prevent a despot from displacing freedom.

Even today and with the imperfections of the Constitution, if we had only individuals of high character who showed the wisdom of the Founders, our liberties, our security, and our prosperity would not be under serious attack. Of course, looking back, a few clarifications placed in the Constitution (clarity, for example, that the government may never extend beyond its enumerated powers) might have diminished today's nitpicking over what the original intent was. But when the prevailing attitude of a current generation is to promote centralization of government, not even improved wording in the Constitution can make a difference.

A growing number of Americans are disgusted and frightened by current conditions, both economic and political. Talk is now frequently heard about interposition, nullification, a new Constitutional Convention, and even secession. Believers in a strong central government are quick to discredit any such talk as preposterous, kooky, and driven by dangerous motivations. As the economy continues to deteriorate and our freedoms are further undermined, there will be a lot more talk about getting out from under the heavy hand of the central government and its failures.

Those who charge the defenders of state sovereignty as being un-American and unpatriotic reflect an ignorance of history and the Constitution. Those same individuals did not condemn the breakup of the Soviet Union, nor do they ridicule the principle of self-determination. But as soon as it's argued that the states deserve the right to reject unconstitutional federal mandates through nullification or interposition, mayhem breaks out.

These principles have been used throughout our history to some degree. Fugitive slave laws were frequently ignored by law enforcement officials in some nonslave states, and rightly so. Juries were known to find innocent, regardless of the evidence, those charged with protecting slaves who had fled slave states.

Refusing to enforce bad laws against American citizens by "oath keepers" would have been helpful and moral during the civil rights struggle of the 1950s and '60s. The beatings and arrests couldn't have occurred if law enforcement officials refused to comply. If the military personnel involved in the Kent State killings on May 4, 1970, had refused to participate in the shooting, a much better outcome might have resulted.

Most of the Founders were supportive of nullification and interposition to protect the independent nature of the states. Many believed that if the state legislatures knew that the option of nullification, interposition, and even secession would be met with a civil war killing more than six hundred thousand Americans, the Constitution would have never been ratified.

Both Jefferson and Madison obviously assumed that nullification was permitted under the Constitution. Jefferson's defense of nullification in the Kentucky Resolution of 1799 was similar to but stronger than Madison's view expressed in the Virginia Resolution of 1798. Even with these early confirmations that this was a legitimate process for limiting federal government's abuse of power, it never became a generally accepted doctrine.

Nullification was used by the South Carolina legislature in 1832 in strong objection to the viciously unfair Tariff Act of 1828. If the ordinance had been entirely successful in nullifying the act that became known as the Tariff of Abominations, the odds of avoiding the bloody Civil War would have been enhanced. The tariff caused prices of manufacturing goods to soar and imports from Britain to disappear. This, in turn, made it more difficult for the British and others to buy Southern cotton. These were good reasons for the South to be furious, and thus the conflict between North and South escalated.

The Founders and the doctrine of common law provided the ultimate obstacle to unconstitutional laws passed by the House and the Senate, signed by the President, and permitted by the courts. That is the principle of jury nullification. This too has unfortunately been undermined. No longer are juries notified that they have a right to judge both the facts and the laws in rendering a verdict. Judges now can remove jurors if they believe in this right, or a person can be prohibited from serving if it becomes known that a potential juror believes in the principle.

Why is there such serious talk about these issues dealing with state sovereignty? It's not just an academic discussion; it's a serious practical debate on how we got ourselves into such a mess and whether or not the federal government is about to implode with an unbearable debt burden. People no longer believe promises of a free lunch. A refreshing review of our history and the original intent of the Constitution regarding a monstrous central government is occurring. Citizens are now questioning our government's authority to make war at will, tax and borrow endlessly, and print money when it's needed.

The debate is healthy and it's not just a "Southern" thing. Even some Vermonters, as they did early in our history, are participating in the discussion of state sovereignty.

The odds are near zero that legislation will be passed to clarify and endorse the state's authority to reject laws passed by the federal government that are unconstitutional and that injure state sovereignty. No constitutional amendment will be passed to explicitly permit nullification or secession. The Civil War was fought to keep all states under the thumb of a powerful central government. Yet through a new relationship evolving out of current political and economic chaos, something approaching this goal is about to come.

It's already known that a significant number of American families can't make it with the current tax system and have escaped it by joining the underground (real) economy and operating off the books. It's less complicated that way and brings down wages, profits, and prices; jobs are more easily found. The more authoritarian a society, the greater is the incentive to participate in the black market. At the height of Soviet power, the underground economy thrived. This is not unique and it's virtually impossible to stop, though many will be severely punished. The effort to survive provides a strong incentive for individuals to escape the heavy hand of government. This process actually helps in the long run.

Once necessary reforms are implemented, having a significant number of people with wealth that can be used in the rebuilding of society is beneficial.

If we continue on the current path, just as individuals walk away from tax and regulatory systems that drive them into poverty, states too will start ignoring federal mandates once it's clear the government has no more largesse with which it can bribe and coerce the states into submission. The federal government will become less significant and maybe inconsequential when the empire collapses and the welfare state becomes irrelevant. In the midst of a currency crisis, just printing dollars and running up more debt can no longer provide the pretense of a cure; it only makes matters worse. Under these conditions de facto interposition and nullification and the relationship between the states and the federal government could approach secession.

The threat will come under the heavy hand of government power, which will struggle to hold the empire together by brute force. Welfare programs will disappear long before the domestic military presence used to "keep the people safe" from the dangers of anarchy is humbled.

It's a shame that it could come to this, but power is indeed corrupting and intoxicating to those who want to rule others for their own good.

The outcome of this effort to demand adherence to the Constitution and the Tenth Amendment hopefully will be positive. The people for too long have been complacent and overly tolerant of government abuse because our wealth seemed to be guaranteed and government benefits became more desired than independence and liberty. Now, with the enlightenment gained from the financial crisis, the people are making up for their complacency. The anger expressed by the Tea Party people is a sign of how serious the conditions have gotten. And we're still in the early stages of the crisis.

If their energy and anger can be channeled in a positive manner, and so far most of it has been healthy, good things can come of it. So far the noise comes mostly from those who are demanding more freedom, not more handouts; that sentiment has to prevail. Socializing an economy on the brink from too much central economic planning can hardly be the solution to our problems. The stakes are high; the answers are obvious.

———————

Woods, Jr., Thomas E. 2010. *Nullification: How to Resist Federal Tyranny in the 21st Century.* Washington, DC: Regnery Publishing.

STATISTICS

The statistical collection that went on in the eighteenth century was the same as in the ancient world. The government counted people, and that's about it. I don't like the intrusiveness of the Census. I believe that people should not be harassed or prosecuted for refusing to fill out a census form or answer intrusive questions posed by hired agents of the state. Perhaps if people held a benign view of the state, based on actual evidence, they would be more willing to cooperate.

Regardless, the Census is nothing compared with the vast statistical collection apparatus maintained by the federal government. Bureaus are everywhere, collecting and reporting every conceivable bit of information they can think of to collect and report. And for what purpose? The push for this came in the 1930s, and the results were to be used for economic planning. The idea was that if the planners had enough information, they could better manage the country, same as a store manager who needs information on inventory, customers, cost accounting, and the like. It hasn't worked. No matter how much data the government collects, it still can't improve on market operations. Mostly they just use collected data to collect more data, until everything is on file.

Statistics are seriously limited in at least three respects. First, their validity depends entirely on the way they are collected, what is being collected, and how they are presented. Second, statistics do not interpret themselves, and so their meaning is easily manipulated by politicians. Third, statistics can tell us nothing about cause and effect; therefore, they really do not address the crucial issues we should be asking about public policy.

The data are of course very useful for political purposes. Governments of all political persuasions resort to statistical "evidence" to promote their cause. Sometimes the statistics are used for political spin, and other times their use involves gross distortion of economic reality. Statistical distortion used in combination with political spin doctors can temporarily deceive the market, but only for a limited time.

When the money supply statistic called M3 was thought to reveal too much evidence of the flawed Federal Reserve policy, the Fed suspended reporting it. For a long while, M3 was revealing the Federal Reserve policy of excessive monetary inflation during the period in which most economists of all persuasion now agree that interest rates were held too low for too long.

Government unemployment statistics are virtually worthless in describing the seriousness of the economic downturn. The most astounding deception is that if a discouraged individual quits looking for work, he or she is no longer listed as unemployed. When a significant number cease to list themselves as seeking employment, the percentage of unemployment can actually go down.

Free market analysis reveals that unemployment is actually over 20 percent, and even by some lesser reported statistics collected by the Bureau of Labor Statistics, it's over 16 percent. Yet we hear is that unemployment is under 10 percent. How is this possible? It all depends on the way you collect and report.

The Gross Domestic Product numbers are always a favorite statistic of financial markets and are generally used by politicians to brag on an improving economy. The politicians want credit and also help in the next election. But the GDP, even without fudging, is a deeply flawed statistic.

In a recession, the government increases spending by borrowing, by printing money, or by raising taxes, regardless of what the money is spent on; this spending will raise the GDP. This borrowing, printing, and taxation is a negative for the economy in itself, a fact not revealed, given the way the data are collected. In reality, higher government spending lowers economic growth. Blowing up bridges overseas and rebuilding them raises our GDP by counting bombs and planes produced, but none of this increases America's wealth. It would be more accurate to subtract government spending from the GDP rather than adding it to it. I tend to look suspiciously at all government statistics since the really harmful ones are never mentioned.

Personally, I enjoy looking at all forms of statistics that the government collects, but I'm also aware that privately collected statistics are a necessary check on government data. I don't follow the statistics to legislate better but only to gain some glimpse into what kind of damage government is doing.

Statistical collection has helped to provide bogus "scientific evidence" that government is doing great good for the country. It is no different from a fortune-teller who pretends to know all truth by looking into a crystal ball. We are being asked to trust something that requires a serious leap of faith and defies all good sense.

In the end, there is no substitute for clear thinking, logic, and common sense. The more you swim in an ocean of government-generated data, the more confused and disoriented you can become. A better path to enlightenment involves reading and thinking for yourself.

SURVEILLANCE

Each of us is caught on a camera quite a few times every day. Most of the time, we don't worry about it. We are taped getting money from a cash machine, buying things at the convenience store, shopping at the grocery, or just driving around a parking lot. Our data are collected even as we browse online. I don't see this as an inherent problem, since most of us agree to this kind of surveillance. When it is done by the private sector, it serves a social function and leads to more security and better service.

Private security cameras on private property can be quite useful in performing a task that government can't and shouldn't be responsible for. Protecting individual plants, businesses, homes, apartments, or condos with cameras should be the prerogative of the property owner. We would all rather not deal with this, but we can also appreciate the benefits. Such surveillance enhances security and deters theft.

The private use of video cameras is not my concern. In fact, they can be used to promote freedom. They allow people to film law enforcement personnel when they get out of line.

More police brutality has been caught on film than ever before, which serves the interest of all of us. I also note that most government agencies are now barring citizens in government offices from carrying cell phones, and there can be no doubt about the reason. Government doesn't want to be watched and filmed.

Meanwhile, the government's own use of surveillance cameras is out of control. Cameras at traffic lights are pervasive throughout the country. Many cities have been sold on the idea, supposedly for safety reasons, but the reality is that the cameras are installed with the goal of raising revenue. The companies that put these cameras in are motivated because they share in the profits. Challenging the charges in court is frequently not even permitted.

All public places now are subject to government cameras: roads, streets, buildings, and who knows where else. The excuse is always the same: They are providing safety for us. But unlike in the private sector, this is not really believable. Government much too often violates our privacy and at the same time is fanatical in protecting its own secrecy.

Not only are the government's cameras proliferating, the government itself is turning even the private camera into a threat it otherwise would not be. Under the Patriot Act, private cameras, as well as cell phones and the Internet, are vulnerable to an aggressive federal government.

Everyone theoretically can be a potential threat, a possible friend of an "enemy combatant," and therefore can be under surveillance one way or the other. We're constantly reminded we live in a dangerous time and we're at war, so be ready and willing to sacrifice your liberty so we can all be safe and secure.

Whether surveillance is good or bad really depends on the institutions that use it and what the film is used for. Nothing good can come out of permitting government to film our every move. It strikes me like a scene out of Orwell's *1984*. What I would like to see is the very opposite: citizens who film ever more government activity, a live camera in every government bureaucracy that can be seen by all citizens, a monitor on every bureaucrat that can be watched by every person who pays the bills. This would be a great way for the citizens to take back control. We need to protect citizens against government intrusions even as we curb the ability of the government to operate in total secrecy.

TAXES

"Taxes are the price we pay for civilization," according to Oliver Wendell Holmes. This claim has cost us dearly. Civilization comes about through economic, moral, and social development. Freedom is a precondition. Taxes and the power to tax have been destructive to civilization and all progress. The whole notion of running the economy and the world and paying for it through forcibly extracting taxes from productive individuals violates the principle of natural rights, and when carried to an extreme, destroys the means of production and the wealth of the country.

Throughout the late eighteenth and the nineteenth centuries, Americans were largely untouched by any taxes. Federal revenue was provided by the tariff—a regrettable form of indirect taxation but one that didn't actually attack the property rights of the citizens directly. The Sixteenth Amendment to the Constitution changed that. After income could be taxed, the whole structure of the relationship between government and the citizen changed. Now we had a different philosophy at work, one that presumed that government had a claim on the productive efforts of every worker.

Though taxes begin low, human nature is such that the politicians and the recipients of government largesse see to it that taxes inexorably rise. Though most think only of the harm done by excessive income taxes, there are many other taxes as well. Sales, property, school, county, city, state, excise, and inheritance taxes all take their toll.

The greater the government taxes, the greater the need, since government management is inferior to individual management and the money is always misallocated. As long as people believe the nonsense that taxation is a blessing and any objection to it means opposition to civilized society and is morally wrong and unpatriotic, we will see a continued decline of civilization. The early American patriots understood the destructive nature of taxation.

People tolerate taxes for a while because they have previously accumulated wealth. As the tax burden grows and productivity falls, tax revenue falls and the only answer seems to be higher taxes. If the people can no longer tolerate higher taxes, government merely borrows and creates new money, and then the inflation tax is paid with higher prices. The whole process destabilizes the political system and eventually becomes a threat to civilized progress.

The idea that it's a fair exchange when citizens "pay" taxes and receive the benefits of a compassionate government can do irreparable harm to a civilized society. Depending on government to take care of us sharply diminishes any desire for assuming responsibility for oneself. Government spending is unwise and interferes with the wisdom of the market on how capital should be allocated. The only people who benefit are the politicians, bureaucrats, and the special interest recipients of government spending programs. The country becomes poorer and anger is generated.

For a long time, people claimed the wonders of taxpayer funding of free public education for the masses. The results today are now being seriously questioned as more Americans are moving their children into private schools and participating in homeschooling. Our public schools are grossly inefficient, and very costly. The costs are spread around in ways that do terrible economic damage and waste resources.

Government control of health care paid for by taxation has not been successful and yet the American people are demanding more of the same. Increased taxation hardly provides a more modern and civilized system of medicine.

Sometimes there can be a false sense of security with a taxpayer-funded program's partial success. But we need to ask, what would be the alternate way of offering the program, without government taxation? The dollars spent on government-provided services like medical care don't disappear if taxation is limited or abolished. They would just be spent elsewhere and more efficiently without corporate and government bureaucrats placed between the doctor and the patients.

Many people forget that regulations act as a tax, and we have plenty of those. People believe that without massive government regulations society would deteriorate into an uncivilized mess. A system that is absent a huge bureaucracy and high taxation is not anarchy. Rules of contract, property rights, honest money, and voluntary exchanges with the necessary bankruptcy laws provide order and efficiency.

As bad as is the economic harm done by giving government blanket authority to tax, the greatest uncivilized consequence of this power is to finance senseless war and provide largesse to the military-industrial complex. Using funds from a system of taxation and inflation, and wars being fought without declaration have created a dangerous situation for all of us. Our presence around the world in more than 130 countries could not be maintained without the power to tax. Our policy of preventive war around the world makes the world a perilous place—a threat in itself to civilization.

Taxation is realized only by force and threat of force. This always means a violation of civil liberties and the Constitution. Freedom suffers from it. Yet the freer a country is, the more productive and civilized it becomes. Taxes are a hindrance to both.

The philosophy of big government generates the need for revenues. The bigger the government, the more revenues required, which threatens economic and political stability.

The argument for big government and unlimited taxation is collectivist in nature. A system of private property ownership, free market exchanges, and a sound monetary system doesn't require high taxation. A minimalist approach to government and taxation places an obstacle to wars abroad and waste at home.

Groups and individuals that justify high taxation and big government automatically reject constitutional restraint of federal government activities. They cannot be champions of personal liberty and at the same time promote government interference in our economic and personal lives. Nor could those who champion military adventurism overseas maintain credibility when they talk about personal liberty and balanced budgets.

Once the politician embarks on militarism or welfarism the spending becomes even a greater problem than taxation to pay the bills. Politically, there are limits on the degree of taxation that the people will tolerate, but the appetite for government spending is never diminished. That is why borrowing and debt continue and grow exponentially, ultimately leading to the inflationary tax to be paid at a later date. If we as a nation continue to believe that paying for civilization through taxation is a wise purchase and the only way to achieve civilization, we are doomed. It's a bad deal for the cause of liberty.

———•◦•———

Chodorov, Frank. 2007. *The Income Tax: Root of All Evil.* Auburn, AL: Mises Institute.

TERRORISM

I t is very likely that young people today believe that terrorism is a new kind of problem, something that emerged as an issue sometime after the end of the Cold War. In fact, terrorism has been around my entire public life. Cracking down on terrorism—defined very loosely as non-state violence perpetuated for political reasons—was a priority during the Clinton years, the Reagan years, and all the way back to the early 1970s, when law enforcement agencies first named it as a serious problem in need of a solution.[1]

The use of the term "terrorism" in relation to political violence has much earlier origins, tracing most directly to the French Revolution, when the Reign of Terror wrought mass violence in the name of political obedience. During the Cold War, U.S. officials would frequently speak about communists and their penchant for terrorism.

---

1. National Advisory Committee on Criminal Justice Standards and Goals, Task Force on Disorders and Terrorism, *Disorders and Terrorism* (Washington DC: GPO, 1976).

Of course, what is and is not called terrorism is ultimately determined by the point of view. The United States has bombed dozens of countries in the name of retaliation, but innocent people in those countries are more likely to think of U.S. actions themselves as a form of terrorism. The United States might call resisters against a U.S. occupation terrorists, while the resisters might regard their own violence as an expression of patriotism. It all depends on the perspective.

Even so, there is no question that terrorism of the sort we most often think of—violence against innocents to punish the United States for its foreign policies—is a serious issue that requires a response. If Americans do not feel safe abroad, or are willing to subject themselves to humiliating searches at airports just to avoid it, our very liberty is at risk from the terrorist threat.

Whenever this subject comes up, I always urge that we look more carefully at the problem than most people are willing to do. We need to ask what drives anyone to criminality. This is an important consideration for all efforts at law enforcement. We must examine the roots to understand the actions. If we want to end violence, we surely need to look at what gives rise to it, especially if it is of a political nature. If we neglect to do that, we usually end up making the problem worse rather than better.

If we listen to what the terrorists themselves say, the message is very rarely about religion or some irrational desire to slaughter the innocent. Rather, it is usually very specifically about U.S. foreign policy in the Middle East and elsewhere. It is about our occupations of Iraq and Afghanistan, our involvement and troops in Saudi Arabia, our subsidization of the border expansion of Israel, and our sanctions and war belligerence in other countries. This is not to say that changing these policies would engender a universal brotherhood of peace and love, but it is to draw attention to the undeniable reality, the plain fact, that most terrorism is not irrational, but rather driven by specific grievances. We would do well to examine those policies and consider their costs before plunging into even more wars that make a bad situation far worse.

This leads to the very important subject of why there is an al Qaeda, and why people are motivated enough to commit suicide in the service of a political goal. They are motivated because our troops are in their country. So what do we do? We send more troops in order to send a signal that there will be no tolerance for dissent. The problem is that this has not worked throughout history. Plainly speaking, when we fight terrorism by exacerbating the very reasons *for* that terrorism, we increase the violence against us.

This should not really be any surprise. Whenever government wages war on anything (poverty, drugs, illiteracy, etc.), it is likely to make the problem worse. Of course, government has no incentive to discover the problems created by its wars because the wars themselves enhance the power of the government, bring in more revenue, provide a good excuse for bureaucratic expansion and violations of liberties, and keep the population whipped up in a state of fear and thereby easier to control. I have my doubts that, just as with the war on poverty or communism, the government really desires to win.

The incentives are exactly the reverse: The worse the problem becomes, the more excuse there is for government power.

Robert Pape, a researcher at the University of Chicago, did a study of six years and 2,200 terrorist attacks that was based on ten thousand records from publicly available databases. He concluded: "We have lots of evidence now that when you put the foreign military presence in, it triggers suicide terrorism campaigns...and that when the foreign forces leave, it takes away almost 100 percent of the terrorist campaign." He has written a book explaining his thesis.[2] Such studies help vindicate what I've been saying my entire public life: Invading other countries is a bad idea, especially if the goal is to stop terrorism; quite the opposite will be the result.

The government is incapable of doing what it's supposed to do. A job like the provision of security is something best left to private institutions. Airlines are a good example. They should be required to deal with their own security needs. Of course, some airlines like all of the responsibility to fall to the government, so if anything goes wrong, it's the government's fault. But when we leave the job to private companies, they handle it creatively. Think of how efficient an armored car company is in protecting the money in those trucks, and nobody has to worry about it. Or think of a jewelry store or a bank. They all have security issues but handle them through private means.

If we really wanted to put a huge dent in the problem of terrorism, there is a way to do it. We should start withdrawing

---

2. Robert Pape and James Ke Feldman. *Cutting the Fuse: The Explosion of Global Suicide Terrorism and How to Stop It* (Chicago: University of Chicago Press, 2010).

troops from foreign countries. We should not go to war without a declaration. We should not go to war when it's an aggressive war. We should take an honest look at all the ways in which U.S. policy incites desperate people to take extreme measures as retaliation for U.S.-sponsored political violence.

TORTURE

P olls show that anywhere from half to two thirds of Americans support the power of government to use torture. Few just say: "I support torture." The words are minced to make it sound less barbaric. President George W. Bush started calling it "enhanced interrogation technique," but everyone knew what that meant; it was agreed on that in polite company it was not to be called torture.

In recent years, especially since 9/11, a majority of the American people have been brainwashed into believing that our national security depends on torture and that it's been effective. The fact is, our Constitution, our laws, international laws, and the code of morality all forbid it. Civilized societies, for hundreds of years, have rejected its use.

When Americans endorse torture they think they are endorsing rough treatment of militant terrorists guilty of committing violence against us. They would rather not think that they are talking about innocent people, or people not convicted or ever charged with a crime, including American citizens who are the recipients of this heinous act.

There's no desire to know that people die during torture and that some commit suicide. And now we read of evidence that some of those whom our government has claimed committed suicide actually were murdered by American torturers—usually CIA agents.[1] The agents who destroyed evidence of their torture did nothing wrong, according to the Obama administration, and will not be prosecuted.

The old ruse is to ask what if you knew someone had vital information that, if revealed, would save American lives. But this is purely hypothetical. One can never know that for sure. If you had a strong suspicion that there might be such evidence, using persuasion and a justified approach is preferable. The evidence shows the odds are greatly increased that vital information is more likely to be gained in this manner.

The question that supporters of torture refuse to even ask is, If one suspects that one individual out of 100 captured has crucial information, and you don't know which one it is, are you justified to torture all 100 to get that information? If we still get a yes answer in support of such torture, I'm afraid our current system of government cannot survive.

Many terrorist suspects arrested in the past ten years have been caught because of paid informants. Accusing your enemy of terrorism gains you a bonus check from the U.S. taxpayers and lets the agents of torture have a field day. Of course they claim falsely that this can only happen on individuals captured outside the United States and held in indefinite detention without counsel and without the right of habeas corpus.

1. "Elite Club Conceals CIA Torture Cells." ABC News, November 18, 2009.

Quickly the argument then becomes: These aren't people or citizens deserving the protection of our Constitution; they are enemy combatants. And who defines an enemy combatant? The President or the Attorney General can do it without judicial overview, and this applies to American citizens as well. Though only a couple of American citizens have been thusly treated, a precedent has been set just in case there's political disturbance in the United States.

It's not difficult to believe that American citizens might become vulnerable to the charge of supporting terrorists for merely challenging our foreign policy and claiming to understand why thousands, if not millions, of Muslims around the world would like to do us harm.

It looks like secret prisons, clandestine rendition, unlimited detention, and torture are all still part of our policies. No effort has been made by the new administration to investigate charges of misconduct in the previous administration. Protecting state secrets is just as strong a policy today as it was in the last administration.

The supporters argue that we must not be rigid in protecting the civil liberties of those who have been arrested as suspects; such information is of tremendous benefit in preventing attacks in the United States. The protorture fanatics were outraged that Umar Farouk Abdulmutallab, the twenty-year-old from Sudan, was not tortured to extract vital information regarding any future plans to attack us. Subsequently, though, the Obama administration said that they were getting information from him with less violent means.

The odds of extricating any significant information from him were utterly remote. The evidence is clear that information obtained from torture is rarely if ever of any value. Those suffering severe mental or physical pain will say whatever they think the torturers want them to say. There is concrete evidence that a more humane method of persuasion yields more information than physical torture does.

The real tragedy is that sadistic cruelty is contagious and dehumanizes those who employ torture. Sadism begets sadism. The "need" for torture and the acceptance of it comes from unabashed fear, insecurity, and ignorance. For a single individual like the "underwear bomber" to intimidate an entire nation demanding his torture is not an encouraging sign for the future of our country. Yet there was no torture, and so far no events could have been prevented by employing it.

For those who still care about our laws and international law (United Nations and Geneva Conference), all torture is illegal. The American government claims that the rules are different because we're in a "battle zone" and any information is urgent. Of course today the war, though undeclared, is everywhere in the world, which allows capture and a chance of torture in any country in the world, including the United States.

It is this argument that provides that anyone—including an American citizen—can be declared an enemy combatant and thus be denied any rights of habeas corpus and eventually tried in a military court.

The image of Americans torturing prisoners at Abu Ghraib and Guantánamo circulated around the Muslim world has done unbelievable harm by the hatred it generated against all Americans. It's going to take a lot of time to alter that sentiment, and it won't happen without a change in our foreign policy and our assumption that we can arrest anybody any-where in the world at will.

General Barry McCaffrey, not exactly an outsider, com-mented on our torture program: "We tortured people unmerci-fully. We probably murdered dozens of them during the course of that, both the armed forces and the CIA." The ACLU and many news sources estimate that at least 100 detainees died as a result of torture while in American custody. Our government has tried to downplay those deaths as suicide. So far there's been no effort to hold accountable the individuals responsible for this travesty.

For a society that condones torture of suspects involved in fighting our occupation of their country, it is not a great leap to accept torture of any criminal gang member here in the United States. The door has been opened more than a crack for this attitude to spread. What I fear is if or when the political system deteriorates due to a growing economic crisis, the cries for strong law-and-order policies could cause secret renditions and torture to come to the United States.

The clandestine activities of the FBI, the CIA, and all six-teen of the intelligence agencies is something that is so mas-sive and secret even presidents have a hard time understanding to what extent they operate. To oppose their authority is con-sidered by many in DC as unpatriotic and un-American. This is not a good sign for America. A better understanding of civil liberties is urgently needed in all levels of our government. The message should be that torture is simply wrong and doesn't work. Torture is more un-American than those who oppose it.

Paul, Ron. *A Foreign Policy of Freedom.* Foundation for Rational Economics and Education, 2007.

Salon Staff. "The Abu Ghraib Files." March 14, 2006. Salon.com.

TRADE POLICIES

Protectionism is related to military Keynesianism in that many supporters of militarism are also champions of sanctions and blockades. True, a lot of protectionists thoughtlessly push protective tariffs purely as a job program meant to protect noncompetitive domestic industries and do not support them for military reasons. But what they don't accept is that trade and friendship diminish chances of war with other nations, and protective tariffs are actually harmful to the American consumer. The moral hazard of protectionism is that the less efficient will not be motivated to become more efficient in order to survive. Complacency and inefficiency set in.

Sanctions and blockades are extremely dangerous and should be considered acts of war. This policy was a prelude to our unwarranted and illegal invasion and occupation of Iraq. There's reason to fear the same will result from our trade barriers against Iran.

Blockading the Palestinians in Gaza has proven to be a dangerous and inhumane policy that has precipitated a worldwide condemnation of Israel. The result has been to make the region much more dangerous. It has undermined the Israel-Turkey friendship that has served both East and West for decades. My contention has always been that our interventionist foreign policy in the Middle East is good neither for us nor for Israel. I'm now more convinced of that than ever.

Sanctions and protectionist measures are always a catastrophe. Believing they are beneficial leads to complacency and false expectations for their success, both economically and for solving geopolitical problems. Many members of Congress falsely believe that strong sanctions are an alternative to war instead of a precursor. Even members who are part of the unofficial antiwar coalition almost always support sanctions, even though they see themselves as strongly opposing war as a solution.

What they fail to see is that blockades for whatever reason can be enforced only through violence and even killing. This moves the countries involved closer to outright war. Iraq is a good case in point: Sanctions were imposed through the 1990s and then the real war followed. Trade and friendship moves the opposing nations in the opposite direction.

International trade organizations such as the WTO, NAFTA, CAFTA, and others are supported by many proponents of free trade and are universally opposed by protectionists and labor unions. The stated purpose of these organizations is to set rules and arbitrate trade disputes between members with the goal of minimizing trade restrictions and tariffs. And there is evidence that some tariffs have been lowered through these agreements. There's also strong evidence that the trade organizations just as often give permission to retaliate against another country for certain trade infractions.

I consider myself the most "radical" free trader in Congress, but I do not vote for these international trade organizations. The process by which these agreements are passed is flawed. Generally, fast-track legislation is passed by Congress, and congressional authority over foreign commerce is transferred to the executive branch. The office of the President then negotiates with groups of other countries the details of how to lower tariffs or gives permission to retaliate against another member for unfair trade practices.

The only way the executive branch should be directly involved is to draft a treaty to be ratified by the Senate. Generally, this is an obstacle if the President is required to get two thirds of the Senate to agree. It's easy to get a majority of each party to give approval to fast-track legislation. Since the Constitution is clear that Congress has the responsibility for foreign commerce, I don't believe the President should even attempt to regulate foreign trade by treaty. The President already has vast authority with veto power over what Congress might pass.

These trade agreements become instruments for international government entities to regulate trade without explicit consent of Congress. They literally undermine our national sovereignty, and that of our states as well, with rules. Too often the rules handed down can be beneficial to large international corporations while harming or ignoring the small companies unable to defend themselves against the giant bureaucracy serving the special interests.

Too many supporters of organizations like the WTO are not true free traders even though some groups who pride themselves on free market economics are strong defenders of these organizations. Countries that won't lower tariffs hurt their own people more than anyone else, since tariffs are a tax. If a foreign country subsidizes a product and goods become cheaper than our own, it's an economic boon for the domestic country. Our country then has more money left over to increase our standard of living by purchasing other products. The political challenge, of course, is that our domestic industries must adapt. But in a free market economy they are required to adapt for all kinds of reasons that might enable their competitors to be able to produce at a lower cost and provide cheaper goods for the consumer. The consumer is the "special interest" in a free market—not protected corporations or big labor.

Many of the professed free traders in Congress who get their credentials by supporting all trade agreements are frequently the strongest supporters for sanctions against countries such as Cuba, Iraq, Iran, and Korea. This position mocks the principle that nations that trade with each other are less likely to go to war. The truth is, some may well understand this and believe in this principle, but it's war they seek. Too often, that is what they get. Stopping all flow of oil to Japan in early 1941 was a significant factor in the attack on Pearl Harbor later that year—something most Americans are not interested in hearing.

I personally like to defend free trade in much more direct manner. I believe everyone has a right to spend his or her own money any way they see fit, whether it be on foreign or domestic goods. If tennis shoes from China cost $20 but $100 if manufactured in the United States, why punish the poor for the sake of protecting domestic industries?

Many will complain that China (or others) uses "slave" labor and for that reason we shouldn't allow their products to compete with ours. But that is hardly accurate. Chinese production uses low-cost labor for sure, but they're jobs that working-class Chinese eagerly seek; they are never forced to work as slaves. All they have to do is compare their current standard of living to the standard of living they had just a few years ago under communism. What many here don't want to admit is that much of our labor is priced artificially higher as a consequence of minimum wage laws, unemployment benefits, and compulsory unions, while prices are pushed higher as a consequence of excessive regulations, taxation, and government-caused inflation.

Protectionist measures don't solve the problems; they only protect the status quo that keeps us from being competitive in many industries.

Unions

U nions came into being in a significant way during the industrial revolution but gained a major foothold in American economic life during the Depression of the 1930s. The National Labor Relations Act of 1935 was, until that time, the most important labor law passed in the United States. It established minimum wages and maximum hours of work and many government regulations on all businesses and labor agreements.

This act, also known as the Wagner Act, passed for the purpose of helping labor, significantly contributed to the deepening and prolongation of the Depression. When an economy corrects from a Federal Reserve–generated bubble and malinvestment, all parties involved must retrench, eliminate the mistakes, and cancel out the errors made during the boom phase of the cycle.

My first exposure to union power came as a young person after World War II. My dad ran a small retail dairy business back when milk was delivered daily to customers' homes. The maximum number of trucks we ever had was about twenty.

Our drivers were nonunion, treated well by my dad, and never agitated to join a union. The fact that we were nonunion allowed my four brothers and me the flexibility to fill in as summer and weekend relief drivers for vacations time and days off—a job that helped us all pay for our college education. A union contract would have never allowed this. Our drivers' wages were commensurate with union wages, and even then they received medical benefits. At that time, before government-managed care took over, true medical insurance was reasonably priced.

Even with this good relationship with our drivers, regional strikes by union truck drivers affected our business as well. During the first strike that I became aware of, my dad pulled all his trucks off the road. I couldn't understand it and thought my dad might be sympathetic, so I quizzed him on this.

He quickly explained to me that the threat of union violence against us was significant if our trucks delivered milk during the strike. He explained that our trucks could easily be damaged and in some cases turned over and destroyed by union strikers.

Union power, gained by legislation, even without physical violence, is still violence. The laborer gains legal force over the employer. Economically, in the long run, labor loses. Whether it was featherbedding in the railroads or union intimidation for milk-truck drivers or car workers, the eventual result is the loss of jobs. It continues until this day.

Today, of course, no one has the service of having their milk delivered to their house, nor do we have any private railroad companies running passenger trains. All this has come about as a consequence of labor laws intended to protect workers' interests. In fact, the laws do the opposite. If only it were so easy to help the working class. Just dictate wages and everyone will be financially better off. Unfortunately, this leads to disastrous results, whether it's the prolonging of the economic mess as it did in the 1930s or the tragic results in American industry that we're witnessing today.

What good is it to mandate a $75 per hour wage if there are no jobs available at that price? What good is a minimum wage of $7.50 if it significantly contributes to overall unemployment?

The reaction to the economic argument explaining the shortcoming of labor unions and minimum wage laws is that it's heartless and unfair not to force "fairness" on the ruthless capitalists. But true compassion should be directed toward the defense of a free market that has provided the greatest abundance and the best distribution of wealth of any economic system known throughout history.

Once power is given to government to set wages higher than the market rate, it also has the power to fix wages at lower rates as Nixon did in 1971 with wage and price controls. Roosevelt and Truman did the same thing. They claimed it was in the country's best interest due to the war effort. Think of the absurdity: for ten years during the Great Depression, the government tried to raise wages, and then, when the war came, the government forcibly lowered wages. The whole endeavor is crazy and dangerous. In a free society, setting wage standards is not ever a prerogative of the government in times of war or peace.

Working people should always have a right to voluntarily organize and negotiate with business owners. It's the use of force or privileges that militant unions demand from government that distorts the true cost of labor. Compulsory unionism, protected by law by a majority vote, violates the principle of protecting minority rights. Making workers pay dues to be represented by an organization they disagree with is hardly fair or just. Coercing businesses to accept contracts with unions at the risk of being closed down is not a voluntary agreement. Workers who are willing to work at a lower than union wage are subject to violence by militant union workers.

In a free society unions would not be banned but the employer would only deal with unions voluntarily. In a truly free society there may well develop competing unions (in highly specialized skill areas) to vie for contracts and argue their case for productivity and safety habits. If they prove their case, workers' wages would be maximized for economic reasons. What many people don't even realize is that in a free market economy, labor becomes scarce and the businessman must seek the best workers by offering higher wages.

Even before the current economic crisis, starting in 2008 in certain areas, labor was scarce, which was a great incentive for illegal aliens to come here for construction jobs that were going begging. They were, for the most part, making more than minimum wage but less than the union wage.

It was not infrequent in my congressional district for farmers, builders, fishermen, hospital administrators, and others to come to my office asking for help to increase the number of work visas to help solve their labor shortages. Many also complained about illegal immigrants being a financial burden on the taxpayers by getting free education and medical care in our emergency rooms.

It is true that illegal aliens place an economic burden on the American taxpayer, but it's doubtful that legal or illegal immigration is the cause of unemployment for American citizens. With the recession, illegal immigration is down because the demand for labor is down. Immigrants weren't undercutting American workers' salaries; jobs went begging because American citizens either didn't want or need the jobs badly enough to take the ones that were offered.

Jobs are always available, even in weak economies—it's just that many refuse to take them because wages are seen as being too low. And when compared to what one can get from unemployment benefits or welfare, the incentive to take a job is significantly diminished.

Once labor gets special protection by labor law, we entrench the principle of government interference. This prepares the way for wage control, and the government can also declare wages to be too high. It also invites controls like antitrust, and restriction on campaign participation by both labor and business. If union dues were obtained strictly by voluntary means, this would not be a problem. Unionized workers, getting special favor from federal laws, should never be allowed to hold the taxpayer hostage with threats of a strike or interfering in the election process or lobbying for legislation designed to perpetuate the overpaid and excessive bureaucracy.

There are, I'm sure, many who support labor unions who would disagree with these points. What they don't understand is that once special privileges are granted for one group, others will compete for political influence as well, to benefit themselves. In this case, big business will have the funds to influence a pliable system with cash outlays for all forms of corporate welfare benefits: special loans, grants, contracts, easy money, financing the military-industrial complex, special tax benefits. In the end, the money talks and the principle of intervention endorsed by the pro-union workers is used to a greater extent to subsidize and aid businesses over labor. It would be best to have a government that would cater to neither group.

In a free society, neither business nor labor gets special benefits from the government; not giving benefits to either equalizes the process, which then would be a benefit to labor. The best way for labor to gain more economic clout is for the free market to thrive and good workers to become a premium, creating a higher demand and higher wages.

It's generally thought that big labor and big business are always at loggerheads, but this is not so. When large corporations, especially those in the military-industrial complex, are artificially subsidized, permitting huge profits, it provides an opportunity for unions to maximize their wages. In instances like this, the unions and businesses frequently work together to obtain obscene contracts from the government. These companies rarely go bankrupt, and if in trouble get bailed out. Even before the recent crisis, corporations like Lockheed and others were taken care of by Congress, with pressure on the Republicans coming from the corporations and on the Democrats by the unions.

The recent bailout of General Motors was a lot messier, but I'm sure there were some who thought the best answer would have been for General Motors to get some military contracts to manufacture tanks or other government vehicles. This was one of the things done in 1979 to bail out Chrysler—the first time—with a contract for the army's M-1 tank.

Interestingly, this Chrysler bailout was one of the first real battles in which I became directly involved in Congress. Even earlier, because Chrysler presented a "need," the Congress responded by taking the contract from General Motors, to whom it had been awarded. The first great switch was pulled off in 1977 by the Secretary of Defense at that time, Donald Rumsfeld.

Billions of dollars have been spent on the M-1 tank over the years and yet there has never been a need for it for the defense of our country—it was purely a military-industrial complex boondoggle to serve the interests of the demands of big business and big labor and to save Chrysler and at that time to stick it to General Motors. But in the end, General Motors got its bailout too.

Not only was the tank not necessary to defend our country; it's weapons like this that encourage our military intervention overseas, resulting in grief and blowback tragedies. This type of spending contributes significantly to our bankruptcy and the drain of capital resources away from productive enterprises.

Though the economic planners claim the Chrysler bailout was a great success since Chrysler paid back the loan guarantees, no one tried or could measure the harm caused by the misdirection of resources inherent in the program. Worst of all, it conditioned Americans to accept the notion that, in tough economic times, the role of the U.S. Congress is to bail out corporations by protecting unearned profits and high union wages.

Sadly, the Chrysler bailout of 1979 set up the unimaginable bailouts of today. It was erroneously concluded that spending on military weapons—even those we don't need—can help a company or even an entire economy recover from a government-caused downturn. Unbelievably, I hear of talk in Washington that the only way to get out of a deep recession or depression is to get into a war, as FDR did.

Instead of arguing that spending money on bailouts of bankrupt, inefficient companies is helpful, it should be seen as wasteful and something that cannot provide an incentive for the companies to clean up their act. It actually encourages the opposite. Besides, direct loans, guaranteed loans, or cash subsidies always harm some unidentified investor or company that was denied access to credit or may even have been taxed to pay for the bailout of their competitors.

The Chrysler bailout was supported by big government, big business, and big banks and big labor; the little guy was stuck with the bills. No one should be surprised that today it's not only Chrysler, it's General Motors, Goldman Sachs, and many others who lined up at the Treasury and Fed and were also bailed out.

After Ronald Reagan took office, in the first budget debate in 1981, a few cuts were made (only) in the previously proposed increases to some domestic welfare programs. Liberal Democrats screamed bloody murder and demanded a sharp cut in the Export-Import Bank, seen as a form of corporate welfare. The amendment to cut passed easily, with greater than 100 votes. It was a big political event and the report of the debate and vote made the front page of the *Washington Post*.

Representatives of Boeing and other big American exporters who lived off export subsidies were quoted as saying that the vote, instead of being devastating to them, gave them an opportunity to "show their clout." And indeed they did.

The following day, since the final passage of the appropriations bill had not occurred, the same vote was repeated. This time it was defeated easily, with approximately 100 members changing their vote. The unions worked the Democrats, big business lobbied the Republicans, and the Export-Import Bank was protected from any cuts in its budget.

The next morning, the *Washington Post* had a follow-up story regarding the impressive reversal in the vote. A House member from Louisiana was asked if his vote was up for sale, since he was one of the members who switched his vote. He was quoted as saying, "No, it wasn't for sale but it was for rent." This episode confirmed my cynicism regarding the way Congress worked nearly thirty years ago.

But the pressure by government workers is still significant. In the midst of the severe economic crisis most of the new jobs are in the public sector—usually federal, since only the federal government can print the money it needs to pay wages, unlike state governments. There are jobs now commanding salaries vastly higher than similar ones in the private sector. Instead of these jobs being a positive for the economy, they are actually a negative—denying the private sector of needed resources and capital to generate economic growth.

Minimum wage laws, mandating union contracts (closed shop), and Davis-Bacon rules are all designed to help a small segment of workers gain economic advantage while actually hurting unprotected workers. And long term, even the beneficiaries suffer from the unemployment that excessive wage demands bring about. It's not a coincidence that Detroit workers suffer more severely than those who are employed in the states where arbitrary union power is held in check by right-to-work laws. High wages are great, but if there are no jobs they become meaningless.

In a free society with free markets, workers should always negotiate for the highest wage, while businesses should always strive for maximum profits. And if left to the market, the consumer will decide which businesses thrive, the profit levels, and the wage rates. By deciding which product to buy, consumers vote constantly on quality, service, and price, which affect wages and profits. Efficiency and productivity determine success or failure.

When labor is efficient and productive, wages must go up, not because of coercive legislation but because under the circumstances there would be competition by businesses to seek out the best workers and reward them with the best wages. Coerced union wages, dictated minimum wages, and prevailing wage laws like Davis-Bacon also grossly distort the market process and contribute to the malinvestment initiated by the Federal Reserve policy and guarantee that in the correction, wages must come down.

When wages are not allowed to come down, the agony of the depression or recession is intensified and prolonged, as occurred in the 1930s. In March of 2010, the Obama administration proposed a unique way of avoiding the government's prohibition of sending contracts directly to companies with union workers. By executive order the President planned to circumvent this restriction by sending $500 billion in annual contracts only to companies that pay high wages and very generous benefits—i.e., union workers.

This effort would have also included government discretion in directing contracts that follow government-mandated labor standards. This change would further expand government control over business-labor relationships and guarantee higher unemployment and slower recovery. These changes would make the Davis-Bacon principle of mandating prevailing wages much worse. Davis-Bacon was passed in 1931 and made the unemployment problem of the 1930s much worse. The outrage is that Obama plans to make these changes simply with an executive order.

Keynes actually understood the need for real wages to go down but opted for the reduction of real wages by decreasing the purchasing power of the dollar through inflation of the money supply. This obviously only made the economic problems worse.

A free market grants no authority or privileges to labor unions or business. All contracts between workers and businesses must be mutually agreeable and without government mandates. No one is forced to work, no one is prevented from quitting, and the wages are to be set by mutual agreement. All workers are free to organize and collectively negotiate with employees. Employees have a right to participate or not. Government workers have no power to force obscene wages on the taxpayers and should not be given a contractual right to strike and hold the taxpayers hostage.

It seems strange that the idea of voluntary associations and personal choices are so readily accepted by individuals of both progressive and conservative persuasions, yet when it comes to setting wages it's assumed that only an all-knowing, all-coercive government has the wisdom to know what the proper wages should be.

If the system of government interference in worker and

business relationships produced a prosperous society with all workers making huge salaries and businesses thriving with huge profits, one could understand the endless blind acceptance of coerced wage controls. But the opposite is true, because the artificially high wages significantly contribute to unsustainable debt in government and business, making the Federal Reserve's generated business cycle that much worse.

Ignorance in economics contributes to this blind acceptance of government regulations over the free market. It also reflects an unwillingness to recognize and defend the principle of individual liberty. In a society that honors individual liberty, the use of force to make people better off or an economy fairer is rejected. The great irony is that, when the goal is liberty, prosperity flourishes and is well distributed. When economic equality is the goal, poverty results.

Petro, Sylvester. [1957] 2008. *The Labor Policy of a Free Society*. New York: The Ronald Press; Auburn, AL: Mises Institute.

ZIONISM

More than two thousand years after the Jewish Diaspora began, in the eighth century BC, and especially following widespread Jewish assimilation into national groups in the eighteenth and nineteenth centuries, a worldwide movement began to recapture a universal Jewish identity, culture, and faith. Part of this mission was for Jews to return to the Middle East (Palestine) and establish a single homeland. But this was not the only issue. The leaders of the Zionist movement, as it came to be called, wanted to preserve the Jewish identity, language, and religion, in the face of acculturation.

Nathan Birnbaum, an Austrian political activist, is credited with coining the word "Zionism" in 1891, from the name of a hill in Jerusalem. It is not in its cultural, religious, or language aspirations that Zionism has inspired the most controversy but rather in its political goals of securing a geographic homeland. The timing of the movement's most notable victory, the establishment of the State of Israel, coincided with a widespread reaction against the violence of anti-Semitism in Europe.

There is no doubt that Jews have a historic claim on the land itself. The Bar Kochba revolt in AD 135 against the Roman Empire prompted a large number of Jews to be exiled from the area now known as Israel. Some historians report that the Jewish population of 300,000 was further reduced to a thousand families during the Christian Crusades in the Holy Lands.

From the 1890s until 1948, when Israel became a sovereign nation carved out of Palestine, immigration was mostly voluntary, gradual, and accomplished with due respect for existing land titles. Zionism, during the first forty years of this movement, was not about taking land by force nor was it about militarism. A continual peaceful transformation would probably have occurred except for the political actions after World War II in which the United Nations turned a local and demographic issue into an international and highly politicized one.

One of the first decisions made by the UN was when the UN General Assembly accepted the Security Council's recommendation in 1947 to partition Palestine. The same year, the United Nations also got involved in the partitioning of Korea. By June 1950, under a UN resolution, America was back at war siding with South Korea against the Soviet Union and China, which supported North Korea.

The partitioning problems of Palestine and Israel and North and South Korea persist to this day. Considering the lives lost and the money spent, it doesn't say much for the

UN's peacekeeping efforts or our own foreign policy of the past sixty years.

Though I was not active in politics in high school or college, I recall attending a Rotary Club meeting in the early 1950s with my father. The speaker was a college student from Palestine studying in the United States. Her story was about how her family had been forced from their property, which had been in the family for centuries, but was then used for Israeli settlements. I can recall thinking at the time that this did not seem fair to me, and it doesn't seem fair to me today.

This taking of land from one group for the benefit of another has been criticized by most Muslims, many Christians, and Jews as well. The entitlement argument that this new arrangement was ordered by God and reflects ancient ownership by the Jews is not an easy case to make. This belief inspires those who support the use of force to achieve an expanding geographic presence for a greater Israel, including most of the Middle East.

Zionism as a movement has accomplished wonderful things for the Jewish people and Jewish faith. It inspired Jews the world over to recapture their language, and to do so in a period of time that was nearly miraculous. It helped restore the Jewish faith as a living presence and heighten consciousness of Jewish identity and purpose. It is tragic that the political agenda has been so divisive for the Middle East and the world, especially given that the entire mission of creating a homeland might have been accomplished without the use of force.

Historian Juan Cole has pointed out that Jerusalem

(Palestine), through the many centuries, was under Jewish rule for only about 170 years. In other words, there are many competing claims for the same land, and it is impossible to decide between them. Dozens of other regimes occupied the land for much longer periods of time. For instance, Muslims ruled Jerusalem for 1,191 years.

Factual history is not much help in sorting out the emotionally charged religious and secular arguments over who should live in and rule over this region. It seems that there should be a statute of limitation on ancient claims of ownership. Those still in possession of titles to land and homes should not be cavalierly dismissed out of a sense of justice.

Even with recognizing the ruthless way some American settlements uprooted both Mexican and Indian occupants, I'm certain I wouldn't be too happy to give up without compensation any property I now own to those with claims just hundreds of years old, let alone thousands. Religious interpretations of God's desires are subjective and can never be settled through reason, no matter how logical some would like to make the debate.

Though the fighting has gone on for literally thousands of years, and control of the Holy Lands has shifted back and forth among Muslims, Romans, Christians, Jews, and others, there have been examples when the people were left alone, for relatively long periods of time. With less government involvement, different religious groups were quite capable of getting along together peacefully. Intermarriage regardless of religious beliefs was not unusual. My advice: Leave the young people alone and they'll find out that they prefer lovemaking to warmongering and are more anxious to get along with one another than the older generations who stir the pots of war.

Give government any kind of foothold and it will figure out a way to force or incite young people into war making. The old saying is true: Old people and governments start the wars and young people must fight and die in them for all kinds of cockamamie reasons.

Today, the Israeli political lobby is a powerful political force. Two to three hundred nuclear weapons, under Israel's control, make Israel more powerful than all the Arab and Muslim countries put together. But that's not where the real power lies. The UN can labor tirelessly in "controlling" one nuclear weapon (in Iran) that doesn't exist while the international community does not put pressure on Israel to sign the Nuclear Non-Proliferation Treaty. In contrast, the world community rarely even admits that Israel's nukes exist—and at the same time Iran has never been ruled in noncompliance with the NPT. The fact that Muslim nations become annoyed with this policy is written off by most in the West by charging anti-Semitism.

Meanwhile, within Israeli politics, there is a great deal of debate and diversity of opinion. The Liberal party in Israel often raises questions about the apartheid conditions that Palestinians are subjected to. Even newspapers in Israel are willing to discuss this issue openly, but it is essentially never permitted in the United States. Former President Jimmy Carter is now persona non grata for raising the question in his most recent book, *Palestine: Peace Not Apartheid*. J. Street, a new pro-Israel Washington PAC, is challenging AIPAC's monopoly control of the discussion of U.S.-Israeli relations in the United States. The group Peace Now also strives to change the tone and essence of the debate.

Other American Jews have spoken out against Israel's treatment of the Palestinians as well. The American Council for Judaism is growing in influence in the American Jewish community, especially with the younger generation. Though it's argued that Jews are motivated to immigrate to Israel because they were exiled from Palestine, only a small fraction of American Jews ever moved to Israel.

Even given all of this, my position on Israel is the same as my position with regard to any other country. I favor a non-interventionist position, consistent with what the American Founders favored and what the Constitution enshrines. I would like a policy of peace, friendship, and trade—and no intervention in any country's internal affairs.

I'm convinced that this would serve Israel's best interest. Since we generously subsidize Israel, the potential of stopping our aid means that Israel must get tacit approval from the United States for its policies toward its neighbors. We have been known to hinder friendly outreaches by Israel in the Middle East, as well as Israel's use of force to protect her borders. Israel is not a truly sovereign nation as long as it depends on getting U.S. permission to do what it sees is in her best interest.

But this is a two-way problem. If Israel would be so bold (something that I do not believe it will be) as to attack Iran without explicit approval of the United States, we'll be blamed anyway, and if war spreads to include Iran, we'll be in the middle of it as long as today's conditions persist.

A principled stand against all foreign aid is a net benefit to help Israel. Foreign aid breeds dependency and sacrifice of sovereignty and removes an incentive to promote a free market economy. We subsidize and protect Arab nations with money and weapons, and many of those are not even close to Israel in supporting democratic elections. No aid means Arab Muslim nations suffer more, giving Israel a military plus. But unfortunately, that will never happen because we must protect "our" oil and we will remain in the region for the foreseeable future.

Our strong support for Israel practically eliminates any desire for it to work out differences in the region by direct negotiations with organizations like the Arab League. Alliances among moderate states to maintain peace and in opposition to the radical mullahs would be more likely than when we control the whole process. And when we do achieve a peace agreement like the Camp David Accords between Egypt and Israel, it costs the American taxpayers plenty—in perpetuity. This bought peace has cost us well over $150 billion since 1979, and yet friction remains. Artificial peace treaties hinder the need for all involved to rely on commerce and trade to improve the standard of living for both sides and to work out their differences locally.

An alliance between Israel and moderate Arab nations may well have developed to deal with Saddam Hussein. That type of a solution would have been a blessing to all Americans.

Voluntary support for Israel either by joining its army or sending money there is quite different from taxing, borrowing, and inflating to pay for the additional debt burden to support both sides of this constant fight in the Middle East.

Zionism and the politics of the entire Middle East are

international. The wars in Iraq and Afghanistan cannot be separated from the general acceptance of our two major political parties that our obligation to support Israel at all costs is deeply embedded in our political culture. The threats toward Iran and the sanctions come at the constant urging of the Israeli right-wing government and their supporters here in the United States. The dissidents who speak out in Israel are rarely quoted here in the United States, and any opposition arising in the United States is rarely reported in our media.

As historically controversial and emotionally charged as the Middle East is, logic is not likely to prevail and allow a peaceful solution anytime soon. Misplaced religious passion of the three great religions—which are theoretically supposed to worship the same God—prohibits the universal sharing of the Golden Rule, love for our fellow man, and desire for peace.

But first, we must see more admission of mistakes made as Ronald Reagan did after the Marines were killed in Beirut in 1983. In his memoirs, he admitted he did not realize how complicated Middle East politics were and that he had made a serious error. That is why he went against his own proclamation that he would never "turn tail and run," because he decided that it was in the best interests of the United States to change a failed policy.

If we were to stay out of the Middle East, militarily and politically, I'm convinced it would be most helpful, in that a "neighborhood" solution would more likely occur without us stirring the pot and jeopardizing more Americans being killed in wars yet to come. This policy, I am certain, would be in the interest of Israel and the United States and world peace.

Carter, Jimmy. 2007. *Palestine: Peace Not Apartheid*. New York: Simon & Schuster.

Saenz-Baillos, Angel. 1996. *A History of the Hebrew Language*. New York: Cambridge University Press.

Slezkine, Yuri. 2006. *The Jewish Century*. Princeton: Princeton University Press.

AFTERWORD

M any people are deeply discouraged at the state of affairs in America. They look at goings-on in Washington and see graft, power grabs, senseless regulation and spending, and a government completely out of control, having grown far beyond the size and scope that a free people should ever permit. They are confused about ongoing wars around the world. They are puzzled by the dampening of economic opportunity. People are worried about the future.

These people are right. Some are active in politics and trying to make a change. Others are discouraged to the point of utter cynicism. There is a third path here that I highly recommend, and that is the path of winning hearts and minds through education, first of the individual, and then of others through every way possible.

We must recapture what it means to be free. By this I do not mean that we should all become policy wonks or waste our time studying the details of this or that political initiative or sector of life. I mean that we need to form a new approach to thinking about society and government, one that imagines that we can get along without such central management. We need to become more tolerant of the imperfections that come with freedom, and we need to give up the illusion that somehow putting government in charge of anything is going to improve its workings, much less bring on utopia.

To embrace the idea of liberty is not a natural condition of mankind. In fact, we are disposed to tolerate far more impositions on liberty than we should. To love liberty requires an act of the intellect, I believe. It involves coming to understand how all the things we love in this world were given to us under conditions of liberty.

We need to come to see government as it is, not as we wish it to be and not as the civics books describe it. And we need to surrender our attachments to government in every aspect of life. This goes for the right and the left. We need to give up our dependencies on the state, materially and spiritually. We should not look to the state to provide for us financially or psychologically.

Let us give up our longing for welfare, our love of war, and our desire to see the government control and shape our fellow citizens. Let us understand that it is far better to live in an imperfect world than it is to live in a despotic world ruled by people who lord it over us through force and intimidation. We need a new understanding of what it means to be a great nation; it should mean, as George Washington said, that our nation is a beacon unto the world, not that we conquer the world militarily, impose our will on everyone, or even remain number one in the GDP rankings. Our sense of what it means to be great must be defined first by morality.

We must come to imagine liberty again, and believe that it

can be a reality. In order to do this, we do not need songs, slo-gans, rallies, programs, or even a political party. All we need is access to good ideas, some degree of idealism, and the cour-age to embrace the liberty that so many great people of the past have embraced.

Liberty built civilization. It can rebuild civilization. And when the tides turn and the culture again celebrates what it means to be free, our battle will be won. It could happen in our time. It might happen after we are gone from this earth. But it will happen. Our job in this generation is to prepare the way.

APPENDIX

The ten principles of a free society:

1. Rights belong to individuals, not groups; they derive from our nature and can neither be granted nor taken away by government.
2. All peaceful, voluntary economic and social associations are permitted; consent is the basis of the social and economic order.
3. Justly acquired property is privately owned by individuals and voluntary groups, and this ownership cannot be arbitrarily voided by governments.
4. Government may not redistribute private wealth or grant special privileges to any individual or group.
5. Individuals are responsible for their own actions; government cannot and should not protect us from ourselves.
6. Government may not claim the monopoly over a people's money and government must never engage in official counterfeiting, even in the name of macroeconomic stability.

7. Aggressive wars, even when called preventative, and even when they pertain only to trade relations, are forbidden.

8. Jury nullification, that is, the right of jurors to judge the law as well as the facts, is a right of the people and the courtroom norm.

9. All forms of involuntary servitude are prohibited, not only slavery but also conscription, forced association, and forced welfare distribution.

10. Government must obey the law that it expects other people to obey and thereby must never use force to mold behavior, manipulate social outcomes, manage the economy, or tell other countries how to behave.

Young people, especially, ask me what I read in pursuit of these goals of freedom, peace, and prosperity. I reference many important works, old and new, in this and my other books, of course. But on the Internet, about which I am questioned the most, I especially value Lewrockwell.com, as well as Mises .org, Antiwar.com, and Campaignforliberty.com.